Asian Americans
at the Margins

ALSO BY H. ROY KAPLAN
AND FROM MCFARLAND

*American Indians at the Margins:
Racist Stereotypes and Their Impacts
on Native Peoples* (2022)

Asian Americans at the Margins

A History of Stereotyping, Discrimination and Achievement

H. Roy Kaplan

McFarland & Company, Inc., Publishers
Jefferson, North Carolina

ISBN (print) 978-1-4766-9289-0
ISBN (ebook) 978-1-4766-5478-2

LIBRARY OF CONGRESS CATALOGING DATA ARE AVAILABLE

Library of Congress Control Number 2024046945

© 2025 H. Roy Kaplan. All rights reserved

No part of this book may be reproduced or transmitted in any form or by any means, electronic or mechanical, including photocopying or recording, or by any information storage and retrieval system, without permission in writing from the publisher.

Front cover images: (clockwise from top left) Warner Oland as Charlie Chan (Fox Films); Japanese internment camp in Stockton, California (National Archives); Indian film actress (Adobe Firefly); Sergeant Bhagat Singh Thind (U.S. Army); 19th-century advertising postcard (Boston Public Library); Vietnamese refugees northeast of Cam Ranh Bay, Vietnam (U.S. Navy); South Korean-American actor Ken Jeong (Jesse Chang); Chinese man pulling rickshaw (University of California, Berkeley); Asian boy in 1970s advertising poster (Library of Congress); Vice President Kamala Harris (White House); Japanese anime illustration (Malchev/Shutterstock)

Printed in the United States of America

McFarland & Company, Inc., Publishers
Box 611, Jefferson, North Carolina 28640
www.mcfarlandpub.com

To my mentors:
Gene Piedmont, Curt Tausky,
Singh Bolaria, Bill Wilson,
and Charles Page

Acknowledgments

Writing a nonfiction book depends on more than the creative and organizational skills of the author. Many people helped me in this venture as I scaled the learning curve. I am indebted to Denny Kato for his informative course on the World War II internment of Japanese Americans and his comments on my draft of Chapter 5. The resources made available by the *Densho* organization were invaluable in my work on the internment of Japanese Americans. And I can't forget the way my granddaughter, Maggy, introduced me to manga, and her mom, Tammy, and my son, Ian, greatly facilitated the formatting of my manuscript. My friends at the Committee of 100 in New York City connected me to the wonderful array of resources provided by that organization. I am especially indebted to Charles Zinkowski, in charge of communications for that organization. Niccole Kunshek, with the American Society of Plastic Surgeons, provided me with research materials on Asian American plastic surgery procedures, and Professor Rachel Volberg of the University of Massachusetts Amherst furnished me with material on problem gambling among Asian Americans. Dr. Ko-Lin Chin, professor of sociology at Rutgers University in Newark, was informative through his writing about Asian gangs and during a phone conversation about the present status of Asian gangs in the United States. Interviews with law enforcement officers around the country assisted me in understanding the past and present status of Asian gangs.

The indefatigable work of Stop AAPI Hate must not be overlooked. This relatively new organization, born out of necessity and hardships experienced by Asian Americans in this country in recent years, provided me with tangible evidence that hate is a common denominator of marginalized minorities. Still, as I have endeavored to demonstrate on these pages, our culture and society would be much poorer without the participation of Asian Americans who seek social acceptance in our society. I hope their travail surpasses the stereotype of the model minority on their path to full recognition and participation in the coming years.

Table of Contents

Acknowledgments vi
Preface 1
Introduction 3

1. Who Are Asian Americans? 13
2. Myths About Asians and Immigrants 43
3. Gambling, Gangs and Deviant Behavior 56
4. The Treatment of Japanese Americans in World War II 71
5. Contemporary Struggles: How Asian Discrimination Looks Today 93
6. Persistent Stereotypes About Asian Americans 113
7. The Model Minority Myth 143
8. The Future of Asians in American Society 159

Chapter Notes 185
Bibliography 213
Index 227

Preface

I am writing this as the Israel Defense Forces invade Gaza, and the United States and the world are awaiting the outcome of hostilities in the Middle East. Antisemitism is on the rise, but it is just one form of prejudice directed toward minority groups. Although Christians have been the targets of prejudice and hatred for decades in lands where they are the minority, they have become a resurgent force in the United States, railing against people from different lands and of different cultures and colors, despite the trials and tribulations they have endured. It seems as if humans relish gaining social and psychological advantages over underprivileged groups. Whether through blatant misinformation or microaggressions, majority group members seem to like denigrating and disparaging minorities, blaming the victims for their plight, despite abundant evidence that prejudice and discrimination are the culprits preventing the less fortunate from moving up the social mobility ladder.

Writing about stereotypes that Asian Americans have endured in the United States for centuries has allowed me to glimpse the ways they have been mistreated and denied full access to the American Dream. I was "othered," branded as an outsider, ridiculed for being undesirable as a child because I am Jewish. The ill-treatment I received had a lifelong effect on the way I viewed myself and others, those unwanted castaways who, like India's Dalits, were viewed as disposable accoutrements to society. As sociologist Mia Tuan noted, Asian features have led them to be classified by whites as "others": "an ethnic identity is imposed on them by virtue of their physical appearance, and ultimately they are seen as less authentically American than their white ethnic counterparts."[1] This caste-like system was created through conquest, slavery, and genocide, with white Christians at the top and other groups such as Asian Americans, blacks, and Native Americans relegated through stereotypes and myths to an inferior status as outsiders and others.

Yet history has proven that these supposed outsiders made incalculable contributions to our country, and without the participation of immigrants and the unwanted, we would not be able to survive. They are the "essential workers" who care for our sick and elderly, grow and serve our food, build and care for our homes, and provide the services that have become vital for the maintenance of law, order, and civility. They are also the teachers, social workers, scientists, physicians, engineers, and businessmen and -women whose industriousness and creativity make this society possible.

People of color, ethnic and religious minorities, the elderly, the LGBTIQ community, and people with different abilities are regularly denigrated and disparaged by so-called mainstream Americans. Yet these very groups, when combined, are forming the new majority that is becoming the leading edge of our society. Despite the fears of some white supremacists that they will be displaced by such groups, there is no cohesive strategy behind their ascendancy. Their perspectives and contributions are as diverse as their cultures and colors, and we all have become dependent on Asian Americans and immigrants like them.

The great conundrum that plagues our society surrounds the obstinate perseverance of stereotypes that perpetuate myths about people of color—myths that denigrate, disparage, and prevent non-whites from full access to the society promised in our sacred documents. This promise has been and continues to be elusive to Asian Americans and immigrants who aspire to the "good life" available to the dominant white stratum.

Being "othered" is like being shunned and denied full access to upward mobility. As the reader will see in the following pages, there has been a long and contentious history of interaction between Asians and whites in the United States—a history riddled with racism and exclusion. But times are changing, and the increasing presence of Asians in America, along with their significant contributions to our culture, is a harbinger of systemic changes that will, hopefully, signal the end of their "othering." But the real issue is, what then? Material success, as measured in the high incomes of many Asian Americans, may enable them to compete with affluent whites for life's "goodies," but what kind of life does that represent? The goal of acceptance and financial security that has motivated many Asians to succeed in our materialistic society may be an ephemeral figment of the imagination, one as elusive as the dream of losing the appellation of being "forever foreign." There must be more to creating the good life than financial success and security. It is my hope that the Asian American community will see the day when they are no longer regarded as foreigners and remain committed to creating a more just and equitable society for everyone.

Introduction

The Covid pandemic revealed social and political weaknesses in countries around the world, but the United States was more deeply affected than many nations. Not only did the pandemic take the lives of more than one million people here, it revealed deep flaws in our social safety net. Mortality and hospitalization rates of people of color ran two and three times those of whites. Vulnerable "essential workers," who bear the brunt of caring for the sick, elderly, and young, who harvest and prepare our food and cater to the demands of the more affluent members of our society, succumbed under the pressures of the pandemic, disproportionately dying because they could not afford to miss work.

The pandemic also revealed a dark underside of our society, one nurtured by the desire of some to place blame for the disease. This blame was fed by the racist rants of Donald Trump that rekindled age-old bigotries about Asians. Although the exact origin of the disease has not been ascertained, the former president accused the Chinese government of being responsible and frequently referred to the illness as "the Chinese Flu" or the "Kung Flu."[1] Despite protestations from the Asian-oriented Committee of 100, Stop AAPI Hate, and the ADL (Anti-Defamation League), the former president disparagingly lobbed such phrases and innuendos to his rabid disciples at rallies around the country, with consequential effects. More than 11,000 hate incidents were committed against Asians in the United States between March 2020 and March 2022,[2] but the social and psychological toll against them was much greater, especially since the relationship between Asians and white people in the United States has been infused with painful memories of prejudice and discrimination.

This book reviews the history and contemporary status of Asians in the United States, identifies stereotypes used about them, and discusses Asian Americans' methods for coping with prejudice and discrimination. Chapter 1 presents a discussion of their origins: Who are the Asian Americans? Where did they come from? What kinds of contributions have they made to our society? The chapter presents a synopsis of Asian American groups and what they have done to improve their standard of living and quality of life in this country. Readers will learn that interactions with people "discovered" by Italian explorer Marco Polo in the 13th century have become far more complex, enlightened, and challenging.

Our discussion begins by following the migration of Asians out of Africa more than 40,000 years ago. All humanity has its roots there. The Great Leap Forward migration out of Africa to the vast uninhabited continent of Asia was prompted by a search for food and natural resources that were being depleted in the land left behind. Over thousands of years these migrants adapted to their environment. Evolutionary changes in their bodies occurred, such as a yellow skin hue and an epicanthic fold that narrows the eyes of some Asians (believed to be an adaptation to the cold, windswept region where they lived, as well as a defense against ultraviolet light).

In the 18th century the Swedish taxonomist Carolus Linnaeus published a classification of races that became the foundation for early anthropological racist theories that designated Asians as inferior to white Europeans. When the increasing number of Asian immigrants in the United States began to pose a threat to the white power structure, policies and laws were enacted to restrict Asian immigration and mobility. Even before contemporary attempts to restrict Asian immigration, Western nations, including the United States, sought to engage China and Japan in trade ventures that evolved into wars. These included the Opium Wars of 1839–1844 and 1856–1860 and the Chinese Boxer Rebellion (1899–1901). The English intervention in India—the country that accounts for the second largest number of Asian Americans in the United States—had an important role in anglicizing East Indians and ultimately led to the transformation of that society and its democratization.

Throughout U.S. history, white society has reacted negatively toward immigrant groups, especially males, because of perceived economic and sexual competition. In the case of Asians, especially the Chinese in the second half of the 19th century, a surge of males entered the United States to seek their fortunes mining for gold in California and, later, to work on the construction of the transcontinental railroad. The Union Pacific railroad line recruited thousands of Chinese laborers, almost all males (estimates vary from 15,000 to 20,000). Very few Chinese women were available for mates. This situation created the perfect storm that fueled derisive stereotypes about Asian foreigners:

They worked hard for less wages than Americans, and they sought white women. What a wonderful example of a self-fulfilling prophesy—an image that persists to this day.

Chapter 2 discusses myths about immigrants, especially Asian Americans. It explores commonalities in the way Asian Americans and other immigrant ethnic groups have been and are being treated in the United States. Interrelationships and conflicts between Asians and the white majority are presented, from foreign attempts to pull reluctant mainland Chinese into trade relationships that led to the Opium Wars in the mid–1800s, to laws that aimed to exclude them from the American mainstream. Fueled by the heightened presence in California and eastern cities of Chinese and Japanese immigrants who were willing to work for lower wages under adverse conditions, labor unions sought to prevent further Asian immigration, which culminated in the Chinese Exclusion Act of 1882. This act was the most restrictive federal anti-immigrant legislation ever passed in the United States. Its prohibitions on immigration were not lifted until 1943, when China became an ally of the United States in World War II. The passage of the Immigration and Naturalization Act (Hart–Celler Act) in 1965 removed quotas based on national origins and led to an influx of Asian immigrants to the United States. Asians outnumber all other minority groups living in the United States except Latinos.

Life for Asians in the United States has never been easy. As minorities of color (although at times they have been considered white), they have had to bear insults and indignities from the white population.

As their social status and numbers increased, their growing presence commanded attention, respect, and admiration. Still, many interactions between Asians and whites have been influenced by stereotypical misconceptions that confuse and misinform the dominant white majority. For example, labeling Asians as the "model minority" placed them in the context of being viewed as financially, intellectually, and socially superior, overlooking the discrimination many still experience in the United States and the wide disparities in household income among and within different Asian ethnic groups. Although the types of discrimination faced by Asian Americans can vary by ethnic group, for example, Sikhs and other East Indians versus Chinese, Japanese, Filipinos, Vietnamese, and Koreans, the stigmatization of these groups has prevented them from fully participating in our society. Despite these encumbrances, their contributions to our society in science, business, and culture have been enormous, but no matter how hard Asians have tried to blend into American society, they are regarded by some whites as "perpetual foreigners." Though they are the fastest growing minority in the United States, numbering over 24 million people from more than 19 distinctive ethnic groups, their history in this country has been marked by insults and indignities. Some Asian Americans walk a tightrope between legitimate and illegitimate behavior, achieving status and respectability, but a small segment of the Asian American population has utilized illegal and even criminal methods for obtaining social status, power, and privilege in America.

Chapter 3 focuses on the seamy side of Asian American behavior, from the notorious Chinese tongs (the word means "meeting house"), to contemporary Asian American gangs, and to the criminally oriented Japanese yakuza. Although more powerful abroad (e.g., the triad in China), these groups have managed to gain a foothold here. This chapter also explores the cultural acceptance of gambling among some Asians, the creation of Asian American casino moguls, and the scope and impact of Asian American relationships to so-called victimless crimes. A mystique surrounds contemporary Asians, characterizing some as high rollers—gamblers who lounge in spacious rooms in luxurious casinos and maintain ties to the heart of Asian gambling in Macau.

Some stereotypes about Asian Americans can be traced to the popularity of mahjongg, played in the United States by over half a million people, mostly Asian Americans and Jews. Even early Chinese immigrants to this country engaged in this pastime. Although it has become less popular today, it still commands a wide following around the world.

Chapter 4 focuses on one of the most egregious and racist actions ever embarked on by the United States. Following the Japanese attack on Pearl Harbor, President Franklin Delano Roosevelt ordered the removal of Japanese to camps located in the U.S. West and Southwest. With their allegiance distrusted, 120,000 Japanese (including 70,000 Nisei [second generation] who were American citizens) were interned. This injustice was not rectified until President Ronald Reagan signed HR 442, the Civil Liberties Act of 1988, which apologized for that action and awarded $20,000 to each survivor. A majority of the people confined to the camps were citizens of this country, but the isolation, indignities, and economic losses they endured have been historically minimized. Today, a large segment of our population is ignorant about this event, which is presented in this book through historical research and interviews with camp survivors.

Although the term "concentration camp" has been used by some Asians to refer to these camps, they were largely absent the state-induced starvation and cruelty found in the Nazi system. But shame, isolation, and boredom took their toll on the Japanese who were unceremoniously herded into railroad cars and transported, often without explanation, to harsh environments. Nearly two thousand of them died in these camps, many by suicide. Many young men who lived there were drafted into or volunteered for the U.S. Armed Forces, and fourteen thousand served gallantly in the 442nd Regimental Combat Team—a unit that was also known as the Purple Heart Division because of the high number of casualties its members sustained in the European theatre during the Second World War. This chapter summarizes the events surrounding the enforced relocation of Japanese Americans in World War II and the exploits of the 442nd Regimental Combat Team and addresses the racial implications of the United States' use of nuclear weapons on Japan.

No matter how hard Asians have tried to blend into American society, they are regarded by some whites as "perpetual foreigners." Throughout their time in the United States, they have suffered insults and indignities. Have you ever wondered why many American cities have Chinatowns? The very nature of these enclaves reflects segregation, racism, and discrimination. Aside from the blatant impediments that have been imposed on their immigration and status, such as the infamous Chinese Exclusion Act of 1882, less obvious but pernicious racism barred Asians from living in predominantly white areas. This behavior was reinforced through federal housing policies that impeded home ownership in these areas by blacks and Latinx, too. Chapter 5 provides an overview of prevalent forms of discrimination and hate crimes against Asian Americans, including microaggressions directed toward them. This chapter discusses the "lynching" of Vincent Chin in 1982 and the murders of eight spa workers (six of them Asian) in the Atlanta, Georgia, area in 2021, as well as the dramatic increase in the number of hate crimes perpetrated against Asian Americans during the Covid-19 pandemic, and summarizes the findings of the recent report on hate incidents perpetrated against Asian Americans produced by the Stop AAPI Hate organization.

Stereotypes about Asians are difficult to eradicate, despite the efforts of many organizations to combat them. The Committee of 100 has been publicizing research that demonstrates racial profiling of Asian scientists and its adverse effect on our society. These stereotypes depict Asians as different and deficient, based upon phenotypical characteristics that purportedly reflect personality traits. A common assumption is that they are inscrutable, with docile and passive traits that have prompted some of their adversaries to assume they are easy targets for psychological and physical aggression, which may explain why Asian women have disproportionately been targets of hate crimes.

Aside from physical characteristics that may distinguish Asians from the white population, for example, the shape of their nose and eyes, and the color of their hair (black) and skin (dark or light brown for some and burnished or "yellow" for others), the genders of Asians have been used in labeling females as hypersexualized ("horny"), aggressive ("tiger moms," dragon ladies), and good at doing nails, and males as followers, cheap laborers ("coolies"), undersized yet potentially dangerous (martial arts aficionados), mysterious, inscrutable, and prone to congregate in gangs. Some of these stereotypes are used to stigmatize the entire ethnic group. For example, the attribution of exotic diets (ostensibly eating dogs and cats, smelling of curry) and the assumption that Asians, especially Japanese and Chinese, are unpatriotic and untrustworthy may be countered by the belief among some whites that Asians prepare tasty food and produce gifted students who excel in STEM (science, technology, engineering, and mathematics) subjects. These characterizations are oversimplified generalizations that serve to rationalize the stigmatization of Asians, forcing many of them to evince what the famed African American sociologist W.E.B. Du Bois referred to as "double consciousness." In their attempt to assimilate into white-dominated society, some Asians walk a social and political tightrope, evincing attitudes and behavior of white and Asian society so they may be accepted in both worlds.

Chapter 6 reveals the origin and effects of prevalent stereotypes about Asian Americans as well as the ways policies, laws, and perceptions about them have been influenced by these stereotypes. This chapter also presents examples of prejudice and discrimination toward Asians derived from cultural stereotypes in the media, including personalities such as the evil villain of English novelist Sax Rohmer, Dr. Fu Manchu; the inscrutable sleuth Charlie Chan (played by various non–Asian actors) and his "number one son," Lee Chan (played by Keye Luke); the martial arts master Bruce Lee; and Kwai Chang (David Carradine in the *Kung Fu* television series 1972–1975), as well as a discussion of East Indian Bollywood films and celebrities.

While Asian Americans' scientific contributions to the world and our society have been significant, Asian Americans have also impacted our culture through literature, art, music, and sports. The roster of achievements is long, and the record of their accomplishments is not only noteworthy but also essential for dispelling the myths and stereotypes that continue to contribute to the "otherness" of their group. For example, two of the three founders of YouTube are Asian Americans, Steve Chen (Taiwanese American) and Jawed Karim (Bangladeshi German American). From Japanese origami to anime, from motion pictures to PlayStation and TikTok, and to our cell phones, calculators, and computers, our lifestyles have been altered by the wizardry of Asian-dominated technological giants like SONY, Samsung, ByteDance, and Huawei. These phenomena are addressed as well as the growing backlash against them as competition between the United States and China increases.

Contemporary Asian comedic film stars like Jackie Chan and the creator of the ABC television series *Fresh Off the Boat* (2015–2020), Eddie Huang, are presented as examples of successful Asian American cultural icons and stereotypical models. Amy Chua's *Battle Hymn of the Tiger Mother* and the critically acclaimed motion picture *Crazy Rich Asians* (2018), directed by Jon Chu, are discussed here, as well as the 2021 release of the feature film *Shang-Chi* (starring Simu Liu), which presented the first Asian superhero created by Marvel Studios. Perhaps this presages greater acceptance of Asian Americans in our popular culture as the practice of "yellowface" (using white actors to play Asian roles) becomes passé.

From the time of the first Asians who entered the United States, barriers were erected by whites to prevent Asians from assimilating into our society. Laws were passed to exclude them from full participation, hindering their upward mobility (denying them citizenship; denying them entry into labor unions; preventing them from establishing families by barring Asian women from entering this country; segregating Asians into central core areas of cities; prohibiting Asians from homesteading land; and denying them the right to vote). Spurred on by the desire to become full citizens, they have, for the most part, lived exemplary lives and made significant contributions to American society. Their lifestyles even earned them the sobriquet "model minority," sometimes used as a cudgel against African Americans and Latinx to demonstrate the purportedly superior family and social values of Asian Americans. Despite this, with the desire of many Asian Americans to fit into the dominant white society, the term "model minority" has become problematic because, as explored in Chapter 7, it creates unrealistic and unattainable objectives for some Asian Americans that can lead to anxiety, depression, alienation, and suicide.

Chapter 7 discusses the causes and effects of friction between Asian American groups and whites as well as popular conceptions of Asians as gifted students, researchers, and industrious workers, despite evidence of institutionalized racism in admission decisions and workplace bias resulting in quotas that limit their upward mobility. The "bamboo ceiling" is a fact of academic and business life in the United States. Only 5.6 percent of Fortune 500 and S&P 500 companies are headed by Asians, and fewer than 4 percent of executives and administrators in higher education are Asian. What accounts for these disparities? Korean American writer Cathy Park Hong captured the ambivalence of the "model minority" syndrome when she noted, "Even if we've been here for four generations, our status here remains conditional; *belonging* is always promised and just out of reach so that we behave."[3]

The concept of the "model minority" is intertwined with U.S. government policies that lifted the ban on Asian immigration in 1965, only to allow entry to the most educated and talented, thus creating a self-fulfilling prophesy: "See! Anyone can live the American Dream! they'd say about a doctor who came into the country already a doctor," noted Hong,[4] and she, like many overcompensating Asians, questioned the fairness of a society that pitted them against blacks, Latinx, and struggling whites. "Your only defense is to be hard on yourself, which becomes compulsive, and therefore a comfort, to peck yourself to death."[5]

The "model minority" myth, according to sociologists Rosalind Chou and Joe Feagin, creates pressure to conform to white-dominated society, causing some upwardly aspiring Asians to feel stressed, embattled, isolated, and inadequate. In their zeal to assimilate into white society, they may avoid "rocking the boat" by not reporting racist verbal and physical affronts. Some Asians find that their journey to become "American" induces them to discriminate against other ethnic minorities, for example, Koreans versus blacks, at times paying a heavy price in their self-esteem. But to many white Americans, those who wield the power and privilege in our society, Asians are still outsiders.[6]

Asian Americans have developed techniques for fitting into the dominant white culture in their quest for recognition and acceptance. Some techniques have been cultivated by some Asian Americans for generations, but the lure of "replacement theory" is strong and gaining impetus in the United States and around the world as alienated white people look to scapegoat others for their misfortune.

The writings of Asian American social critics, such as Wesley Yang, Charles Yu, Cathy Hong, Julia Lee, and Jay Caspian Kang, are critical of our social system because it attracts and repels Asian Americans, creating an approach/avoidance conflict for upwardly aspiring Asian Americans.[7] Will they ever become fully accepted here, or will they always be considered "perpetual foreigners"? These questions are addressed in Chapter 8, which discusses the possibilities of full Asian American participation in the United States. More than contributing medical and scientific innovations and the production of food, music, and other popular cultural artifacts, Asian Americans' very presence and history cry out for equality and fairness and the necessity to be welcomed and accepted as full citizens. They deserve no more or less than the dominant whites, who often withhold approbation based on the color of one's skin. As Hong notes, "In our efforts to belong in America, we are grateful, as if we've been given a second chance at life. But our shared root is not the opportunity this nation has given us but how the capitalist accumulation of white supremacy has enriched itself off the blood of our countries."[8]

This chapter also discusses changes that are occurring in our society that will influence whether Asians and other minority groups can ever be truly assimilated—recognized and accepted. Current trends in the United States that represent attacks on Asians and other minorities by far-right and white supremacist groups, such as the Three Percenters, Oath Keepers, Proud Boys, and QAnon, are discussed. Devastating outcomes have resulted from their activities and belief in "replacement theory," the growing fear among some whites that they will be subsumed, devalued, and relegated to an inferior existence as ethnically diverse groups become the new majority in the 21st century. Our discussion focuses on the origin of replacement theory and why white supremacists, as well as many working- and middle-class whites, espouse this position to the long-term detriment of our society. Stereotypes about Asians are used by these groups as recruitment techniques, and they are reinforced using social media. What do Asians have to do to convince white society that they belong, or will they forever be viewed as "foreigners"? As Hong noted, "When I hear the phrase 'Asians are next in line to be white,' I replace the word 'white' with 'disappear.' We are reputed to be so accomplished, and so law-abiding, we will disappear into this country's amnesiac fog. We will not be the power but become absorbed by power, not share the power of whites but be stooges to a white ideology that exploited our ancestors."[9]

A common theme throughout this book and my other works is the desire of Asian Americans and other ethnic minorities to be accepted by the dominant white society. Despite a long list of malevolent actions and policies that have been perpetrated against them by whites, America remains the "Mountain of Gold," the destination of immigrants from around the world—a place of promises and prospects for better lives. This book denotes the types of obstacles Asians have had to overcome in their quest to be treated fairly and to be given the opportunity to demonstrate their desire to become partners in the great American experiment of freedom and democracy.

1

Who Are Asian Americans?

> "Living as a minoritized, nonwhite person in this country is to exist in a perpetual state of shame. It is to be told every day: 'You will never belong. You will never be enough. You will never be American—by which, we mean you will never be white.'"
> —Julia Lee, *Biting the Hand: Growing Up Asian in Black and White America* (New York: Henry Holt and Company, 2023), p. 116.

In this age of heightened social conflict, race is a hot-button topic, emotionally charged, guaranteed to kill a conversation or ignite a spirited debate. But if we accept scientific facts about humans and our ancestors, we can allay some of the misperceptions that are responsible for promoting much of the misinformation and ill will about our species. We are all descendants of a female (some refer to her as Mitochondrial Eve) who lived in Africa about 200,000 years ago and a male (some refer to him as Eurasian Adam) who lived there approximately 60,000 years ago. Although our two ancestors never hooked up, we all contain mitochondrial genetic material from Mitochondrial Eve and males contain Y chromosomes derived from Eurasian Adam. Two million years ago, our ancient ancestors, *Homo erectus,* left Africa and began populating Asia. In fact, the earliest recorded use of fire by *Homo erectus* was in China 2.12 million years ago. The modern version of humans, *Homo sapiens,* made the journey from Africa to Asia between 70,000 and 50,000 years ago. The large size of the Asian population may be due to the historically low migration of Asians to the West and the abundance of fertile arable land there—for example, 520 million fertile hectares in China versus 137 million hectares for all of the European Community. Variations in skin color, hair texture, and the shapes of noses, lips, and eyes are the result of eons of evolution that prompted changes in the human genome as adaptations to a group's environment. Following the migration of people out of Africa, groups of our ancestors developed genetic adaptations to their new surroundings. Still, these variations cannot refute the biological fact that all humans share nearly 100 percent identical genetic material. In effect, we are all cousins.[1] This scientific fact about our common origins and biology not only challenges popular misconceptions about humans, it calls into question the justification for prejudice and discrimination by one group (often whites) toward another (often people of color).

One has only to look at the similarity in appearance and language between Russians and Ukrainians to comprehend the bonds between them. Yet the United States has, for decades, been riven by white supremacist sentiments that falsely exalt the genetic superiority of whites above people of color, lamenting the decline in white fertility and the growth of our population because of an influx of immigrants and a higher birth rate among people of color—what is commonly referred to as "replacement theory."[2] In fact, the 2020 Census of the United States revealed the effects of the continuing trend toward multicultural diversity in this country. But these trends are not the product of a preconceived plan to increase the base of the Democratic Party. They reflect long-standing declines in the majority white population, now consisting of 235.4 million people (a decline of 8.6 percent from the 2010 census), and increases in the number of diverse ethnic groups. The most dramatic increase was recorded in the mixed-race group, which grew by 276 percent from the 2010 census, to nearly 50 million people. Of particular note for us, the second largest increase recorded in the census was among Asians, whose population grew to 24 million (20 million listed themselves as "Asian alone"), an increase of 55.5 percent since 2010, and equal to more than 7 percent of the U.S. population.[3] According to the Pew Research Center, the Asian population will number 46 million people in the United States by 2060.[4]

The scope of the Asian continent is daunting. Spanning multiple countries, Asia is the largest continent in the world, composed of more than 17 million square miles. But to lump all Asian Americans into one category would be to perpetuate stereotypes that they "all look alike." Their cultures are as diverse as the fabric of our multicultural society, reflecting a variety of languages and features that create a panoply of looks and preferences that defy generalizations about them. A closer look at the countries that contribute the majority of Asians to the United States reveals that most come from East and Southeast Asia and the Indian subcontinent (see Table of the Distribution of Asian Americans). We begin our discussion by taking a look at the largest Asian

American ethnic group, people who share similar ancestry, culture, and languages—the Chinese.

Chinese Americans

Numbering nearly five and a half million people, the Chinese account for nearly a quarter of the Asian population in the United States. Despite having as much industriousness and desire to assimilate into the dominant society as other immigrant groups, they have never been fully accepted or assimilated—otherwise there would not be Chinatowns embedded in major cities throughout this country.[5] The first major Chinatown, which was established by Chinese immigrants in San Francisco at the time of the California gold rush in 1850, was a sanctuary for the thousands of Chinese laborers who toiled in the gold fields and later worked on the transcontinental railroad. Initially, Chinatowns provided security for this largely male population of workers, but white resistance to the growing number of Chinese who were willing to do deleterious, backbreaking work for less than the "going wage" increased as the economy deteriorated in the latter part of the 1800s.[6]

From the time of the Venetian explorer and storied traveler Marco Polo in the 13th century, there has been a fascination with the Far East. Polo's tales of wonder about the culture of Chinese society and riches along the famed "Silk Road," which functioned as a commercial distribution hub for the goods produced in that part of the world, led to many myths and misinformation surrounding China and the culture of the region.[7] Pearl S. Buck's widely read book *The Good Earth* no doubt contributed to misunderstandings about Chinese culture.[8] However, as the late historian Stuart Creighton Miller demonstrated, antipathy toward the early Chinese immigrants in contemporary times was not restricted to the West Coast—it was reflected in negative stereotypes and hostile, even aggressive actions by labor unionists and whites throughout the country.[9] The wave of Chinese who came to the United States in the 19th century stemmed from a lack of opportunity for upward mobility in their homeland under the ruling Qing Dynasty. These Chinese entered the United States during the California gold rush and within 30 years numbered nearly a quarter of a million people. The culture of this predominantly male-driven immigrant surge was characterized by frugality and industriousness, as well as a practice, shared by other immigrants, of sending portions of their earnings to their homeland.

Since the bulk of Chinese immigrants were young males, and not notably asexual, they sought female companionship. This behavior strained the already tenuous relationship with the dominant white males who controlled access to white (and black) females and viewed such overtures as an infringement on their sexual territory. This phenomenon was a source of friction between the dominant white male establishment and the nascent Chinese community in this country.

San Francisco was the first major port of entry for the Chinese immigrants who toiled in the minefields, worked assiduously on the transcontinental railroad, and helped build California's infrastructure. But antipathy toward Chinese immigrants was, as historian Miller described, prevalent in American society long before their increased presence here. Western countries, especially Great Britain, attempted to "open up" the Chinese mainland to commerce in the 19th century. Before that, U.S. trade began in earnest with China in 1785 in the hope of cashing in on the Chinese desire for pelts and ginseng. But until 1840 trade with China never amounted to more than 6 percent of our total trade and just 2 percent thereafter (compared to nearly 14 percent today).

Miller attempted to pinpoint the origin of prevalent stereotypes about the Chinese by assessing the historical trends that helped to formulate the attitudes of traders, missionaries, and diplomats. Each group had selfish motives for promoting relationships with the Chinese. Traders were interested in tapping into the enormous market of the Chinese mainland. Missionaries were fascinated by the prospect of bringing millions of heathens into the Christian fold. Diplomats were enthralled by the potential of opening up a "closed" society for the traders, missionaries, and political elites.

Chinese society was old, ancient, compared to modern European countries, and the uniqueness of this civilization was often lost on the ethnocentric traders, missionaries, and diplomats who considered the Chinese uncivilized. These ethnocentric perspectives were fueled by Westerners' inability to comprehend the intricacies and nuances of Chinese culture with its reverence for tradition and obeisance to authority and pacifism, in contrast to the Western values of competition, materialism, and individuality. As international borders were expanding in the 19th century, these values led to stereotypical misconceptions about the Chinese that have persisted to this day.

The missionaries' perception of the Chinese as heathens and idolators was linked to their ostensible lack of interest in Christianity—a paradigm established in the early 1800s as Christian missionaries encountered Chinese intransigence toward their overtures, leading to references to the nation as "the Kingdom of Darkness." As Miller noted, "The nadir of the missionary's despondence was reached when he began to sense total futility in all his efforts and even faltered in his conviction that God wanted China converted to Christianity."[10] Missionaries' degrading depictions of Chinese society were actually designed to enlist greater support for their cause. In a society as large as China, there were abundant diversions that drew the ire of supposedly virtuous Anglos.

The public was warned about the wicked, Satanic, heathen, pagan nature of the Chinese by missionaries and traders, who advised prospective businessmen to be aware that "A Chinaman is cold, cunning, and distrustful; always ready to take advantage of those he has to deal with; extremely covetous and deceitful; quarrelsome, vindictive, but timid and dastardly. A Chinaman in office is a strange compound of insolence and meanness. All ranks and conditions have a total disregard for the truth."[11]

These ethnocentric ramblings were purveyed by the mass media that denigrated Chinese culture by focusing on the depredations on females in Chinese society, including female infanticide and foot binding. Accompanying accounts of torture and public executions were also circulated, with a description of the Chinese appetite for unique cuisine (e.g., eating dogs) and curious medicinal practices. "One Albany, New York, editor reported with horror that the Chinese murdered young girls in order 'to drink certain fluids from their bodies' for medicinal purposes."[12]

The British attempt to open up China, along with its intentional policy of disseminating opium in exchange for Chinese goods (notably silver and silk), led to the first Opium War, which commenced with an attack on Canton in 1840 and ended with the Treaty of Nanking (1842).[13] This endeavor received support from U.S. merchants who also desired expanded trade with the "sleeping giant." The commercial façade of the British invasion was underpinned by a racist undercurrent that depicted the Chinese as docile, infantile, conceited, depraved, slovenly, heretical, despotic, stagnant, filthy, licentious, cowardly, perfidious, criminalistic, and diseased. The ethnocentric characterization of the Chinese was facilitated through the dissemination of these stereotypes in the 1840s by the "penny press"—a medium that reached wide U.S. audiences and reinforced the Chinese as backward and unwanted.

Some opponents of Chinese immigration in the United States went so far as to imply that low-skilled, low-paid, Chinese manual laborers (frequently referred to as "coolies") would represent a new slave society—one that would replace black laborers freed through the Civil War.[14] Underlying this sentiment was an unmistakable whiff of racism, manifested in the belief of Anglo superiority and the fear of contamination of the white Anglo gene pool by "alien" Mongoloid characteristics.

Known as "The Chinese Question," these sentiments were articulated at the turn of the 20th century by authors such as Madison Grant[15] and Lothrop Stoddard,[16] who were intransigent opponents of immigration based on the pseudo-scientific suppositions of "scientific racism" that were popular at this time. But even President Rutherford Hayes expressed such views decades earlier, when he noted in his diary in 1879, "I am satisfied that the present Chinese labor invasion (it is not in any proper sense immigration—women and children do not come) is pernicious and should be discouraged. Our experience in dealing with weaker races—the Negroes and Indians, for example,—is not encouraging ... I would consider with favor any suitable measures to discourage the Chinese from coming to our shores."[17]

The mid–19th century was suffused with scientific racism, which was the application of Darwin's theories of natural selection to humans. This was facilitated by the English sociologist Herbert Spencer.[18] Proponents of these racist theories held that the Chinese culture and homeland were unalterably opposed to the American way of life—the Chinese could not and *would not* assimilate. Their very presence in our society would create negative implications and gross misfortunes for Anglos. The Chinese were considered biologically unsuitable for America's melting pot, although their inexpensive labor was highly valued by entrepreneurs but despised by domestic workers in the United States, Australia, and South Africa. Chinese laborers, pejoratively referred to as "coolies," were likened to slaves and deemed unwelcome and untrustworthy by labor unions and even some governments.[19] Residues of this phenomenon continue to influence our attitudes toward the Chinese, despite the passage of time and evolution of political forces.

An example of early stereotypical sentiments about the Chinese is contained in the comment of poet and diplomat Bayard Taylor in 1855:

> It is my deliberate opinion that the Chinese are, morally, the most debased people on the face of the earth. Forms of vice which in other countries are barely named, are in China so common, that they excite no comment among the natives. They constitute the surface-level, and below them there are deeps on deeps of depravity so shocking and horrible, that their character cannot even be hinted ... Their touch is pollution, and, harsh as the opinion may seem, justice to our race demands that they should not be allowed to settle on our soil.[20]

(This supposition has been proffered about other waves of immigrants, most recently Latinx at our southern borders,[21] and then, as now, it is specious.)

It should be noted that Sinophobia and anti–Chinese immigration sentiments were not restricted to the West Coast, especially California. Strong opposition to Chinese immigrants on the East Coast was fueled by the mass media, and it provoked negative public sentiments against them, frequently including scurrilous allegations. Aside from outright racist sentiments, labor union protectionism motivated some of the antipathy toward Chinese immigration. For example, a writer for the *New York Times* proclaimed that "Mongolians will gradually incorporate themselves into the blood and being of the country, infusing their foul and mortifying vices."[22]

However, some observers believed that Chinese immigration would result in short- and long-term benefits for both countries because Chinese immigrants would contribute their labor to improve our society and return wealthier to China, where they would spread Christianity. Still, the overwhelming sentiment among the Anglo population was against Chinese immigration, and this was intensified from the moment of their arrival in the East in Baltimore in 1775. Suspicions among Anglos about the "Yellow Peril" (a term popularized by Kaiser Wilhelm II) not only imputed nefarious social stigmata such as licentiousness, sloth, immorality, and debauchery of white females, but the Chinese were suspected of spreading diseases such as cholera and leprosy. (These scurrilous allegations, along with the imputation of transmitting tuberculosis, were made about Vietnamese and East Indians in the 20th century.) Nevertheless, more than a quarter million Chinese immigrants entered the United States in the thirty years following the California gold rush.[23]

Perhaps, but not surprisingly, the greatest opposition to Chinese immigration came from organized labor, and paramount in the fight to prevent Chinese labor were the Irish, who had themselves been targets of ethnic prejudice. "We want white people to enrich the country, not Mongolians to degrade and disgrace it."[24] To incite public opposition to the increasing Chinese presence in our society, outrageous allegations about the supposed immoral habits of the Chinese were made. They were accused of corrupting young white women, ostensibly held captive beneath Chinese settlements, for "crimes that cannot be named." It was contended that "degraded races" such as "Niggers and Chinamen" were incapable of comprehending democratic principles that the Irish had fought for.[25]

One of the chief complaints that organized labor made about Chinese workers was that they worked harder than white laborers and for less. While there was some truth to these allegations, immigrant labor has traditionally greased the wheels of American progress. The influx of southern and eastern European immigrants was encouraged through the establishment of Ellis Island, which became a primary immigration port of entry in January 1892, just ten years after the first Chinese Exclusion Act was passed. The first person processed (there would be 12 million before the facility closed in 1954) was seventeen-year-old Annie Moore, from County Cork, Ireland.

The Chinese vehemently denied allegations about the cut-rate compensation for their labor.[26] Thanks to the diligent labor of Chinese workers, many of whom entered the United States as contract workers whose passage was arranged through a credit-ticket system that indentured them to American labor agents, the Central Pacific Railroad was able to meet its commitments and connect with the Union Pacific Railroad at Promontory Point, Utah, on May 5, 1869. Ninety percent of the twenty thousand men who built the Central Pacific Railroad were Chinese, and the work of Chinese immigrants helped to create the California infrastructure.

In one of the most carefully constructed reviews of the Chinese impact on the construction of the Central Pacific Railroad in the mid–1800s, Stanford University historian Gordon Chang painstakingly delineated the role of the "railroad Chinese" in their monumental contribution to linking the eastern and western halves of the United States.[27] The Chinese toiled in inhumane working conditions and inhospitable climates to link with their eastern counterpart, the Union Pacific Rail Road. Often tunneling below ground, clearing chunks of rock after dynamite blasts, enduring bone-chilling temperatures at some times and scorching heat at others, the Chinese laborers met and exceeded the expectations of their white supervisors. Despite being held in high regard for their speed and workmanship, their pay scale was considerably less than what white workers received for the same job. Although Union Pacific administrators confirmed that Chinese workers outperformed white workers before a Senate committee on Chinese immigration, they still professed a preference for hiring white workers.[28]

Coming primarily from the Siyi counties of China, these young males endured extraordinary physical and mental hardships in their search for better lives in America, or what they referred to as the "Gold Mountain." Historian Chang described an instance of their travail:

> At sixty-seven miles from Sacramento, the train reaches Dutch Flat, and at Shady Run Station, the train reaches the first tunnel, seventy-five miles from Sacramento. It is five hundred feet in length and 4,500 feet above sea level. Plenty of snow still covers the ground next to the track, and soon the train passes through towering drifts, the way cleared by men working with shovels. At more than one hundred miles from Sacramento, the train enters Summit Valley, at 6,800 feet in elevation, and then it reaches Summit

Tunnel, 1,659 feet in length. Great banks of snow, ice, and rock still cap the summit at more than 7,000 feet.[29] [In 1865, Chinese laborers dug 15 tunnels at high elevations in the Sierra Nevada Mountains measuring overall 6,000 feet.]

Lacking contemporary technology, the Chinese laborers used their physical stamina and work ethic to accomplish what many observers thought impossible. More than 1,200 died in the process of linking the North American continent. Earning on the average less than $40 a month, they bivouacked in makeshift housing (frequently tattered tents), worked six days a week, and fought off loneliness and boredom, at times by indulging in opium smoking, by gambling, and by availing themselves of prostitutes who proliferated around their camps. (The Chinese male to female ratio in the mid–1800s in California was approximately 39–1.)

Chinese immigrants did not have the benefit of extended families to assist them with living arrangements, but many received assistance from clan and mutual aid associations known as *huiguans*. These were often found in coastal cities, especially San Francisco and New York. They provided financial and emotional support for many of the isolated immigrants, many of whom came to the U.S. shores from Guangdong province in China. According to Ngai, the first *huiguans* in the United States were created in California in 1851, and they were affiliated with Chinese companies (the Siyi and Sanyi) representing the interests of Chinese immigrants here. In 1882 a coordinating body known as the Zhonghua Huiguan was created to form a Chinese Consolidated Benevolent Association that came to be known as the Six Companies.[30]

Some organizations, known as tongs, offered Chinese immigrants protection and other forms of aid that helped the mostly male Chinese adjust to their new surroundings. Hostility to the wave of Chinese immigrants in the mid–1800s was partially a remnant of the prior antipathy to the influx of nearly half a million Irish men and women who fled their country in the 1840s because of the famine that ensued from the failure of the potato crop (due to *Phytophthora infestans*).

As a reaction to being unfairly targeted in the labor market, the Chinese withdrew even further into the safety of their Chinatowns. Rejection, harassment, and discrimination characterized their lives, establishing a classic case of "blaming the victim." Because Chinese immigrant men could not afford to pay for the four- to six-week voyage of their wives, many were forced to patronize "singsong" girls (prostitutes) and were decried by the dominant society as being licentious and depraved. This pattern of sexual hostility elicited by white men was repetitious of white men's jealousy over sexual access to black women as well as white. Sexual competition and competition in the economy were potent stimuli for creating negative stereotypes about the rise of the "Yellow Peril." These adverse sentiments escalated during the financial recession of 1873, when the stock market collapsed and the cost of the Civil War weighed heavily on the nation's economy. With mass unemployment, the Chinese became a visible target for disgruntled and displaced workers, more so than the hordes of white immigrants who were seeking admission to the "promised land."[31]

The repression and stigmatization that confronted Chinese immigrants in the mid–19th century forced many of them to seek protection from tongs. These organizations operated in cities such as San Francisco and later Philadelphia and New York. They were usually composed of young men (known as highbinders or hatchet men) who sometimes engaged in pitched battles in the streets over territory. In the latter part of the 19th century and the early 20th century the Tong Wars pitted the Hip Sing Tong against On Leong Tong. The tong phenomenon waned after the San Franciscan earthquake destroyed the economic base they depended on, but Chinese American Bill Lee described exploits of Chinese gangs in America in the mid to late 20th century.[32]

The tongs originated in mainland China in the mid–17th century when the Ming Dynasty was overthrown by the Qing Dynasty, and many of the participants in the U.S. tongs came from Guandong Province, a prime source for Chinese immigrants to the United States. The organizations initially began as benevolent associations, but a lack of financial resources led some Chinese immigrants to engage in gambling and prostitution for income. Although they provided social support for male Chinese immigrants, for example, housing and employment, they also exploited the lopsided sex ratio of Chinese males to females by promoting prostitution and sex trafficking. The adverse sex ratio was exacerbated by the Page Act of 1875, which forbade the immigration of Chinese women, and the Chinese Exclusion Act of 1882 banned new arrivals of most Chinese men as well.

Some Chinese females, known as *mui tsais*, were sold into sexual slavery by their parents, while others were deceived by the tongs, who misrepresented their occupational prospects in this country. In 1874, the Occidental Board Presbyterian Mission House was formed to assist Chinese girls and women who were being sexually exploited. Led by Donaldina Cameron and Tye Leung Schutze, more than two thousand Chinese women and girls were rescued from sexual exploitation, with most residing for various times at the Presbyterian Home (later renamed the Cameron House). Cameron died in 1968 at the age of ninety-eight.[33]

In 1882 anti–Chinese riots broke out in California, which was still the epicenter of Chinese immigration. Denis Kearney, the head of the Workingmen's Party in California, openly denigrated Chinese laborers and attempted to blame them for the economic misfortunes of working men during the recession. Under pressure from Kearney and the American labor movement, the Chinese Exclusion Act was passed that year. It was the first time that the United States closed off foreign immigration, and Chinese immigrants were prohibited from becoming naturalized citizens. With the exception of Chinese diplomats, students, and merchants, Chinese workers were prohibited from entering the United States for ten years (a practice that was extended in 1892 in the Geary Act and again in 1902, and ostensibly made indefinite in 1904). It was not until 1943, with the passage of the Magnuson Act, which permitted an annual quota of 105 Chinese, that a change in this tradition was implemented (and this was linked to the political reality that brought the United States and China together as allies in World War II).

The official ban on Chinese immigration had a dramatic effect on the number of Chinese in the United States. According to the U.S. Census, there were 105,465 Chinese in the country in 1880, but the number declined to 89,863 in 1900 and 61,639 by 1920. The Chinese developed illegal methods for circumventing official immigration obstacles. One was the creation of "paper sons"—the attempt to allow young Chinese males to enter the country through forged documents that purported to show they were sons of U.S. citizens of Chinese descent. One might conclude that the Chinese Exclusion Act laid the foundation for subterfuge and illegal immigration into the United States.

In an attempt to retaliate against the Chinese Exclusion Act, China implemented a boycott of U.S. products, but it was ineffectual. In the final analysis, the flood gates could not hold back the rising tide of U.S. imports.[34] Throughout these troubling times, many Chinese used the judicial system to pursue their rights. California lawyer and entrepreneur Frederick Bee was an ardent supporter of their cause from 1882 to 1892, litigating many civil rights cases on their behalf. During these years and the following decades, Chinese immigrants managed to circumvent the official non-entry policy of our government and successfully settled in this country. Nevertheless, it was not until the passage of the Immigration and Nationality Act (Hart–Celler Act) of 1965, signed by President Lyndon B. Johnson, that immigration policy based on race and ethnicity was terminated for the United States, thereby changing the face of immigration and the country.[35]

Stereotypes and prejudice are based on distorted generalizations about the group being stigmatized. They simplify social reality by dehumanizing and denigrating an individual or group to give them a negative aura so they can be rejected or "othered." Despite contributions that the Chinese have made to our society, such as the compass, inoculation, printing, and gunpowder, with images of the evil Dr. Fu Manchu, the inscrutable, stolid Chinese menace to modern society, and the obsequious master crime fighter Charlie Chan (initially played by the white actor Warner Oland), irrational myths and stereotypes frequently overcame benevolent images. That is why the Committee of 100, a nonpartisan leadership organization of prominent Chinese Americans that endeavors to combat prejudice against Chinese and other Asians in the United States, published the report *From Foundation to Frontiers: Chinese American Contributions to the Fabric of America* in 2020 at the height of anti–Asian sentiment in this country. Here are a few findings:

The Chinese population is well educated. A majority of Chinese in the United States have a bachelor's degree or higher, compared to one-third of the general population. However, one-fifth of the Chinese population are not proficient in English. Nearly two-thirds of Chinese in the United States work in professional and business services, health services, leisure and hospitality, wholesale and retail trade, and the education industry. Chinese Americans have a strong entrepreneurial orientation—more than 160,000 own their own businesses. In fact, one in ten businesses that provide food or accommodation services and one in twenty wholesale-trade businesses in the United States are owned by Chinese Americans. The vaunted Chinese laundry developed as a by-product of the California gold rush because enterprising Chinese immigrants took advantage of the need for clean clothes for the fortune seekers. In the absence of women and the reluctance of men to engage in laundering their own clothes, Chinese laundry owners shipped the laundry to Hong Kong for cleaning at a dollar a shirt and later shipped the shirts to Honolulu for $8 a dozen. Chinese owners established the first commercial laundry in the American West in 1851, charging $5 to clean a dozen shirts, and by 1870 there were 1,300 Chinese laundries in San Francisco alone with others following in Denver, Pittsburgh, Chicago, and Philadelphia.[36] This entrepreneurial spirit is echoed today in Chinese American–led businesses such as AMD and NVIDIA, major computer technology manufacturers that generated nearly $18 billion in 2019 and employed more than 25,000 people in the United States and overseas.

As the Committee of 100 report pointed out, another major contribution to the Californian (and later the American) economy was made by Chinese immigrants in agriculture, who took responsibility for reclaiming 88,000 acres of swampland in the Sacramento–San Joaquin

Delta by 1880 and dramatically increasing the value of the land. Their labor wasn't restricted to the delta. By 1880 more than 50,000 Chinese laborers worked on rice and sugar plantations, helping to make California an agricultural giant. The propensity for immigrants to engage in agricultural pursuits continues to this day, with large numbers of Latinx people growing and harvesting our food.

A more recent analysis of Chinese Americans, conducted for the Committee of 100 by the School of Social Work at Columbia University in New York City, revealed that there is much diversity among Chinese living in the United States, and Chinese residents are assimilating into the culture of the United States. Although the sample of 6,481 respondents from around the nation was not representative, it revealed that 57 percent of the respondents reported being proficient in English, and half of them exclusively spoke English at home. Nearly nine in ten said they felt part of the American culture, and they were politically savvy—83 percent were registered to vote and 91 percent reported that they voted in the 2020 presidential election. Nevertheless, while they reported feeling accepted, they experienced high levels of anxiety and discrimination. Nearly two-thirds of the respondents were worried about their safety and were increasingly vigilant, and one-quarter of the respondents did not feel accepted by American society. A quarter of the respondents reported being harassed or discriminated against in the previous twelve months, ranging from vandalism on their homes or property, such as cars, to receiving racial slurs or experiencing physical intimidation and assaults. Their most urgently reported problem was racism, a phenomenon no doubt heightened by increased tensions between the United States and China, with people having higher levels of education recording the highest level of concern about this (52 percent). Significant differences existed among the respondents based on income levels and the utilization of state-supported services, bolstering the perspective that the Chinese American population, like other Asian American groups, is not a monolithic sociocultural block.[37]

As the Chinese became acculturated in America, many focused their energy on achieving high levels of education, and their contributions to our society include those of Tung-Yen Lin, a structural engineer who perfected prestressed concrete for modern buildings, and the late renowned architect I.M. Pei, who designed the John F. Kennedy Library and the East Building of the National Gallery of Art, and Chien-Shiung Wu, also known as the queen of nuclear research and the First Lady of physics, who was elected to the National Academy of Sciences. Today, one in twenty-five members of the National Academy of Sciences and the National Academy of Engineering is a Chinese American. So, too, are Jerry Yang (co-founder of Yahoo), Steve Chen (co-founder of YouTube), and Eric Yuan (founder of Zoom Video Communications). But their endeavors are not limited to the scientific and technological fields. Alfred Lin, a venture capitalist, assisted in the startup DoorDash food delivery service. And Aileen Lee, another prominent Chinese American venture capitalist, has seeded software enterprises.

Fashion design is one of the occupations that has been profoundly affected by the infusion of Chinese Americans. One in twenty fashion designers in the United States is Chinese American. Chinese cuisine is also widely popular in this country, with more than 45,000 Chinese restaurants prior to the Covid-19 pandemic. Chinese American philanthropy continues to reach new heights, with more than 1,300 Chinese American foundations donating half a billion dollars in 2014. Growth among Chinese American philanthropic foundations between 2000 and 2014 was 418 percent, compared to a 195 percent increase for all American foundations.[38] The Cyrus Tang Foundation is the largest Chinese American philanthropic foundation in the United States, with assets around $350 million. The principal beneficiary of Chinese American largesse has been higher education. Like the clans that assisted new Chinese immigrants in the mid–1800s, the Chinese-American Planning Council, the largest Asian-American social service agency, provides services such as education, community health, and family support to 60,000 New Yorkers, not just Chinese. Today, 10 percent of Chinese Americans are employed in the healthcare field in the United States, and the Chinese American community, including more than 690 Chinese American organizations, raised more than $18 million and delivered millions of pieces of personal protective equipment (PPE) to hospitals, nursing homes, police departments, and other social service agencies in the first two years of the fight against Covid-19.[39]

One of the fields that Chinese Americans have excelled in is higher education. As of 2018, Chinese Americans filled one in fifty teaching and research positions at U.S. colleges and universities. Leaders included Yuan-Cheng "Bert" Fung, known as the "father of modern biomechanics," and Chang-lin Tien, who held the position of chancellor of the University of California at Berkeley from 1990 to 1997.

The magnitude of the financial contributions of Chinese Americans to our economy cannot be overstated: In 2019 they supported approximately $304 billion in the U.S. gross domestic product, including $175 billion in labor income stemming from three million jobs. Chinese Americans accounted for 1.2 percent of the U.S. labor force (2.3 million workers) and held executive representation on twenty Fortune 500 companies with a market cap of $1.4 trillion.

Despite attempts of our government to surveil Chinese Americans and Chinese nationals, ostensibly to impute nefarious intentions and link them to un–American activities, one in five Chinese American men served in the U.S. Army in World War II. This phenomenon also occurred among other people of color, such as Native Americans, Japanese Americans, and African Americans, despite pervasive discrimination exhibited toward them at home.[40] Despite harassment and persecution of Chinese Americans because of suspicions about their loyalty to this country, 16,000 of them worked in national security and international affairs in the public sector in 2018 (1.3 percent of all Americans working in these fields), including one in twenty computer and research scientists and one in fifty interpreters and translators working in the intelligence community.[41]

Chinese Americans have also made great strides in the political sphere of our society. On December 1, 2022, Representative Ted Lieu of District 33 in California was elected vice chair of the Democratic Party Caucus—the highest rank ever achieved by an Asian in that party. Even with all of these contributions, Chinese Americans and other Asians in our society are still stigmatized, treated unfairly, and discriminated against. We will return to this theme after reviewing the status of other prominent Asian groups.

East Indian Americans

With more than 4.6 million people, East Indian Americans account for 21 percent of Asian Americans in the United States, but 38 percent of them are not citizens, although about a million and a quarter of them have been born in the United States, and a million and a half have been naturalized. Although Indian Americans are the second largest immigrant group in the United States, and they are financially and educationally well off compared to the general population, they still face discrimination from the dominant white population about their identity and assimilating. One might hope that significant changes in public attitudes have occurred since a 1911 Congressional Report declared that Hindus were "universally regarded as the least race of immigrants thus far admitted to the United States."[42]

The origins of the East Indian Americans are as diverse as the many ethnic groups they comprise. Legend has it that the Indian subcontinent was conquered in 1500 BCE by a nomadic fair-skinned horde who came from Iran and surrounding regions. These supposed conquerors were known as Aryans, but recent research calls into question the veracity of particulars about this event. There is some debate about the methods used by the Aryans to achieve supremacy over the indigenous inhabitants of the Indian subcontinent, notably the Harrapans and Dravidians. DNA research has helped to fashion a much less conflictual representation of the invasion and diffusion of Aryan culture. It was not hostile or even aggressive, but gradually enveloped the region through a combination of cultural improvements used by the Aryans, applied to farming and education.

The most erudite analysis of ancient DNA material in the Indian subcontinent was conducted by Vagheesh Narasimhan et al. (there were 117 original collaborators on this paper).[43] After analyzing the DNA of 523 people who lived in the Neolithic and Bronze Ages, they discovered up to 30 percent Aryan heritage in South Asia. However, the contemporary resident population of the region was found to be composed of a genetic mix combining Indus Valley and Ancestral North Indian civilizations, as well as remnants of Steppe Ancestry (today's Yamnaya Steppe people).

One of the preeminent questions about East Indian culture concerns the origin of the caste system—that constellation of beliefs and practices that defines one's social and behavioral status from birth. Until recently, the Aryans were held responsible for instituting one of the most rigid social and behavioral systems on the planet. In ancient Hindu tradition there were four main groups that Indian society was organized around, known as the *varnas*. Initially discussed in the *Vedas*, the acknowledged holy book of Hindus, the caste system was described thusly:

1. At the top of the hierarchy were the fair-skinned *Brahmans* (high priests and educators).
2. *Kshatrya* (rulers and warriors) followed them in importance.
3. *Vaishya* (landlords and businessmen) were judged to be third in stature.
4. *Sudra* (peasants and workers) were considered near the bottom of the caste system.

All these categories of people with caste designations were said to originate with *Purush*, a primal man. The castes were, according to ancient Vedic thought, said to derive from *Purush*'s body parts: The Brahmans were said to have sprung from his head; the Kshatrya from his hands; the Vaishya from his loins; and the Sudra from his feet. The "untouchables" or *Harijans*,[44] were people who dwelled outside of the caste system (and the group that Mahatma Gandhi sought to liberate in his drive to free India from the dominion of the British until he was assassinated in 1948), were relegated to the lowest status jobs and life in Indian society. Many East Indians do not adhere to the rigid social rules of the caste system, and the geographic dispersal of the population through roughly 600,000 villages with 115,000 containing 2,000 to 10,000 people would seem to mediate against it. Living in small-scale societies infuses social control in the system because people see and know one another, and many Hindus believe in reincarnation. From their perspective, the transmigration of the soul is believed to be related to the life one lives. In essence, good and bad deeds are thought to have an effect on future incarnations. *Karma,* or the way one lives, is believed to determine one's future life.[45]

While the Aryans were thought to be the originators of the caste system in India, recent analyses indicate that the British, in their role as occupiers of the Indian subcontinent from 1858 to 1947, played an important role in rationalizing and enforcing the system.[46] While much of the Indian subcontinent's history is subject to debate and contradiction, the region is characterized by a high degree of ethnic and cultural diversity. India's twenty-nine states have different cultures and languages, but Hinduism accounts for nearly 80 percent of the religious population (1.4 billion people), although there are 204 million Muslims as well in the country. Many East Indians have brought their religious traditions to the United States, which has 2.5 million Hindus.

A representative study of 1,200 East Indian American residents of the United States found that 31 percent of them believed that discrimination against them was a major problem.[47] There might be some solace in the finding that a majority of the respondents believed that Americans discriminated against other groups of Asians more than their group. Today, Indian Americans' standard of living is double that of the median American household, and Indian Americans have twice the national average of bachelor of arts degrees. But not all members of this ethnic group share in this success and affluence—there are pockets of poverty and deprivation among them, and they may face stigma, prejudice, and discrimination.

At times defined as strangers and aliens, and despite the belief that Indian Americans are less often discriminated against than other Asians, racists have brutally attacked them. Confusion, misinformation, and blind hatred have led some white supremacists to target members of this group, especially Sikhs. Sikhs are a monotheistic religious/ethnic group whose male adherents do not cut their hair or shave, and they wear turbans. Guru Nanak taught that Sikhs should honor the earth and believe in one god. Nine other subsequent gurus reinforced these beliefs. Estimates place the number of Sikhs in the world at around 25 million (the fifth largest religion), including 700,000 Sikhs in the United States.

In recent years there have been numerous attacks on members of this religious group by white supremacists. In 2012 a Sikh temple or *gurdwara* in Oak Creek, Wisconsin, was assaulted by Wade Michael Page, a forty-year-old white male, who murdered seven Sikhs and wounded three others (including policeman Brian Murphy).[48] In 2021 eight people were murdered in an Indianapolis Federal Express facility, four of them Sikhs. The FBI has found that anti–Sikh crimes in the United States have risen every year since it began tracking them in 2015. There were 94 crimes perpetrated against Sikhs in 2020 in the United States.[49]

Obviously, Sikhs present a distinct image of "the other" to nonmembers of this group, making them an easy target for the senseless rage of bigots. For most Indian Americans, however, their dress and facial appearance may shield them from the untoward advances of racists. Since many East Indians have Anglo facial features,[50] they may not have to endure the verbal and physical attacks other Asians are subjected to. Indian Americans' skin tones cover a wide range from light to dark, and the texture of their hair, though uniformly black, is not curly like that of African Americans; they do not have an epicanthic fold affecting the shape of their eyes like some other Asian ethnic groups; and having an English accent may confer higher social status on them.[51]

Indian Americans have made significant economic, social, and political contributions to the United States. For example, they have had a major impact on our telecommunications. Satya Nadella, born in 1967, is the chairman and chief executive officer (CEO) of Microsoft. Sabeer Bhatia is the co-founder of Hotmail. Vinod Khosla co-founded Sun Microsystems and now heads a venture capital organization named after him. Ajay Bhatt is a computer architect who helped design and develop the Universal Serial Bus (USB), as well as the Accelerated Graphics Port (AGP) and Express Platform Power Management architecture. He holds thirty-one patents. Padmasree Warrior was Cisco's chief of technology, and prior to that she worked twenty-three years for Motorola, where she was also chief of technology. Shantanu Narayen is the CEO of Adobe Systems, one of the largest software systems in the world.

In the health science fields the contributions of Indian Americans have also been stellar. The American Association of Physicians of Indian Origin (AAPI) has 60,000 members and is the second largest medical association in the United States. Under the first Trump Administration, Seema Verma held the position of administrator for the Centers for Medicare & Medicaid Services. Vivek Murthy was the U.S. Surgeon General in the Obama and Biden administrations. Rajiv J. Shah is the president of the Rockefeller Foundation and was the head of the U.S. Agency for International Development in the Obama Administration. There are also successful physician/authors such as Deepak Chopra, Abraham Verghese, and Atul Gawande, as well as Pulitzer Prize-winning Siddhartha Mukherjee. Rounding out the cultural side is Nina Davuluri, Miss America of 2014, although we should not overlook the impact that Bollywood (Indian) films have had on the movie industry in this country, despite the fact that non-white ethnic groups remain underrepresented in the filmmaking industry.[52] In the field of politics, Indian Americans have been making major inroads, and we discuss this in Chapter 8.

Regarding the topic of loyalty to the United States, there can be little question where the sentiments of most Indian Americans lie.[53] Indian law forbids dual citizenship, but 80 percent of Indians living in the United States would accept citizenship here if it were offered. Like other ethnic minorities in this country, most Indian Americans are dedicated to the principles that provide a framework for our society, and many have become quite successful and philanthropic.[54] In many other ways, Indian Americans reflect traditional American values: Nearly three-fourths of them are married (compared to 48 percent of the general population of this country); they have the highest rate of endogamy (marrying within their own group) of any ethnic group; and, as we have seen, they are highly educated.

The Indian American Attitude Survey found that 41 percent of their respondents believed that maintaining their Indian identity was very important, and an additional 37 percent said it was somewhat important.[55] Indianness was valued less by respondents born in the United States in this study, and they worked assiduously to become integrated into American society—20 percent reported that they performed a community service in the prior year. Even though they made a conscientious effort to assimilate, half the respondents reported being discriminated against in the past year, most often on the basis of skin color (30 percent).

This finding is fascinating in view of the fact that colorism, that is, discrimination on the basis of white skin tone, is prevalent in the mother country, India. Professor Neha Mishra of Reva University in Bangalore, India, has demonstrated the preference for light skin over dark skin among the Indian population. Although the ancient Indian civilization did not evince preferences for skin color, and Indian gods were often depicted as dark-skinned, for example, Lord Ram and Lord Krishna, the arrival of the Mughals in the 16th century and, more importantly, of the British in modern times led to increased societal preference for lighter skin tones. There is a preponderance of light-skinned models, actors, and actresses influencing the public's preference for whiteness in India, despite the fact that a majority of the Indian population has dark skin. One of the most disturbing indications of this phenomenon can be found in the "Want Ads" section of major newspapers where prospective mates advertise the qualities they are looking for. "Fairness" (light skin) is repeatedly listed as desirable. The obsession with light skin has led to a proliferation of skin-lightening products with estimated value of more than $450 million annually. We discuss this phenomenon further in Chapter 6.[56]

Filipino Americans

A majority of Asian Americans were born in another country (57 percent), and many of them came to the United States as immigrants fleeing hostilities in their homelands. This was the case with many immigrants from the Philippines, a series of islands controlled by Spain for 333 years. Located on the rim of the Asiatic Mediterranean Sea, bounded in the west by the South China Sea and in the east by the Pacific Ocean, the islands are adjacent to the Sulu and Celebes seas in the south and the Bashi Channel in the north. They received their name from King Philip II of Spain, who reigned over them. After the Spanish American War, which began in 1898, the Philippines were ceded to the United States and they remained under U.S. control for nearly half a century, through a failed Filipino war for independence and a series of political initiatives designed to "prepare" the Filipinos for self-rule.

Racist stereotypes held by senior diplomats, as well as President McKinley, about the inability of Filipinos to govern themselves were used to rationalize our occupation of the islands for 48 years. It was not until 1946, after a bloody war from 1899 to 1902 that left 4,200 American soldiers dead along with 20,000 Filipino military and 200,000 Filipino civilians (from violence, famine, and disease, principally cholera and malaria), that the United States granted the Philippines its independence. Initially the war was fought by conventional methods, which resulted in strategic defeats for the Filipinos. Tactics were changed under the leadership of Emilio Aguinaldo, who took Filipino insurgents into the mountains for a guerrilla war that lasted three years. The capture of Aguinaldo in 1901 by U.S. forces de-escalated hostilities. President Theodore Roosevelt granted full amnesty to Aguinaldo and all

Filipinos who fought in the war (referred to by the Americans as an insurrection).

Initially, Filipino immigrants, like other Asians who came to the United States, were engaged in agricultural pursuits, especially on the West Coast (California), but they gradually emigrated to other parts of the country and focused on pursuing a better life than the one they had. Their story, like that of other Asian Americans, is one of perseverance in the face of prejudice and a focus on higher education as the means for upward mobility. As a group, Filipinos sent $13.7 billion to the Philippines in 2023.[57] In 2019, it was estimated that Filipinos living abroad sent $35 billion back to the islands, amounting to 10 percent of the country's gross domestic product (GDP).

William Howard Taft became the first head of the Philippine Commission in March 1900, and then Civil Governor until 1904, when he was appointed Secretary of War by President Theodore Roosevelt. Taft began a "policy of attraction" to win over Filipino elites and educate them on the virtues of capitalism. With the implementation of the Exchange Visitor Program in 1948, and the elimination of racial quotas with the passage of the Immigration and Nationality Act of 1965, large numbers of Filipinos emigrated to the United States. Health care in this country was one beneficiary. The shortage of nurses created by World War II led to an influx of Filipino nurses, many of them trained in American procedures and recruited by American hospitals. More than 150,000 Filipino nurses have emigrated to the United States—one out of every twenty registered nurses in this country. There are 1,680 Filipino physicians for every 100,000 persons in the United States.

The Filipino population is the fourth largest immigrant population in the United States (behind Mexico, China and India). More than 4.2 million Filipinos currently live in the United States, with 1.7 million living in California (principally Los Angeles, San Francisco, San Diego, Riverside/San Bernadino, and San Jose). New York State is home to almost a quarter million Filipinos, and New York City has nearly 90,000, with 60 percent living in the Borough of Queens.

The educational attainment of Filipino Americans is high. Thirty-eight percent of them have a bachelor's degree, compared to 20 percent of the general population and 24 percent of all Asian Americans taken together. The median age of Filipino Americans is slightly higher than that of all other Asians (thirty-six compared to thirty-four years old). While 13 percent of the general U.S. population live below the poverty line, only 7 percent of Filipino Americans do. (For all Asian Americans there is a rate of 11 percent living in poverty.) Strikingly, the median household income of Filipinos in the United States is $90,400, about $5,000 higher than all other Asian Americans and about $3,400 higher than the general public in this country. Not surprisingly, unemployment among the Filipino American population is low. Interestingly, foreign-born Filipino Americans have higher educational attainment, a lower unemployment rate, and higher median household income than their United States-born counterparts.[58]

The contributions of Filipino Americans to our society are so numerous that they defy classification. Here are a few individuals[59]: Conrad Gempesaw, Ph.D., the 17th president of St. John's University in New York City; Kevin Nadal, Ph.D., professor of psychology at John Jay College (New York), and past president of the Asian American Psychology Society; Vivian Vasquez, Ph.D., professor of education at American University and author of twelve books on education and literacy; Don Figueroa, comic book artist who helped create the *Transformers*; Michael Janis, award-winning glass artist; Byron Acohido, Pulitzer Prize for journalism, 1997; Cheryl Diaz Meyer, Pulitzer Prize for photojournalism, 2004; Elaine Quijano, CBS News correspondent; Alex Tizon, Pulitzer Prize for investigative reporting, 1997; Jose Antonio Vargas, Pulitzer Prize as a writer for the *Washington Post*, 2008; Noel Francisco, 47th Solicitor General of the United States; Peter Bacho, author of the American Book Award-winning novel *Cebu*; Robert Lopez, composer of "Let It Go" from *Frozen*; Lea Salonga, actress and winner of Tony, Olivier, Drama Desk, and OCC awards; Bobby Murphy, co-founder of Snapchat; Jose B. Nisperos, first Asian Medal of Honor recipient; Benjamin Cayetano, first Filipino governor in the United States (Hawaii); Roman Gabriel, quarterback for the Los Angeles Rams and Philadelphia Eagles, National Football League Most Valuable Player, 1969; Tim Lincecum, major league baseball pitcher, San Francisco Giants and Los Angeles Angels (three no-hitters, multiple Cy Young Awards); Bruno Mars, singer and dancer; Lou Diamond Phillips, actor; Robert Lopez, first Filipino Oscar recipient (music).

Vietnamese Americans

With nearly two and a quarter million immigrants and their descendants, the Vietnamese American population composes the fourth most populous group of Asian Americans and 3 percent of all immigrants in the United States. Vietnam is another in a series of nations that sent a flood of immigrants to this country following a war. The precipitous termination of hostilities between the United States and

Vietnam in 1975 led to a surge of 175,000 Vietnamese immigrants to the United States, and the subsequent arrival of their families in the following years dramatically increased their number. Although their rate of entry into this country has declined (62 percent came before 2000) as their homeland has undergone economic and political transformations, Vietnamese immigrants and their posterity compose a formidable component of the Asian American bloc.

Although the United States was engaged in a violent conflict within Vietnam for more than twenty years (1954–1975) with more than three million service men and women stationed there over the decades and 58,300 losing their lives (compared to 1.1 million North Vietnamese and Viet Cong fighters, between 200,000 and 250,000 South Vietnamese military fatalities, and 2 million civilian deaths combined from both sides), relations between the countries have stabilized, if not normalized. More than $92 billion in trade was conducted between the two countries in 2020, putting Vietnam in the top ten trading nations with the United States, and our trade deficit of $68 billion with Vietnam revealed that they were winning the peace. More than half (52 percent) of Vietnamese immigrants live in two states: California (39 percent) and Texas (13 percent). More than three-fourths (78 percent) of Vietnamese immigrants have lived in the United States for more than ten years.

The Vietnamese have the highest level of English proficiency of any immigrant group. Vietnamese Americans born in the United States have 90 percent English proficiency. While 45 percent of foreign-born Vietnamese immigrants have completed high school, compared to 27 percent of all Asian immigrants, only 10 percent of all Vietnamese immigrants have postgraduate degrees, compared to 24 percent of all Asians in this country. However, that number rises to 18 percent for American-born Vietnamese, and the rate of Vietnamese Americans with bachelor's degrees (22 percent) is higher than that of the general population in the United States (20 percent).

While 13 percent of the general population in the United States live in poverty, slightly less (12 percent) of the Vietnamese American population do, compared to 10 percent of all Asian immigrants. Over three-fourths (76 percent) of Vietnamese immigrants have become U.S. citizens, compared to 59 percent for all Asian immigrants. More than half (59 percent) are currently married. Their annual household income is considerably less than other Asian immigrants ($69,800 compared to $85,800), which reflects their lower median personal earnings ($31,000 for Vietnamese immigrants vs. $40,000 for all other Asians), although their unemployment rate (4 percent) is the same as for other Asian American groups.

Contributions made by Vietnamese Americans to the United States in art, culture, business, science, politics, and sports are too numerous to list. Vietnamese actors have starred in motion pictures like *X-Men: Apocalypse* (Oliva Munn), with Maggie Q in *Mission Impossible*, and Kelly Marie Tran in *Star Wars: The Last Jedi*. Betty Nguyen was with the *CBS Morning News* and was also a CNN anchor. Cuong Vu is a Grammy Award-winning jazz trumpeter and vocalist. Viet Thanh Nguyen won the Pulitzer Prize for fiction in 2016 for his book *The Sympathizer*. Viet D. Dinh was Assistant U.S. Attorney General and drafted the USA Patriot Act, and Eugene H. Trinh was a NASA astronaut and the first Vietnamese American in space.[60]

Korean Americans

As with Vietnamese and Filipino American immigrants who came here following devastating wars in their homelands, a surge in Korean immigrants occurred after the Korean War, 1950–53. Although there has never been a formal peace treaty following the end of hostilities between the warring parties, the Korean peninsula remains divided at the 38th parallel, where the dividing line was initially set by the Soviet Union and the United States following the end of World War II. On June 25, 1950, North Korea, under the leadership of Kim Il–Sung, invaded South Korea. Because the Soviet Union was boycotting the United Nations (UN), and the UN had recognized Taiwan as China (mainland China was not then recognized by the UN), the Security Council of the United Nations created a UN Command (principally of U.S. forces, but ultimately composed of twenty-one nations) to assist the South Koreans, then under the leadership of Syngman Rhee, to repel the invasion.

Initially, the combined UN and South Korean forces were successful in their military engagement with the North Korean invaders, pushing them back near the Yalu River, which borders mainland China. Then, on October 19, 1950, the People's Voluntary Army of China entered the war and forced the United Nations command to retreat, leading to a bloody conflict for the next three years. Officially referred to by President Harry Truman as a "policing action," the conflict proved to be one of the most destructive in modern history, with more than three million fatalities, and with North Korea becoming one of the most heavily bombed countries in history.

During the conflict, several million North Koreans fled, and, along with South Koreans, many emigrated to the United States. Today, there are nearly two million Korean Americans living in the United States.

Los Angeles is home to by far the most Korean Americans with 326,000 residents, followed by New York City with nearly 100,000 (60 percent of them living in the borough of Queens). Their median age is thirty-six years, which makes their ethnic group slightly older (by two years) than the general Asian American population. Four out of five Korean Americans have lived in this country for at least ten years, and their educational attainment is significantly higher than people in the general U.S. population: 35 percent have bachelor's degrees versus 20 percent for all Americans, and 22 percent have postgraduate degrees versus 13 percent of the general U.S. population. This is reflected in the fact that only 11 percent of Korean Americans live below the poverty level in this country, compared to 13 percent of the general population.

Korean Americans have an unemployment rate of only 4 percent, and nearly two-thirds of them (62 percent) are employed. However, their median household income in 2019 of $72,000 was significantly below that of other Asians ($85,000) but considerably above the $69,560 for the general U.S. population. The difference between foreign-born ($68,000) and United States-born ($88,100) Korean American median household incomes is remarkable, perhaps indicating the successful assimilation and upward mobility of Korean Americans.

Philip Jaisohn, also known as Jae-Pil Seo (1864–1951), was the first Korean to become a naturalized citizen of the United States in 1888 following a failed Korean coup he participated in. He was also the first Korean American to earn a medical degree in this country, but many other Korean Americans have emulated his work. Korean emigration to the United States is often viewed as occurring in three waves. The first (1903–1905) consisted of about 7,500 Korean men who served as contract laborers on the sugar plantations in Hawaii. The second wave was primarily composed of women who had married U.S. servicemen during the Korean War. This wave lasted from 1950 to 1989 and involved almost 100,000 women ("internationally married women" or "military brides"). However, large numbers of Korean adoptees, many of them children of interethnic relationships between American GIs and Korean women, also entered the country at this time. More than 107,000 Korean children were adopted in the United States between 1953 and 2007, solidifying the ties between the two countries. Many of these children have made important contributions to our society. The third wave of Korean emigration to the United States began in 1967 as an artifact of the 1965 Immigration Act (Hart–Celler Act) that relaxed quotas on immigrants, allowing family reunification and preferential occupational specialization.[61]

The list of notable Korean Americans is long and demonstrates the ubiquitous presence of Korean Americans in our society and the myriad contributions they have made to the United States. Here are a few: Frank Cho, comic book artist (*Liberty Meadows, The New Avengers*); Dennis Hwang, artist of many Google Doodles; Grace La, designer, professor of architecture, Harvard University Graduate School of Design; Jim Lee, co-founder of Image Comics and now President, Publisher and Chief Creative Officer of DC Comics; Nam June Paik, father of video art; Peter Shin, producer of *Family Guy*; Albert An, former CEO, Tower Research Capital; Nelson Chai, former chief financial officer (CFO) of Uber, Merrill Lynch and New York Stock Exchange and former president of CIT Group; James Kim, founder of Amkor—one of the largest outsourced semiconductor packaging design and testing services in the world (billionaire); Kewsong Lee, former CEO of the Carlyle Group; James Park, co-founder of Fitbit; Gideon Yu, co-owner of the San Francisco 49ers NFL football team; Fred Armisen, comedian (*Saturday Night Live, Portlandia*; paternal grandfather was Korean); Sandra Oh, actress; Juju Chang, ABC News Anchor/Reporter; John Yoo, University of California Berkeley law professor and former deputy assistant attorney general in the Office of Legal Counsel (OLC) of the U.S. Department of Justice; Andy Kim, Young O. Kim, Michelle Steel, Marilyn Strickland (U.S. Representatives to Congress); Major General Sharon K.G. Dunbar, U.S. Air Force; David Kim, concertmaster, Philadelphia Orchestra; Walter Kim, president, National Association of Evangelicals; Dennis Choi, neuroscientist at Stony Brook University, director of the Neurosciences Intitute, and former executive vice-president of Merck; John Chun, automotive designer of 1968-69 Shelby Mustang GT350 and GT500; recently deceased Waun Ki Hong, division head and professor at the M.D. Anderson Cancer Center, University of Texas, a chemoprevention pioneer; Larry Kwak, physician and scientist, specialist in immunology and cancer vaccines (named one of *Time Magazine*'s 100 most influential people in 2010); Jeong H. Kim, former president of Bell Labs; Peter Kim, former president of Merck and member, National Academy of Engineering; David Y. Oh, NASA engineer and flight director of the Mars rover *Curiosity*; Michelle Rhee, former chancellor of Washington, D.C., public schools; Marcus Freeman, head coach of the Notre Dame football team, former NFL player; Hines Ward, NFL player for Pittsburgh Steelers, MVP Superbowl 40; and Emma Broyles, Miss America 2022.[62]

Japanese Americans

The first Japanese immigrant to the United States was a fourteen-year-old boy named Manjiro who was saved by Captain William

Whitfield aboard the ship *John Howland*, after he was shipwrecked about 300 miles from the coast of Japan. The date was May 7, 1843, and Manjiro changed his name to John Mung. Today, there are about 1.5 million Japanese Americans living in the United States, but from the time their ancestors disembarked in this country the Issei (first generation) have received a mixed and often unenthusiastic welcome, including the internment of 120,000 Japanese (70,000 American citizens) during World War II. Following the attack on Pearl Harbor on December 7, 1941, which led to the near devastation of our Pacific fleet and the death of 2,403 military personnel and civilians, intense anti–Japanese emotions gripped this country, but no person of Japanese ethnicity living in Hawaii or on the U.S. mainland was ever convicted of committing sabotage during the war. (See Chapter 4.)

For their part, many members of the second generation (Nisei) and their children (third generation or Sansei) have, like other Asian Americans, made major contributions to our society. While the flow of Japanese immigrants to the United States increased dramatically following the discovery of gold in California in 1849, the pace of their immigration was slowed when white American workers perceived them as a threat to their survival because of their willingness, like the Chinese, to perform squalid work for low wages. Frequently working alongside Chinese laborers, and later toiling in the sugar cane fields in Hawaii and on farms for pitiable wages, the Japanese in general quickly adapted to the American culture and recognized, despite cultural and legal barriers, that industriousness and education were tickets to success. While 34 percent of Japanese Americans have completed bachelor's degrees (almost double the rate of the general U.S. population), their rate of people who have completed some postgraduate work (18 percent, vs. 13 percent for the general U.S. population) is significantly lower than the 24 percent rate for all Asian Americans as a group. Still, there are fewer Japanese Americans living in poverty (8 percent) than for all other Asian Americans (10 percent) and all other non–Asian Americans (13 percent).

Most Japanese Americans are located on the West Coast of the United States. California with 393,000 (Los Angeles 177,000) is home to the most Japanese Americans. Honolulu, with 190,000, has the most of any city in the United States. The only major Japanese American population on the East Coast of the United States is found in New York, with 56,000. Since the Japanese have resided in the United States longer than other Asian groups, their average age is significantly older than the others. (Their median age is forty-one, compared to thirty-four for the entire Asian group of immigrants.) Their unemployment rate of

3 percent is lower than for the general population. The median household income for Japanese born in the United States (approximately $89,000) is significantly higher than the general non–Asian average. The Japanese American Citizens League creed of 1940 extolled the virtue of living in this country ("I am proud that I am an American citizen of Japanese ancestry, for my very background makes me appreciate more fully the wonderful advantages of this nation ... I pledge myself ... to defend her against all enemies, foreign and domestic"), but the treatment of Japanese and other Asians by European Americans has been, over the decades, despicable.[63]

The behavior of subsequent generations of Japanese Americans after such mistreatment is even more remarkable. The list of Japanese American notables is too long to enumerate here. As with other Asian Americans who assimilated into our culture, the longer their ethnic group remained in this country, the greater the scope of their contributions has been in our society. From arts and literature, to science and sports, Japanese Americans have left an indelible stamp on the fabric of our society. Beginning with George Shima (originally Ushijima Kinji), the first Japanese American millionaire in the United States, who was the object of racism despite his success as "the King of Potatoes" in California, Japanese Americans have made enormous contributions to our society. While breaking down ethnic and color barriers was a major challenge to the first generation, their children and grandchildren were able to break through entrenched racist obstacles to achieve success. Here are a few notable examples: Yoko Ono, widow of Beatle John Lennon, artist, musician, author, and peace activist; Hiroaki Aoki, founder of the restaurant chain Benihana; Francis Fukuyama, economist, philosopher, historian; Robert Hamada, former dean, University of Chicago Graduate School of Business; Wayne Inouye, former president and CEO of Gateway, Inc.; Darren Kimura, founder of Sopogy, inventor of MicroCSP technology; Kevin Tsujihara, former CEO of Warner Brothers; Sessue Hayakawa, late actor and Academy Award nominee; Seiji Ozawa, conductor of Boston Symphony, 1973–2002; George Takei, actor (playing Sulu) in *Star Trek*; Ann Curry, former anchor, NBC News and *The Today Show*; Harry B. Harris, Jr., retired four-star admiral and former commander of the U.S. Pacific fleet; Daniel Inouye, deceased World War II Medal of Honor recipient and U.S. Senator from Hawaii (for thirty-nine years); Susan K. Mashiko, retired major general, U.S. Air Force; Paul Nakasone, four-star general, commander of U.S. Cyber Command and former director of the National Security Agency and chief of the Central Security Service; Richard Aoki, civil rights activist and early member of the Black Panther Party; Bruce Harrell, mayor of Seattle; S.I. Hayakawa, late California State Senator and linguist; Michio Kaku, theoretical physicist; Syukuro Manabe, Nobel Laureate in physics (2021); Ellison Onizuka, first Asian American astronaut—died in the *Challenger* disaster, 1986; Bryan Clay, gold medal in Olympics decathlon (2008); Tommy Kono, two-time Olympic gold medalist weightlifter; Kyle Larson, 2021 NASCAR Cup Series Champion; Mike Lum, first Japanese American baseball player; Wally Kaname Yonamine, first Japanese American in the National Football League.

The Asian population in the United States will be 46 million people by 2060, a far cry from the 63,000 Asians in the 1870 census. The groups mentioned on the preceding pages comprise the majority of Asians living in the United States, and most of these people or their ancestors arrived after 1965 when quotas were lifted through the Hart–Celler Immigration Act. Today, nearly 20 million people in this country claim to be entirely of Asian descent, with another four million classifying themselves as combinations of Asian, Latinx, white, black, or

TABLE 1: COMPOSITION OF ASIAN AMERICANS

	Percent
Chinese	24
Indian	21
Filipino	19
Vietnamese	10
Korean	9
Japanese	7
Total	90
All Others as of 2019 (in thousands)	10

Pakistani	(554)
Thai	(343)
Cambodian	(339)
Hmong	(337)
Laotian	(254)
Bangladeshi	(208)
Nepalese	(198)
Burmese	(189)
Indonesian	(129)
Sri Lankan	(56)
Malaysian	(38)
Mongolian	(27)
Bhutanese	(24)
Okinawan	(14)

Table of the Distribution of Asian Americans (Abby Budiman and Neil Ruiz, "Key Facts About Asian Americans: A Diverse and Growing Population," Pew Research Center, April 2021, and Wikipedia, "Demographics of Asian Americans," en.wikipedia.org/wiki/Demographics_of_Asian_Americans).

some other variation. More than 7 percent of our population (7.2 percent) is composed of Asian Americans, and they face an increasing wave of anti–Asian discrimination based on centuries-old stereotypes that depict them as outsiders who are unwilling and unfit for assimilation.

As with many Asian Americans, intermarriage between ethnic groups, notably whites, blacks, Latinx, and Asians, has produced a generation of people who have battled racist stereotypes and survived to make considerable contributions to improving the quality of life in our society. Looking at the success of Asian Americans reveals how much we depend on the infusion of the creativity and ingenuity of immigrants, yet white supremacists cling to a vision of our society that flies in the face of history. We explore that phenomenon in the next chapter.

2

Myths About Asians and Immigrants

> "You're here, supposedly in a new land full of opportunity, but somehow have gotten trapped in a pretend version of the old country."
> —Charles Yu, *Interior Chinatown: A Novel*
> (New York: Vintage, 2020), p. 58.

When a Church of England priest, Thomas Malthus, published his *Essay on the Principle of Population* in 1798, he believed that population growth, if left unchecked, would outpace our ability to produce sufficient food to sustain humankind. Without preventive checks, such as limiting births, human population growth would eventually outpace our ability to sustain the population explosion. From his perspective at the end of the 18th century, food production increased arithmetically, while population growth increased geometrically. As a nascent economist, Malthus's doomsday scenario stamped the discipline as "the dismal science" because he predicted that positive population checks like war, pestilence, famine, and disease would ultimately limit the growth of humanity.

Fortunately, things have changed since he wrote his ominous treatise more than two centuries ago. Agricultural methods for increasing crops through improved cultivation of land have improved harvests. So, too, have genetically modified seeds that resist drought and disease while producing larger, more nutritious food crops, such as varieties of rice and other grains. While humankind is still plagued by Malthus's positive checks such as war, famine, and disease, these have not fundamentally altered what seems like our inexorable path to overpopulation.

The world's present population is approaching 8 billion. Despite the toll taken by wars in the last century (108 million people),[1] and 70 million deaths from famine,[2] the so-called "positive checks" that

Malthus believed would arrest population growth have only attenuated the world's population. The seemingly inexorable Malthusian journey toward overpopulation and extinction hasn't happened. Even though the casualty rate from war and famine seems staggering, diseases have claimed a large number—6.5 million people have died as a result of Covid-19 as of this writing, and more than 80 million people died in the 20th century from infectious diseases, notably smallpox, malaria, and tuberculosis.[3] Our ability to conquer and suppress infectious diseases has meant that the mortality rate of humans from such diseases has dropped precipitously while longevity has increased, with some exceptions, such as now from the effects of Covid-19.

What this means is that technological innovations have enabled humans to support increases in population despite the continued ravages of wars and other human conflicts that continue to wreak havoc on societies, such as the Russian invasion of Ukraine, and the outbreak of novel infectious diseases such as the new coronavirus that has plagued humans for several years. Despite human suffering from the maldistribution of goods and resources (positive Malthusian scourges), these just aren't sufficiently lethal to derail the human journey toward population oblivion.[4]

But there is one form of human behavior that holds the promise of avoiding the destruction of our species. Commonly known as "the technological imperative," it is the tendency of societies to experience lower population growth as the educational level of the populace increases. This phenomenon has been observed in the 19th and 20th centuries, most notably in Europe, England, and the United States. For example, at an annual growth rate of 4.64 percent, Syria is experiencing the fastest population growth in the world, and its population can be expected to double in less than eighteen years. Niger, with a population annual growth rate of 3.66 percent, can expect its population to double in around twenty years. Angola, with the world's third fastest annual population growth rate of 3.4 percent, will also double in size in about twenty years, as will the populations of Benin (3.39 percent) and Uganda (3.35 percent). On the other hand, Jamaica, ranked by the Central Intelligence Agency at 200th in the world for its negative population growth (-.08 percent), and Russia (-.17 percent), Germany (-.2 percent), and Poland (-.2 percent) will all see a decline in their populations (although Poland's population is presently increasing because of an influx of Ukrainians as a result of the conflict with Russia).

For purposes of comparison, the United States' annual population growth rate of positive .71 percent places it at 135th among the nations of the world in population growth, while India with an annual growth rate of positive 1.09 percent ranks 94th in the world and will double in size in about 70 years. China, with a population growth rate of positive .29 percent, is projected to see a decline in its population within the next quarter century,[5] primarily from its previous draconian population policy that emphasized having only one child. And Japan, experiencing an annual population decline of -.29 percent, is experiencing an aging and shrinking population.

Looking at the range of population growth across the world, one can readily see the correlation between technological development and the rate of population growth. There is an equally strong correlation between the technological development of a nation and the rate of infant and maternal mortality, as well as life expectancy and income.[6]

Generally speaking, a country's population will double according to the following projections: 1 percent annual growth = 70 years; 2 percent = 35 years; 3 percent = 23 years; 4 percent = 18 years. But there are outliers and contradictions to the technological imperative, and correlation does not prove causation. We should not assume that the past is necessarily going to predict the present or future. Part of the problem is related to the influence of prevailing values and norms that may prevent (or hasten) the adoption of technological innovations. Social scientist William Ogburn labeled the tendency for a culture to be reluctant in adopting technological innovation a "cultural lag"—that is, there is a conflict between prevailing cultural values and technology, preventing the diffusion of ideas.[7] Two prominent illustrations of this phenomenon are the Catholic Church's opposition (and that of other "right to lifers") to abortion and contraception as well as comprehensive sex education in schools, and our precarious relationship with nuclear weapons, which are still used as a "sword of Damocles" hanging over nations that have or aspire to have them.[8]

We should not become complacent about our prospects for avoiding a population disaster. There is no ironclad proof that the technological imperative is unalterable or infallible. Humankind is confronted with a conundrum: As long as humans have egos and scarcity exists because of living in resource-poor, organizationally backward, or governmentally deprived environments, humans will strive to maximize their advantages and situation over their perceived adversaries. While some astute writers have disparaged the folly of this zero-sum game, including the growing self-sustainability movement around the world that focuses on slow or no growth,[9] most economic thought continues to revolve around assumptions that emphasize the virtues of population growth and its attendant generated increases in gross domestic product (GDP, the sum of all goods and services generated by a country's economy in a given year). Since the human proclivity for using, consuming, and disposing seems insatiable (and is incentivized through government policies and corporate greed personified in advertising campaigns to stimulate acquisitiveness), new products and services are continually developed to stimulate demand among the population.

Birth rates of technologically advanced societies have been steadily decreasing; hence the need for new entrants into the labor force, that is, immigrants, to provide labor and creative energy to unleash the industrial and technological forces that ostensibly provide for the well-being of the population. As long as economies function on the basis of maldistribution and scarcity of resources, the model that accentuates growth will persist and will depend on the infusion of immigrants to maintain the viability of technologically advanced societies.[10]

Enter the Asians ...

The immigration experiences and success of Asian Americans defy stereotypes about them. Obviously, the longer an immigrant group resides here, the more assimilated its members become, and the greater their contributions to this country. In 2019, median household income for Asian Americans was $85,800, compared to $61,800 for non–Asian households. Many of the arguments, federal policies, and stereotypes that have been used against Asian immigrants were used against virtually all other immigrant groups, going back to the founding of our nation. The Irish and Germans encountered prejudice in the mid–1800s when hundreds of thousands of them emigrated to this country. The ranks of Irish immigrants swelled concomitantly with anti–Catholicism as the Irish fled their country because of the potato crop failure that led to destitution and famine.[11]

The tactic used by affluent whites was to pit one group against another, especially whites against non-whites, and against later immigrants from southern Europe in the late 1880s and of course, before them, Asians.[12] Before that, genocide was practiced against Native Americans, the indigenous people whose land was stolen from them by white settlers who swarmed across their land like locusts, using, consuming, and disposing of the natural resources that Indians stewarded and cherished.[13] At the tip of the anti-immigrant spear, one of the primary sources of hostility directed toward immigrants (initially blacks and then Asians) was labor unions who jealously defended the "right" of white workers to toil in the factories of this nascent manufacturing dynamo. Preservation of labor turf, the right of white workers to be exploited by America's gilded captains of industry, led to the rise of racist memes that stereotyped workers of color as less skilled, less capable, and less deserving of work, despite the demeaning and dehumanizing characteristics of such depictions.

Casting blacks and Asians as intruders into the world of work had a concomitant ideological frame that depicted them as undeserving of the "fruits of their labor"—rhetoric that was used to not only denigrate and disparage workers of color, but also to justify their mistreatment. They were willing to toil and persevere in adverse environmental climates (e.g., Chinese and Japanese laborers did most of the work on the Pacific side of the transcontinental railroad, recruited for these jobs when white workers refused to take them). At times, but not always according to prevailing stereotypes, they worked for lower rates of pay than the predominantly white union workers demanded.

To this day, stereotypical memes about immigrant laborers depict them as little more than uncivilized animals willing to forgo "modern," safe working conditions with livable wages. Yet in 2020, in the United States 4,764 workers died on the job, 3.4 per 100,000, but the death rate for Black and Latinx workers was 4.5 per 100,000 according to the Bureau of Labor Statistics. These figures mean that 13 workers die on the job every day in this country.[14]

The Truth About Immigrant Labor

Much confusion surrounds the purported impact that immigration has on the native workforce. Criticism of immigration with its supposed negative impact on employment and wages was particularly acute following waves of immigration associated with the influx of foreign workers fleeing conflict, as in World War II, the Korean and Vietnamese wars that produced surges in Asian immigrants, and, more recently, the wave of Latinx, especially Mexican, immigrants following the civil and economic unrest associated with the Great Recession and the rise in drug-related crime in Central America. However, considerable research on the effects of immigration on employment and wages on native workers, much of it conducted during the recent spike in Latinx immigration to the United States, conclusively demonstrates that negative effects are inconsequential.

Giovanni Peri, an economist at the University of California, Davis, conducted an analysis of 27 studies between 1982 and 2013 that measured the effects immigrants had on native workers' wages and concluded that among the industrialized countries in his study (e.g., the

United States, the United Kingdom, Spain, Canada, Austria, Israel, and Germany) there was little or no effect on wages between immigrants and native workers.[15] In fact, Peri reported that while immigration may slightly lower the wages of less educated workers, immigrants who are highly skilled actually may enhance productivity and improve the economy of their host country. He concluded that "More open immigration policies which allow for balanced entry of immigrants of different education and skill levels, are likely to have no adverse effects on native workers' wages and may pave the way for productivity growth." Our previous discussion of the contributions of Asians to the United States demonstrates the veracity of his conclusions: Immigrants stimulate the economy of their host society through their physical and intellectual contributions, which improve the quality of life of everyone.

One conclusion we can draw from this discussion is that living in a society dominated by white values and standards of beauty has created a desire among Asian Americans to become part of the dominant society in looks as well as behavior. This sentiment is prevalent among other immigrant groups. Although they have been stigmatized as being lazy, research indicates that Asians, as well as other ethnic minorities, journey to America to improve their socioeconomic position, not to get public assistance. While white working-class opposition to immigrants has been a consistent theme based on the fear of competition for jobs, despite the overtly oppressive nature of some working conditions, threats to the livelihood of working men and women were bolstered by ideological and racist memes that denigrated and disparaged immigrants. Paramount among these memes were the allegations that immigrants, especially Asians in the latter part of the 19th century through the mid–20th century, were willing to work for less than the "going wage." Such sentiments were buttressed by the large number of Asian workers (primarily Chinese and Japanese) who helped construct the transcontinental railroad and the California infrastructure. Accusations that Asian immigrants (and today's Latinx immigrants) gladly toiled in harsh, even deleterious work environments were linked to the racist trope that they came from non–Western cultures, looked different (external features such as skin color, eye shape, and hair), and were biologically, as well as socially and psychologically, inferior to whites and hence less deserving of admission to our society and sharing in the social and economic opportunities available to whites.

Bolstered by late 19th- and early 20th-century eugenicists such as Madison Grant, Carl Brigham, and Lothrop Stoddard,[16] popular white culture in the United States became increasingly insular and isolationist as a reaction to the influx of immigrants. Although hostility toward

Asian immigrants and black workers had been endemic to white society for decades,[17] the American manufacturing engine needed an infusion of industrial laborers in the early to mid–20th century, and as the late historian Tyler Stovall pointed out, Ellis Island, the entry and processing point for more than 12 million migrants (mostly whites from Eastern and Southern European countries), was emblematic of "white freedom."[18] These aspiring millionaires, who fled autocratic, tyrannical, and inhospitable environments in their countries of origin, came to the United States fueled with dreams and illusions, only to find that the streets were not paved with gold and the living conditions in tenements were squalid. However, being white, they could learn the language and assimilate, something that blacks and Asians (and later Latinx) had difficulty doing.

"By the Sweat of Thy Brow, Shall Thou Eat Bread"

Another widely held misperception about immigrants is that they come to the United States to obtain welfare and associated social services, such as health care, food, and rent subsidies. This charge had been leveled against Asians for over a hundred years, and Donald Trump expanded on the bogus theme by accusing immigrants of using "chain migration," that is, the practice of immigrants following relatives to a place—in this case the United States. Immigration law allows green card holders (people who have been given permanent resident status to live and work in the United States) to bring family members (hence the practice is also known as family unification) here to join them. Visas may be granted to one's family and are given primarily to green card holders' spouses and minor children. If citizenship is granted (which can take many years), then married children, parents, and siblings may be allowed to emigrate to this country, but all individuals must prove they have a means to support themselves financially upon arrival. The number of immigrants allowed to enter this country is capped for each immigrant group, but there is a backlog of more than eight million requests, despite more than 800,00 applications being denied in a recent year.[19] Although this country has benefited from the physical and creative energy of immigrants, Trump remained intransigent about admitting them, especially non-whites who came from what he crudely called "shit-hole countries," and Muslims. He even proposed violating the tenets of the 14th Amendment, which gives citizenship to everyone born in this country.[20]

The United States remains a favorite destination for immigrants in search of better lives, and the number of people displaced by conflict, climate change, and unstable or autocratic governments is increasing around the world, estimated to be more than 100 million in 2022.[21] As we have seen, Asian immigrants to the United States were primarily male, a phenomenon reinforced by federal policies, such as the 1875 Page Act, but while male immigrants exceeded females in the past, female legal admissions to this country have been increasing in recent years.[22]

One persistent myth about immigrants to the United States is that they come here so they can access our public assistance programs. The Clinton Administration eliminated "welfare" in 1996 and substituted Temporary Assistance to Needy Families (TANF), which overhauled the public assistance program. The poor and immigrants were traditionally suspected of having a deficient work ethic, and stigma was heaped on them, ostensibly for being morally depraved. Their assumed propensity for using public assistance was a way of isolating and labeling them as social lepers. Ironically, studies show immigrants are less likely than native citizens to use public assistance programs. (The reader should be cognizant of the fact that only legal tax-paying permanent residents are eligible to qualify for public assistance programs after having lived here for five years, yet nonresident immigrants must still pay taxes and they are not able to access these services.)[23]

The libertarian Cato Institute reported that immigrant households living in poverty consumed less public assistance than native citizen households living in the same conditions.[24] For example, Cato Institute researchers reported that adult immigrants used Medicaid (health assistance for the medically indigent and needy) at a lower rate (20 percent less) than U.S. citizens, and their children were less likely to use the CHIP (Children's Health Insurance Program), 16 percent less, and SNAP (Supplemental Nutrition Assistance Program, formerly known as food stamps), 18 percent less. Even when immigrants qualified for public assistance programs, the cost per capita was lower than for native citizens—for example, 42 percent less for the use of Medicaid and two-thirds less for immigrant children in the CHIP program. While this pertains to documented immigrants, it is estimated that undocumented immigrants, who are not eligible for public assistance programs, pay billions of dollars a year in taxes.

The Institute for Taxation and Economic Policy reported that undocumented immigrants paid $11.7 billion in state and local taxes in 2013.[25] This included $7 billion in sales taxes, $1.1 billion in income taxes, and $3.6 billion in property taxes. California, New York, Texas, Illinois, New Jersey, and Florida received the most revenue from taxes from undocumented immigrants. Undocumented immigrants paid a higher percentage of their earnings in taxes than the top 1 percent of taxpayers (8 percent versus 5.4 percent).[26]

Records indicate that between half and three-quarters of undocumented immigrant households file income tax returns using Individual Tax Identification Numbers, and many who don't file returns pay taxes through paycheck deductions as well as sales and property taxes (even if they rent, because it is added to their rental fee).

Tax scholar and law professor Francine Lipman identified the many ways undocumented immigrants pay for services they do not receive in this country. She estimated they pay tens of billions of dollars every year in local, state, and federal taxes that help keep our nation solvent. In Social Security taxes alone, Professor Lipman estimated that undocumented immigrants paid more than half a trillion dollars between 2000 and 2007, and they will pay an additional $611 billion to the Social Security system over the next seventy-five years. Many undocumented immigrants have mismatched Social Security numbers or don't understand how to file requests for refunds of federal taxes. Consequently, they overpay them, amounting to a "fiscal windfall" for states and the federal government.[27]

In 2019, undocumented immigrants paid an estimated $492 billion in taxes in the United States,[28] and they would earn and pay much more if they had temporary or permanent legal status. As it is, immigrant spending power is estimated to be $1.3 trillion annually.[29]

Undocumented immigrants also contribute more to public benefit programs than they consume. This is understandable since some work without valid Social Security numbers, and undocumented immigrants are not eligible to receive Medicaid, CHIP, SNAP, TANF, and SSI (Supplemental Security Income), nor were they eligible to receive benefits from the $2 trillion Coronavirus Aid, Relief, and Economic Security Act (CARES Act) even if they filed federal tax returns. In fact, welfare expenditures per immigrant in 2016 were $3,718, which was 39 percent less than the $6,081 for the average value of welfare benefits received by natives residing in the United States.[30]

Illegal Immigration and Crime

Another popular myth about immigrants, especially undocumented (illegal) immigrants, is that they are criminally disposed and violent. Professor Alex Nowrasteh, one of the most prolific researchers about the relationship between immigration and crime, conducted a review of studies that assessed this situation and concluded that "immigrants are less crime prone than natives or have no effect on crime rates."[31] On the contrary, Nowrasteh reported that "increased immigration does not increase crime and sometimes even causes crime rates to fall."

A more current analysis of this phenomenon by Light, He, and Robey used data from the Texas Department of Public Safety. Texas is the only state where every jurisdiction is required by law to report all class B misdemeanors or higher. Class C offenses are ineligible for prison in that state, and many are resolved through citations. In Texas, there is a 96 percent compliance rate with the law and, consequently, little missing data. Texas reported more noncitizens arrested in recent years than any in other state except California.

The researchers found "no evidence that undocumented immigrants are more heavily involved in property or drug offenses in Texas."[32] They concluded that the data demonstrated undocumented immigrants had a substantially lower crime rate than native-born and legal immigrants for felony offenses. United States-born citizens were twice as likely to be arrested for violent crimes, two and a half times more likely to be arrested for drug offenses, and four times more likely to be arrested for property crimes. The arrest rates for undocumented immigrants were stable to decreasing over the study years (2012–2018).[33]

Despite popular assumptions that undocumented immigrants are lawbreakers, and the fact that our federal government spends more on immigrant enforcement than all other criminal law enforcement combined, the data do not support these illusions. Obviously, immigrants (legal and illegal) do not wish to interact with law enforcement because this may result in their deportation. Immigrants may even be reluctant to report being victimized because that might bring unwarranted attention to them.

The "healthy immigrant thesis" attempts to explain the relatively low rate of criminal activity among immigrants. From this perspective, many immigrants come to the United States in search of jobs so they can work, not commit crimes. We explore these phenomena later in Chapter 7 in a discussion of the social and psychological implications of Asians being labeled as the "model minority."

Immigrants and Illness

One of the most pernicious stereotypes about immigrants, and one used against Asians today, is the allegation that they bring diseases into the United States. This meme has been used to isolate and stigmatize foreigners for over a century, and it is linked to racist tropes that portray immigrants from non–Anglo countries as dirty, disease-ridden, and unassimilable. The Chinese and Japanese were the targets of such racial animus in the 19th century, because of physical and cultural differences in appearance between them and the dominant white Anglo majority.

The pursuit of industrialization in the later part of the 19th century and early part of the 20th century in the United States precipitated a concomitant increase in white supremacist rhetoric, manifested in the eugenics movement and the writings of Grant, Stoddard, and Brigham.[34] Native-born white workers resented the intrusion of foreign labor, prompting an unremitting cascade of barely veiled racial epithets hurled at immigrants. Initially, in the later part of the 19th century, the visibly different Asians bore the brunt of discrimination. Later, during the influx in the early part of the 20th century of immigrants from southern and eastern Europe (Jews, Italians, Greeks, Poles) who fled their countries in search of better social, political, and economic lives in this "promised land," the ire of labor unions and public apprehension about the intrusion of "different" kinds of people into our society shifted to them. The promise was temporized by their mistreatment at the hands of unscrupulous landlords who piled them into tenement houses, and social opprobrium fueled by the isolationist and racist belief that the introduction of their genetic material would contaminate and degrade the gene pool of the white Anglo stock of this nation. While others such as de Gobineau and Chamberlain had earlier decried the alleged despoliation of Anglo/Nordic/Aryan genes by the introduction of "alien" genetic material,[35] the profusion of eugenic thinking in the early part of the 20th century had a dramatic impact on popular stereotypes about immigrants.

The principal focus of public scrutiny and disaffection for immigrants was rooted in the false assumption that they were not only socially undesirable but unhealthy and transmitters of disease. In their important analysis of this phenomenon, Markel and Stern[36] clearly demonstrated the fallacy of this purported association. Despite the widespread belief that immigrants spread diseases, they noted that the perception of infected immigrants was "typically far greater than the actual danger."

Historically, in the United States, there has been a preference for "old" immigrants (from England, Ireland, Scotland, Belgium, Denmark, France, Germany, the Netherlands, Sweden, Norway, and Switzerland) over "new" immigrants (from Russia, Poland, Austria–Hungary, the Balkans, Greece, Italy, Spain, Portugal, and Turkey). Looking at major waves of immigrants to the United States, Markel and Stern linked public health concerns to political considerations that influenced public opinion and governmental policies more than public health facts. For example, although immigrants (primarily those "old" and poorer ones who travelled to this country in steerage quarters on ships) were given medical exams upon arrival, the exams were often perfunctory, although somewhat intrusive and abusive. The ostensible prevalence of the infectious eye disease trachoma, which if left untreated could lead to blindness, was investigated at Ellis and Angel islands, often by flipping the eyelids of incoming immigrants to search for signs of redness and scarring.[37]

Mexican and Chinese immigrants, people who didn't conform to the stereotypical assumptions about "healthy" individuals, were more carefully screened than other immigrants (whites and especially those coming from Anglo countries). Ellis Island (on the east coast of the United States), the destination of immigrants from predominantly white countries, recorded a rejection rate of 1 percent between 1891 and 1924, while Angel Island (on the west coast of the United States), the principal debarkation point for Asians and Mexicans between 1910 and 1940, recorded a 17 percent rejection rate for health reasons. Although the Chinese comprised 1 percent of all immigrants in these years, they accounted for 4 percent of all immigrants being annually deported. Unlike for immigrants at Ellis Island, stool samples were demanded of Asian and Mexican immigrants, ostensibly looking for hookworms, which were purportedly widespread in these groups. One can easily discern the racist stereotypes used for immigrants from these groups: swarthy, unclean, criminally minded, degenerate, parasite-riddled, lousy, defective, feeble, infected.

The prevalence of such physical labels evolved into a preoccupation with political labels as the United States became embroiled in a Cold War with the Soviet Union and China. The tenor of anti-immigrant rhetoric focused on the necessity for restricting immigrants who might be politically subversive of our culture and society because of possible communist ties that posed an existential threat to our capitalistic social system. This line of reasoning was personified by the junior senator from Wisconsin, Joe McCarthy, who made a dubious career based on allegations about his political enemies from 1947 to 1957. Such reasoning permeated the Immigration and Nationality Act of 1952 (also called the McCarran–Walter Act) and led to the practice of medical inspections of foreigners prior to their embarkation by plane for the United States.[38]

As Markel and Stern noted, "The number of 'diseased' immigrants has always been infinitesimal when compared to the number of newcomers admitted to this country." This statement pertained to the influx of Asians following the liberalization of immigration after 1965 with the passage of the Hart–Celler (Immigration and Nationality) Act. Much of the angst over the increased immigration of Asians and others following the liberalization of U.S. immigration policies was attributable to blatant jingoistic, racist statements of policymakers who attempted to stigmatize immigrants by using medical labels to justify excluding them from this country. Frequently used terms and stereotypes associated with the alleged infection of the native population by immigrants were contagion, mental disorders, unclean, contaminated, and impure.

It was not uncommon for politicians to assume a link between the purported inferior physical health of immigrants and their supposed social and moral deficiencies to exclude people of color, notably Asians and blacks. While such thinly veiled attempts to exclude immigrants of color from our society have waned in recent years, this did not prevent Donald Trump from stigmatizing them,[39] or former CNN business host Lou Dobbs from falsely alleging in 2007 that immigrants were responsible for increasing the prevalence of leprosy (Hansen's disease)—a position he retracted when confronted with the facts. Still, the allegation contributed to his dismissal from CNN, although he found a home at the Fox Business Network until his show was canceled in February 2021.[40]

While the negative policies and rhetoric directed against immigrants subsided during the decades following World War II, the AIDS epidemic that began in the 1980s precipitated a new and socially toxic anti-immigrant sentiment in our society. With Angel and Ellis islands closed, the predominant new ports of entry were John F. Kennedy, O'Hare, Miami, San Francisco, and Los Angeles International airports. But as Markel and Stern note, with improvements in public health, maternal and child health care, vaccinations, and drug treatments, today's immigrants are healthier than their predecessors and pose little public health challenge to our society. Nevertheless, such facts have not dissuaded political leaders, even Trump, from denigrating Asians and labeling them as responsible for spreading Covid-19, or as he was fond of saying, "the Chinese flu."

After reviewing the relationship between the spread of disease and immigrants, Markel and Stern concluded that "more often than not these arguments have been motivated by and closely intertwined with, ideologies of racism, nativism, and national security rather than substantial epidemiological or medical observations."

3

Gambling, Gangs and Deviant Behavior

> "'Contrary to stereotypes about Chinese people, quite a number of us are not meek, passive, law-abiding citizens.'"
> —Bill Lee, *Chinese Playground: A Memoir*, San Francisco: Rhapsody Press, 1999.

It's rather paradoxical that this chapter is devoted to a topic that denotes deviancy about a group of people from diverse ethnicities who, for the most part, are paragons of virtue. Asian Americans have a long history of abiding by the laws, policies, and regulations that order our society. As most immigrants know, the quickest path to being deported or forfeiting one's freedom is to violate group norms. For most of their time in the United States, Asian Americans have tried to blend into society and avoid behavior that might accentuate their differences. Asians, Hawaiians, and other Pacific Islanders account for only 1.6 percent of all crimes reported by the FBI, and only 1.4 percent of total arrests for persons under eighteen years of age.[1] The very concept of "model minority," which we explore further in Chapter 7, reflects this phenomenon.

Despite their attempts to pass as American, some of their physical attributes, such as skin color and eye shape, have been used to distinguish them from the Anglo mainstream, causing some Asian Americans to refer to themselves as "perpetual foreigners." One of the recurrent stereotypes about Asian Americans is their penchant for gambling, reinforced through literature that references their preoccupation with such activities. This is also reflected in public statements of anti–Asian immigration advocates in the 19th and early 20th centuries and expressed in anti-immigration (particularly anti–Asian) laws such as the Chinese Exclusion Acts that began in the late 1800s.

Some evidence points to a higher prevalence of problem gambling among Asian Americans than other ethnic groups, but the conditions that are conducive to fostering illicit gambling behavior, especially poverty, unemployment, blocked educational opportunities, prejudice, and discrimination, affect the mental health outlook of us all. When people are deprived of legitimate means for upward mobility or perceive that the path to their progress is blocked, they may choose to engage in illicit or extralegal methods for obtaining success. Turning to gambling and gangs is, from the perspective of people who are denied equality of opportunities through legitimate means, an alternative method for becoming successful in a social system perceived as rigged against them. Much as some people may embrace prayer, religion, or magic, gambling and gangs may be perceived as a way out of one's plight—a path to success and security unobtainable through work and individual initiative because of societal barriers that limit one's opportunities.

We have seen that most Asian American immigrants worked tirelessly and under adverse conditions to achieve the American Dream. Diminishing their efforts and attempting to attribute a propensity for gambling overlooks the learned, cultural component of such behavior. We must look at the historical social influences that shaped Asians' and Asian Americans' interest in gambling. To do this, we begin by assessing the extent and nature of gambling in Asia prior to the flight of immigrants to the United States.

Gambling in Asia: Past and Present

Gambling has deep roots in Asia, especially in China, where evidence of an ancient lottery dates back to 2300 BCE.[2] Many modern games of chance have their roots in ancient Chinese games, for example, keno, which may have been based on the Chinese game of *baige piao* (white pigeon ticket) that was related to the use of homing pigeons and helped to fund the Great Wall. The first evidence of playing cards can be traced to China in the 9th century CE. The late anthropologist John A. Price noted that gambling flourished in China after 1000 BCE.[3] Other Asian nations such as Thailand, Burma, Malaya (today Malaysia), and the Philippines were also places that entertained gambling activities.

According to Price, early Vedic hymns in India described gambling for cattle and chariot races and the use of dice, and the story of the struggles of King Nala, who reputedly gambled away his kingdom using loaded dice and then regained it using "honest" ones, became legendary. Wagering on contests between animals was a common form of gambling in the ancient world. Cock fighting was observed in the Indus Valley as early as 2000 BCE, and all sorts of contests were conducted using everything from fighting fish to dogs, even crickets. While Islamic countries have a lower rate of gambling than other nations in the Asian region because of religious strictures against it, gambling among all social strata in Asia is, today, rampant. Even though communist countries such as mainland China outlawed gambling in 1949, it thrives among all strata of society as a remnant of culture and tradition.

The tradition of gambling in China is reflected in the popularity of such games as *liu-po*, a dice game that was popular during the Han Dynasty. Some contemporary interest in gambling is evidenced in the popularity of daily numbers games such as *chap ji kee*, which was popular in Singapore until the late 1960s, and also reflects the Chinese interest in luck, numerology, and superstition. *Sic bo*, an ancient Chinese dice game where the dealer rolls three dice and players wager on possible outcomes, was brought to the United States in the beginning of the 20th century by Chinese immigrants.

An illustration of the cultural tradition of gambling and its influence on people is found in the former Portuguese city of Macau, which became the world's gambling mecca prior to the spread of Covid-19. In 1999, when the city of 680,000 residents became a special administrative region of China, it entertained 39 million visitors, generating $36 billion (six times that of Las Vegas, which has 90 percent more land). Gambling was legalized in Macau by the Portuguese in 1847, but since the clampdown on gambling activities there in 2012 by Xi Jinping, the President of China, and the devastation wrought by the Covid pandemic, visitors have dwindled to less than 6 million, and revenues to just $300 million, compared to $535 million in Las Vegas, for 2020. Still, gaming accounts for 80 percent of tax revenues in Macau, and efforts to diversify Macau's economy have not been particularly successful.[4] The opulence of the gambling city is perhaps best represented by the Venetian Macau, the seventh largest building by floor area in the world. At approximately ten million square feet with 640 gaming tables and 1,760 slot machines, it also boasts three thousand guest suites and thirty restaurants. Despite hard times brought on by the pandemic, there are still about forty junket operators in the city, as well as numerous online wagering opportunities (begun in 1994) to cater to high rollers and compulsive gamblers around the world, and post–Covid gambling activity has increased.

Contemporary Gambling Among Asians in America

A prominent stereotype about Asian Americans is the assumption that they are obsessed with gambling. Stories abound about their propensity to engage in and wager on games. Historical cultural tradition is used to explain the prevalence of gambling behavior among Asian Americans going back to the 1800s when they toiled in the western mountains of the United States in pursuit of gold and silver and worked indefatigably constructing railroads, but one must be careful not to paint the diverse group of Asian Americans with a broad brush.[5] While some Asian cultures emphasize the role of luck, chance, and fate in one's success in life, numerous ethnic groups comprise the Asian American category, and diverse attitudes and behaviors exist among these groups that defy generalization about their gambling. The problem related to the use of stereotypes is one of generalization. While there may be a kernel of truth at the core of a stereotype, it is unwise and unfair to characterize an entire group as representative of the stigmatized trait. Keep this in mind as we summarize some studies about gambling behavior among Asian Americans.

One of the largest epidemiological studies ever conducted in the United States was a representative survey of adults eighteen years and older residing in households during 2001–2002. More than 43,000 people were questioned about their use of alcohol and related conditions.[6] The researchers based their conclusions about problem gambling on 11,153 people who gambled five or more times a week. They found that Asian Americans had the highest rate of gambling among the groups reporting, 2.3 percent, compared to 1.2 percent for white respondents and 2.2 percent for blacks. Noting that cultural differences, access to gambling, and acceptability, that is, tradition, figured prominently in the diverse rates, the researchers labeled pathological gambling as an "impulse control disorder." But the findings and conclusions about Asian Americans must be tempered by the fact that only twenty-four Asians were included in the study and this small number of people was merged with an equally small number of respondents (fifteen) who were Native American. Nevertheless, the findings point to higher rates of gambling than in other groups in our population, and they have been borne out by other studies, especially of college students.[7]

Asian college students have been found to have problems with gambling in the United States. Luczak and Wall reported that one of the most significant predictors of problem gambling among their subjects was being a Chinese or Korean male.[8] Chan et al.[9] found more problem gamblers among Asian college students than among white college students. A study of 3,058 college students at a large Southern university in the United States found a larger proportion of Asian students than of white, black, and Hispanic students met the criteria of being problem gamblers, and the researchers proposed policy changes to address this situation.[10]

After reviewing the literature on problem gambling and interacting with patients and staff, Nam and Hicks,[11] who were on the staff at the Maryvale Treatment centers, concluded that Asian Americans are prone to problem and pathological gambling. While there appears to be some evidence indicative of cultural traditions that might predispose to high participation in gambling activities among Asian Americans, studies have actually shown that gambling prevalence is lower among Asian Americans than among white Americans.[12] Further examination of the data reveals that Asian Americans appear to have higher rates of problem and pathological gambling than the general population (as much as three times that of whites) when they abuse this activity.

Analyses of multiple studies of gambling behavior in different countries reveal that Asians, especially males, are more likely to engage in gambling than other ethnic groups (one study reported they are seven times more likely than whites), and they experience higher rates of financial hardship, domestic violence, and suicide than the other ethnic groups studied.[13] Despite the occurrence of these phenomena, Asians are less likely to seek professional aid for gambling problems than are members of other ethnic groups. This situation may be related to denial of social and family problems, an attempt to avoid shame and "save face," and/or lack of knowledge of and access to treatment facilities.

The Lure of Mah Jongg

The only time I saw pineapple as a kid was when my mother had her friends over to play mah jongg. It was a weekly ritual for her, and I'll never forget the sound of the tiles and boisterous chatter as they called out the symbols on the little rectangular tiles they stacked on the playing table. Mah jongg, a table game that includes 144 or 136 ceramic tiles, was invented in the early 1800s in China, where it was called pinyin (sparrow), and has some commonalities with the card game gin rummy. Usually played with four people arranged around a table, the winner is the first person who matches fourteen themed tiles that correspond to printed symbols on them, for example, directions, flowers, seasons, dragons, and dots.

The game became popular in China and other Asian countries and was imported to the United States in the 1920s. Abercrombie and Fitch sold twelve thousand mah jongg sets in 1920 during the first American infatuation with the game, and Joseph Babcock published his "Rules of Mah-Jongg" (the Red Book) at that time, although the rules were later simplified and altered. The game was so popular in the United States that the Original Memphis Five recorded the song "Since Ma is Playing Mah Jong" and entertainer Eddie Cantor sang it.

Interest in the game fizzled out in the United States, but it remained popular in China and other Southeast Asian countries. In 1949, the Communist Chinese government derided mah jongg because it was thought to create problem gambling, but it enjoyed a resurgence in the United States in the 1930s, especially among Jewish women. In 1937 the National Mah Jongg League was formed and created the first American mah jongg rulebook: "Maajh: The American Version of the Ancient Chinese Game." In 1999 a second organization, the American Mah Jongg Association, was formed, and a resurgence of interest occurred in the game.

Mah jongg is the preeminent table game in Japan, with nearly 8 million players and approximately 9,000 mah jongg parlors in 2020. The game is treated as a sport with teams, logos, and nearly 2,000 professional players who receive salaries and vie for supremacy in playoffs. Today, "Mahjong Trails" is one of the top-grossing games on Facebook. Currently, it is estimated that more than half a million people play the game in the United States, and although many of them are not Asian Americans, the game is still popular among them, although interest in it is being replaced by high-tech wagering and casino gambling.

Cultural Components of Asian Gambling

Whether it's a matter of betting more frequently or wagering more money, common stereotypes about Asians and Asian Americans are that they like to gamble, are "high rollers" in casinos, and generally enjoy gambling more than other ethnic groups in our society. The prevalence of these stereotypes has led the casino industry to target Asian Americans from all socioeconomic levels. The Lunar New Year, a joyous time when Asians celebrate households, deities, and ancestors, and when bad luck of the old year is replaced by good luck in the new one, has been coopted by some casinos to entice Asians to journey to Nevada for the celebration. For example, the Lucky Dragon Casino in Las Vegas was the first Asian-themed resort designed to attract Asians, but it failed and was sold in 2019 for $36 million to become the Ahern Hotel and Convention Center—a nongambling institution. However, reporters have noted the presence of Asian liaisons (especially Chinese) in assisting patrons in casinos, providing buses to transport Asian Americans (especially elderly patrons) to casinos, featuring Asian entertainers and karaoke nights, and even advertising in Asian newspapers about trips to nearby casinos, as well as providing stipends to elderly gamblers. Paul Osaki, the executive director of the Japanese Cultural and Community Center of Northern California, once remarked, "An astronomical amount of money leaves the Asian community for gambling industry coffers."[14] Attempts to snag Asian American players in casinos even include the promotion of traditional Chinese games such as pai gow (a form of poker introduced in the United States in 1985).

Professors Mathews and Volberg have noted the toll that gambling behavior takes on Asians and their families,[15] and a review of twenty-five articles from 1840 to 2008 encompassing nearly 13,000 Chinese community participants from seven countries found that social gambling was widespread among them; that prevalence rates for problem gambling increased in the ethnic group over the years; and that they were reluctant to seek professional help for their problem.[16]

Whether from attitudes that are conducive to promoting gambling and risk-taking behavior or, as some researchers contend, from the availability of games and opportunities that may predispose Asians to participate in gambling, cultural determinants such as early exposure and involvement in gambling activities have been shown to be risk factors for problem gambling among Asians as well as non–Asians. In fact, as researcher Wooksoo Kim concluded, after reviewing twenty-four studies of gambling behavior among Asians in the United States, Australia, and Canada, the availability of and access to gambling activities is a greater risk factor than cultural (learned) attitudes that may influence the level and frequency of gambling among Asians.[17] As we have shown, Asian American immigrants, especially those people who are economically disadvantaged, and elderly people who seek stimulation from interaction with others and escape from daily monotony through risk taking are candidates for problem gambling and have been targeted by gambling enterprises as prospective customers, creating a self-fulfilling prophecy that perpetuates the stereotype about the propensity of Asians and Asian Americans to indulge in gambling activities.[18]

The Role of Gangs in Asian Life

A call came in to the manager of the Great Wall Chinese restaurant on 4th Avenue in St. Petersburg, Florida, warning him that a trio of shakedown punks would be arriving soon to demand $200 a week to "protect" him from problems at the business. Earlier in the day, the three Asian young men had made stops to collect their bounty at two other Chinese establishments on the street where nine Chinese restaurants were located. But this time, thanks to the warning, the manager was ready for the thugs. Brandishing a gun and handcuffs, he shot out the tires of their car and, with help from other staff, held the would-be extortionists until the police arrived. They were charged with extortion and armed robbery.[19]

Ironically, thirty years after this incident, all of the nine Chinese restaurants on 4th Avenue in St. Petersburg, Florida, are out of business, more as a result of failed economics than extortion, but the pattern of this series of crimes is eerily reminiscent of criminal behavior that threatened, and in some ways continues to threaten, the social and economic status of Asian Americans and defies the stereotype of the "model minority" and the strict upbringing of Chinese children described by the late Professor Betty Lee Sung: "Disobedience [of children] is not tolerated and corporal punishment is freely meted out [by the mother]."[20] According to Professor Sung, "The Chinese child is taught that when he does wrong, it is not a personal matter between himself and his conscience, he brings dishonor and shame upon his family and his loved ones."[21] Although she stated that the upbringing of Chinese children focused on character building and dignity, with Chinese children taught that "forbearance, patience and sacrifice are virtues and that self-interest must be subordinated to the larger good,"[22] some youthful members of Chinese communities around the United States obviously didn't get that message. While Sung presented evidence indicating that it was rare for Chinese children to appear in court for criminal offenses in the 1950s, increasing immigration of Chinese and other Asian youth following wars in Southeast Asia and the liberalization of immigration policies accompanying the Hart–Celler immigration law in the mid–1960s ushered in a flood of new, impetuous, and aggressive Asian youth who proved to be willing allies of the criminal underworld in cities around the United States.

According to one source, there are more than 33,000 gangs in the United States with a million and half members.[23] Most gangs are found in urban areas and today are Black and Latino. Gang behavior among Asians in the United States was more prevalent in the 1970s, 1980s, and 1990s. Gangs were linked to the growth of tongs in 17th-century China, when they were devoted to overthrowing the Manchu-Qing Dynasty. Then a group of Taoist monks tried to lead an insurrection against the ruling elite without success. It wasn't until 1911 that the Chinese monarchy, which had survived for 2,132 years, was overthrown and the Republic of China was proclaimed on January 1, 1912. But the allure of the tongs persisted in China and later in this country, as Chinese immigrants made their way to the United States.

A distinction must be made between the tongs, which began in the 12th century in China, and triads. Traditionally, tongs were a place for Chinese people of the same ethnicity, trade, or industry to assemble for social interaction, engage in recreational activities, settle disputes, and provide mutual assistance and support for one another. Tongs were legal entities, whereas triads, which began as the Hung Mun Triad or society in the 17th century, bound participants by oath and pledges to overthrow the Qing Dynasty. According to Lo and Kwok,[24] the original triad did not begin as a criminal enterprise but evolved into one when China became a republic. Then dozens of triad societies emerged, many of them criminally disposed. The two world wars and the Japanese invasion of China propelled the triads into Hong Kong, which became the epicenter of triad activity. By 1960 it was estimated that one in six people (500,000) were members of triads there.

Originally, there were four large triads: 14K, the Wo Group, the Chiu Chau Group, and the Big Four. Each of these was controlled by an administration that had a headquarters and branches. During the Chinese Civil War (1927–1949), community organizations in Chinatowns were often divided into pro and anti political factions in support of sides, that is, pro–Kuomintang (Sun Yat-Sen and Chiang Kai Shek) versus the communist government. The contemporary Chinese Consolidated Benevolent Association (CCBA), which is pro–Taiwan, is often in opposition to the communist government on the mainland.

The triads were joined and linked to local gangs, such as the Big Circle Gang and the Hunan Gang, which were prominent in the 1990s. As Rutgers University sociology professor Ko-lin Chin[25] deftly described, tongs operated openly in the United States and were affiliated with business organizations, and they often had an affiliation with triads. Tongs made their entry into the United States in the 1850s in San Francisco's Chinatown when local government failed to provide needed social services such as job referrals, housing, networking, and entertainment to Chinese immigrants. They also served as mediators in conflicts and liaison between local governments and Chinese communities. Their power increased because of the exclusion and discrimination against Chinese in this country, and while tongs are legal entities, some have, as Professor Chin described, resorted to illegal activities such as gambling, prostitution, drugs, and human trafficking.

Professor Chin conducted his analysis of Asian youth gang

behavior in the early 1990s in New York City. His team conducted 603 interviews with Asian entrepreneurs in the city, as well as seventy interviews with former gang members, fifteen with community leaders, and twenty-three with members of law enforcement. Although cognizant of the potential risks surrounding the nature of his research, he was still able to delineate the structure and function of Chinese gangs in the city.

While Chin observed that Vietnamese gangs, such as Born to Kill, were among the most vicious, youthful Chinese gangs were far more abundant in the city, and they were intricately associated with tongs. It was not uncommon for adult organizations like tongs to hire youth gang members as "street soldiers" to enforce territorial boundaries and police the area. These "hatchet men" were used to protect illegal activities such as gambling and prostitution. One of the primary sources of revenue for the youth street gangs was extortion. Chin was able to catalogue weekly and monthly payoffs to youth gang members, who occasionally extorted "lucky money" (gratuities paid to enterprising lone wolf youths who intimidated businessmen), foisting goods on local entrepreneurs, and the theft of merchandise in lieu of or in addition to cash payments for protection. Chin estimated that Chinese youth gangs were generating large sums of money from extortion; for example, the Flying Dragons' leader was receiving $3,400 per week from one gambling house, while the leader of the Ghost Shadows reportedly was receiving $10,000 a week from extortion activities. (This was in the 1990s and would be equivalent to double that amount today.)

Most of the money was paid for protection, but more than half of his entrepreneurial respondents reported that they were forced to sell items by gang members, and 41 percent said they gave youthful gang members "lucky money." Chin concluded that extortion was widespread in the Chinese community in New York City, although he found that most victims were exploited no more than three or four times a year. Typical payments for these activities at the time varied from $100 for protection to $20 for "lucky money" and $50 for coerced purchases. While the practice of extortion was rampant, the average annual cost of victimization was $688, with half his respondents paying just $120 annually. When considered in a larger context, for example, compared to rent, many of the respondents viewed the payments as a minor business expense. Although recalcitrant business establishments and owners might be assaulted or even murdered for refusing to ante up, Chin reported that physical abuse was rare—threats, harassment, and intimidation were the most likely form of aggression perpetrated against them (reported by a third of his respondents). Only two people in his sample reported being physically assaulted, and nearly three-fourths of his respondents disclosed that they were able to negotiate decreases in payments.

Contemporary Asian Gang Activity

From the time of Frederick Thrasher,[26] social scientists have speculated about why people join gangs. Membership in Chinese and other Asian gangs in the United States is obviously linked to achieving respect and being protected from real and perceived external threats. Historically, ethnic minorities, including blacks as well as Latinx, white ethnics (Irish, Scots, Italians, and other Eastern Europeans), and Asians, have sought refuge in gangs to protect themselves from predations and discrimination emanating from majority group members. Indeed, the very existence of tongs in San Francisco, the first major destination of Asians in the United States, can be linked to their role as a source of camaraderie, protection, and social services for new immigrants who often found themselves in need of friendship, jobs, housing, and associations in their communities. For youth who joined gangs associated with adult organizations like the tongs, ties to the community were realized, helping to overcome isolation and alienation. Gangs can also be a source of jobs and income through illegal or extralegal activities, and they may confer security and prestige on members, as well as offering protection from other, potentially hostile, gangs. When gangs assume legitimacy in Asian communities, either because Asian community members are reluctant to seek assistance from legitimate law enforcement agencies or from fear of retribution, the gangs may become institutionalized and serve as acceptable alternative sources of conflict resolution, and even as mediatorial agents in business conflicts.

The liberalization of immigration laws following the implementation of the Hart–Celler law in 1965 precipitated an increase in Chinese street gangs, just as the conflict in Southeast Asia resulted in increased gang activity in the latter part of the 20th century. An increase in Asian gang activity was recorded in Boston, Chicago, and New Orleans, as well as in New York City, San Francisco, and Los Angeles. The Flying Dragons in New York City became allied with the Hip Sing tong in New York City and Philadelphia, and the Sun Ye On triad was engaged in smuggling in members from Hong Kong to the United States. One may expect an increase in such activities considering the recent turmoil in Hong Kong, as the mainland government imposes restrictions on the island.

Certainly, some criminal and quasi-criminal enterprises such as

3. Gambling, Gangs and Deviant Behavior

youth gangs, triads, and tongs were formed to provide residents, especially new immigrants, with shelter, comfort, and camaraderie. They also condoned the use of weapons, along with a rationalization for their use as a necessary evil that promised safety, security, and sustenance. Although Professor Sung, mentioned in the preceding section, was initially skeptical about the growth of Chinese youth gangs, she presciently observed that control over Chinese children was waning because Chinese mothers frequently left home in pursuit of employment in the middle of the 20th century. This led to reduced discipline and a laissez-faire home environment. She also noted that American-born Chinese (ABCs) were more likely to reject traditional ways in favor of American values, which could lead to lower family stability, social disorganization, and a decline in parental authority, as values of the East and West clashed in the transplantation of people from one continent to another.

According to interviews and police reports in major American cities, it seems that the heyday of Asian gangs has come and gone, at least for the time being. Professor Ko Lin Chin attributes their demise to the ill-fated *Golden Venture*, a ship that ran aground on Rockaway Beach in New York on June 6, 1993. The ship carried 286 undocumented Chinese (Fujianese) who had been traveling for 222 days over 17,000 miles in search of a better life in the United States. Ten of the hapless smuggled passengers died in a vain attempt to seek refuge here, while the Clinton Administration confined 260 of the passengers to Immigration and Naturalization facilities, where many remained for four years until President Clinton pardoned fifty-three of them. Although the case of *Yang v. Reno*, alleging abnormally stringent application of immigration law against the undocumented immigrants, was thrown out in 2002, it provided the impetus for federal and local prosecution of Asian, especially Chinese, gangs that were involved in human trafficking. Using the Racketeers Influenced and Corrupt Organizations Act (RICO), local, state, and federal (FBI) law enforcement successfully prosecuted many of the leaders of these gangs, who were sentenced to lengthy prison terms.[27]

Although some criminal activities are still engaged in by Asians in the United States, the indictment, conviction, and incarceration of many of the Asian gang leaders in the 1990s essentially emasculated the Asian gang movement. Inquiries to police departments in major cities across the country about current activities of Asian gangs revealed a dramatic decline in their presence.[28] While some illicit activities may still be engaged in by latter-day descendants of these gangs, their scope has been curtailed and, as Professor Chin noted in the case of Chinese gangs, the tongs dissociated themselves from the excesses of the gangs to maintain their credibility and status within the Chinese and mainstream culture.[29]

We would be remiss if we did not address the Japanese group known as yakuza or *gokudo*. This unique set of organizations originated in the 17th century and took on the role of a semi–Robin Hood perspective with its stoic code of conduct reflective of a right-wing conservative philosophy. From 1958 to 1963, membership in the yakuza reportedly rose by 150 percent to 184,000 and included more than 5,200 gangs. Today, the yakuza, much smaller in numbers, have extensive ties to illegal and extra-legal activities, and, according to Japan's National Police Agency, number about 24,000 (out of a Japanese population of 126 million). They are still recognized by some segments of the Japanese public as legitimate. Their code of ethics stresses respect for human dignity, a prohibition on stealing from ordinary people and on using drugs, chivalrous behavior, and hands off the partners of fellow members. But members of the three principal groups (the largest being the Yamaguchi-gumi) have dabbled in activities such as loan sharking, extortion, gambling, money laundering, arms smuggling, and human trafficking, in Japan, the United States (especially Hawaii), China, Taiwan, the Philippines, North and South Korea, the Pacific Islands, and other parts of Southeast Asia.

Even more perplexing is the yakuza's penchant for engaging in legal and quasi-legal real estate activities. They have been known to pressure stockholders into expanding the scope of developments by intimidating them at meetings. While their code of conduct precludes involvement in the drug trade, the second largest yakuza organization, Dojin-kai, has been heavily involved in trafficking methamphetamines. While the yakuza have been registered by the Japanese government as semilegitimate organizations, Japan's Securities and Exchange Surveillance Commission listed more than fifty companies with ties to organized crime in recent years.[30]

These criminal organizations have extended their reach into the United States, at times collaborating with Chinese triads, penetrating into Las Vegas, Seattle, Los Angeles, San Francisco, Chicago, and New York City. With their traditional belief in fealty toward mentors (the father figure or boss in the relationship between a neophyte and established yakuza is known as *oybun*, and the neophyte as son or *kobun*), the emphasis is on satisfying the wishes and demands of the senior member. If the neophyte offends his mentor, he is obliged to follow the ritualistic practice of *yubitsume*, amputating the left pinky at the joint and sending it to the *oybun* as a sign of remorse.

In addition to such signs of subservience, many yakuza have

ornate tattoos, sometimes even full-body engravings that were created by painstaking individualized artistic renderings over many years, without the aid of commonly used electronic devices.

Over the years, some yakuza members, such as Shimizu Jirocho (1820–1893), achieved a level of respect and even became renowned folk heroes. Many motion pictures have been made about their exploits, even graphic novels (manga) for children, as well as video games such as *Judgment* used in PlayStation 4. The allure of the yakuza fascinated some members of Japanese society because of their history of being outcasts. Although membership in these secret societies has declined since an act targeting them in Japan was passed in 1992, there remains a hard core of members who are viewed as underdogs by some people, tracing their history to the domination and exploitation of their predecessors, the Burakumin, who were alienated and ostracized as far back as Japanese feudal society, hundreds of years ago. In fact, 70 percent of the Yamaguchi yakuza organization are Burakumin, and a significant portion (perhaps 10 percent) are of Korean descent. Not unlike the formation of other gangs in the United States, yakuza members may have been drawn together out of shared interests, protection, and camaraderie in the face of societal pressures directed against them. The yakuza are still active in the United States and other countries, as witnessed by the

Yakuza men (*Wikimedia*).

recent arrest (April 2022) of several people in New York who were purportedly involved in an arms and narcotics plot.[31]

The social changes that followed Asians to the shores of this country precipitated the efflorescence of mutual aid societies (tongs). The hostile reception that awaited them in the land of the Golden Mountain and beyond, as well as a decline of parental control, contributed to feelings of alienation and created a climate that recognized the communal needs and camaraderie proffered by gangs. These offered participants economic, social, and psychological acceptance and protection against the vagaries of living in a hostile world. But age and extended time to contemplate the wisdom of one's errant ways led to the mollification of the survivors of youthful gang violence. Their testimony can be seen on YouTube—a reminder of the folly and foibles of youthful intransigence and indiscretion.

4

The Treatment of Japanese Americans in World War II

> "Throughout history, our ties to a worldwide web of other Asians has been used against us: to question our loyalty and patriotism, to attack and condemn us for the perceived sins of overseas doppelgangers, to exclude and isolate us in our home."
> —Jeff Yang, Phil Yu, and Philip Wang, *Rise: A History of Asian America from the Nineties to Now*, New York: Mariner Books, 2022, p. 423.

One of the most racist events in the checkered history that characterizes interactions between the majority white population of the United States and Asian Americans occurred during the early years of the Second World War. Following the Japanese attack on the United States' naval base in Pearl Harbor, Hawaii, on December 7, 1941, which decimated the U.S. Pacific fleet and left 2,403 military personnel dead, including sixty-eight civilians, and 1,178 wounded, President Franklin Delano Roosevelt addressed Congress and declared war on Japan. Nineteen U.S. navy ships were destroyed or damaged, although three U.S. aircraft carriers were out to sea and unharmed. Japanese Admiral Isoroku Yamamoto, who conceived the plan for the attack, rightly feared that the United States would be able to recover because the fleet wasn't totally destroyed. Within six months the rejuvenated U.S. Pacific fleet dealt a crushing defeat to the Japanese at the Battle of Midway, sinking four Japanese aircraft carriers and beginning the territorial reclamation that eventually led to the defeat of the Japanese.[1]

While many Americans associate December 7, 1941, as "a day which will live in infamy," in President Roosevelt's words, fewer people recall February 19, 1942, the day President Roosevelt issued Executive Order 9066 creating the War Relocation Authority (WRA) that facilitated the subsequent relocation of 120,000 Japanese Americans, labeled "evacuees," to ten camps in the western and southern parts of the United States. Although most of the inhabitants of these camps are deceased, and, as described in the following, reparations were paid to survivors, the swiftness with which the Japanese were shuttled off to the camps combined with the camps' isolated locations and initial rudimentary state of development led many camp survivors to refer to them as concentration camps, although they were not designed to torture or exterminate the internees. I was aware of this labeling dispute, but taken aback when I saw a monument to the residents of the "concentration camps" when I was walking one morning in Honolulu. Nevertheless, the camps are usually referred to as "concentration camps," often with the caveat that they were not as brutal as their Nazi counterparts.

Nearly all of the major camps were located in isolated areas. There are differing estimates of the number of people who were relocated, with the most common number around 120,000. Nearly all of the detainees were from the West Coast of the United States, principally California. Two-thirds of the people sent away were American citizens, either born

Map of detention camps for Japanese (National Park Service).

in the United States or naturalized. Those relocated were given little notification of their impending journey and many did not even know their destination.

First-generation Japanese immigrants are referred to as Issei, the second generation as Nisei, and the third generation as Sansei. As we have seen, many white Americans held Asians, primarily Chinese and Japanese immigrants and their families, in contempt, stemming from historical competition between the groups for jobs, property, and mates. Antipathy toward these groups was apparent, especially in California, where numerous laws were enacted forbidding Asians, especially Chinese and Japanese, from owning land.

So-called "alien land laws," often in the western part of the United States where the majority of the Japanese and Chinese population resided, were designed to limit their presence and permanence. Arizona, Arkansas, California, Florida, Idaho, Louisiana, Minnesota, Montana, Nebraska, New Mexico, Oregon, Texas, Utah, Washington, and Wyoming all had laws that barred or restricted Asians from owning land. Since many Asian immigrants coming to the United States had an affinity for agricultural pursuits, such prohibitions were particularly onerous for them. These laws were enacted to protect the jobs and income of white citizens and prevent Asian encroachment into the agricultural sector, but many Asians managed to circumvent them.[2]

The first targets of these laws were the Chinese, when Oregon's constitution in 1859 stated that "no Chinaman" could own property in the state but protected the rights of "white" foreigners, giving them the same rights as native citizens. The Washington state constitution of 1889 specified that one had to be eligible for naturalization in order to own land, and since the Chinese Exclusion Act of 1882 forbade the naturalization of Asians, they were formally excluded from property ownership. But the Japanese kept coming to the United States. Finally, in 1907–1908 a "gentlemen's agreement" was reached between the United States and Japan. The Japanese government agreed to limit the number of Japanese immigrants to the United States, and in return, the U.S. government granted admission to the wives, children, and other relatives of Japanese immigrants who were already here.

California passed its own version of legislation excluding Asians from property ownership in 1913, the Alien Land Law, which prohibited Asians from owning land and entering into long-term land leases if they were not citizens. However, some Chinese and Japanese conceived of a way around such restrictive legislation by purchasing land in the name of their Nisei children, who, by virtue of citizenship conferred on them by the Fourteenth Amendment to the U.S. Constitution, were born here and hence citizens. In 1923 the Supreme Court of the United States ruled that laws restricting the rights of "aliens" to own property were not a violation of the Fourteenth Amendment. By 1920, Japanese immigrant farmers controlled 450,000 acres of farmland in California and accounted for more than 10 percent of crop revenue. It was not until 1952 that the U.S. Supreme Court voided alien land laws, in *Sei Fuji v. California*.[3]

The children of immigrants born in the United States, in this case the second generation of Japanese, the Nisei, were automatically citizens according to the birthright clause in the Fourteenth Amendment: "All persons born or naturalized in the United States, and subject to the jurisdiction thereof, are citizens of the United States and of the state wherein they reside." The Japanese comprised an infinitesimal segment of the American population (there were approximately 400,000 in the United States around 1930), and about half of them were U.S. citizens. (The Fourteenth Amendment also states, "No State shall make or enforce any law which shall abridge the privileges or immunities of citizens of the United States; nor shall a State deprive any person of life,

"Japs Keep Moving" sign (densho.org/campu/campu-rocks).

liberty, or property, without due process of law; nor deny to any person within its jurisdiction the equal protection of the laws.") Apparently, racist animosity among white Americans overwhelmed their sense of respect for the Constitution when the "relocation camps" and mass deportations of Japanese Americans were implemented after the attack on Pearl Harbor.[4]

It's estimated that the incarcerated Japanese lost over $400 million (equal to over $6 billion in today's currency), according to Professor Gwen Jensen, 75 percent of their personal property.[5] Although Congress later gave the survivors $38 million (followed by an apology and individual reparations of $20,000 in 1988), that hardly served to recompense the people swept up in the web of hysteria and racism. Many internees had little time to sell their personal property and businesses and didn't even know where they were being transported. Initially, some leaders of the Japanese communities were arrested and interrogated because civilian and military authorities were suspicious of their loyalty to the United States and feared they might commit acts of sabotage or espionage. No person of Japanese ancestry living in the United States was ever convicted of a serious act of espionage or sabotage during World War II.[6] Conversely, as historian Joan Miller pointed out, widespread espionage and sabotage were conducted by German agents in the United States, primarily directed toward the transportation of war materials to the Allies and against America's military and industrial production. Fortunately, according to Miller, "German espionage operations in America were replete with mistakes, bad organization, involved poor agent selection, and ultimately fulfilled few of the expectations of the Third Reich's spymasters."[7]

Prior to people arriving at the camps, holding facilities such as racetracks and fairgrounds were used to detain the Japanese. Historian Renee Romano interviewed a detainee who recalled that she and her family were held at Santa Anita racetrack in a small stall, while the famous racehorse Seabiscuit was housed in two stalls near them.[8]

Conditions in the holding centers and camps were deplorable, especially in the early months of relocation. Yet misinformation was spread in the public that implied the Japanese American inmates were being coddled and receiving foodstuffs denied to the general public. Surrounded by barbed wire and armed soldiers with guard dogs, many of the camps, officially designated as war relocation centers, were barely livable. The initial occupants were frequently pressed into service, assisting the authorities in finishing their construction. Since many of the camps were located in desert areas, there were frequent sandstorms, and sanitary conditions at the camps were complicated by inclement weather conditions. Dysentery was a common malady linked to contaminated food and water. Nearly two thousand (1,862) people died from medical causes in the camps, and there were long-term health consequences, especially cardiovascular disease and psychological anguish. Historian Gwendolyn Jensen verified a 2.1 times greater risk of cardiovascular disease, cardiovascular mortality, and premature mortality among camp survivors compared to non-interned counterparts.[9] She also found that California Nisei who experienced the internment situation died 1.6 years earlier than their non-interned Hawaiian counterparts.

A persistent effect of the internment process was the deteriorating emotional/psychological state of the survivors and their children. The loss of personal property carried with it long-term ramifications for the survivors' sense of worth and well-being. Dr. Nobu Miyoshi, a social worker and physician who studied survivors of the camps, noted that they were "permanently altered in their attitudes, both positively and negatively, in regard to their identification with the values of their bicultural heritage; they remained confused or even injured by the traumatic experience."[10] This conclusion was confirmed by the research of Professor Donna K. Nagata of the Psychology Department at the University of Michigan. She found that Sansei (third-generation) Japanese felt the incarceration affected their lives in "significant ways," including a loss of self-esteem and an accelerated loss of Japanese culture and language under the pressure to assimilate to the majority/dominant white culture.[11] Testimony by a woman who had been interned at a camp years before supports this: She was "suddenly aware of what being of Japanese ancestry was going to be like. I wouldn't be faced with physical attack, or with overt shows of hatred. Rather, I would be seen as someone foreign, or as someone other than American, or perhaps not be seen at all."[12]

George Takei, one of the original cast in the television series *Star Trek* (he played the helmsman, Sulu), highlighted his experiences at the Rohwer Relocation Center on the eastern edge of Arkansas in his recent graphic memoir *They Called Us Enemy*. He vividly recalled the date, October 7, 1942, when armed guards forcibly removed his family from their home in California and dispatched them and 8,500 other Japanese Americans to the smelly confines of the relocation camp, which lacked privacy and felt like a "furnace." Takei, only five years old at the time, never forgot the anguish he, his brother, his sister, and his parents experienced as they passed through a system that degraded and dehumanized them.[13]

One of the most disastrous consequences of the internment was the accelerated suicide rate among the internees, as much as four times

4. The Treatment of Japanese Americans in World War II 77

A Japanese man sitting alone by his farm (ddr.densho.org/ddr-densho-151-269).

higher than prewar levels. Boredom and idleness were their constant companions. Many internees were adherents to a strong work ethic, which was circumscribed by the isolation they experienced. Suffering from racist allegations that questioned their loyalty, as well as losing their personal wealth and property, along with the enforced negativity of their surroundings, led to short- and long-term negative impacts on their mental health. The accelerated suicide rate of internees was double that of the general population at the time of their incarceration.

Food in the camps was initially quite poor and was consumed in large mess halls that frequently separated families. Inmates were given foods they were unaccustomed to eating, such as mutton, and it was not uncommon to find maggots and mold in the meals. Many of the camps sought to capitalize on how little they spent on food—below

Manzanar Relocation Camp (Library of Congress).

the allocated WRA thirty-five cents per person a day. Inmates were fed a variety of organ meats, horse, and spaghetti. Vegetables began to appear after they managed to grow them in nearby areas. Initially, potatoes were a staple, but the Japanese successfully lobbied for more rice instead. Authorities were often suspected of pilfering supplies ostensibly meant for inmates, and this, along with the lack of privacy and other restrictions and deleterious conditions, led to unrest and revolts in some facilities.

Latrines lacked privacy and were overcrowded, inadequate, and rudimentary. Women were often victims of sexual assaults, and either refused to make the journey to latrines at night or went in groups for protection. Many families resorted to "chamba" (chamber) pots—pails that were used during cold nights when temperatures hovered between −2 and +27 degrees in Minidoka, Idaho, for example.[14]

As Hana and Noah Maruyama, hosts of the *Campu* podcasts about the camps, summarized:

> "Living in the camps was humiliating. The loss of freedom, being suspected of being the enemy and the ever-present threat of sexual assault that never went away—the big things. Then there were the latrines with no partitions. Food poisoning. Neighbors hearing your every move, word, and … fart. A gross undignified, anxiety-inducing nightmare. Waiting in line in the heat of summer with a belly full of tainted macaroni salad. Carrying the chamba down Sewer Lane, hoping its unspeakable contents didn't slosh onto you.

Winding your way around ditches of raw human waste that formed in the streets."[15]

While the U.S. government cited national security as justification for the internment of Japanese in the relocation camps, the entire project was not only antithetical to American values—it was unconstitutional. Many of the interned Japanese realized this fact and refused to participate in official activities that would have normalized this aberrant behavior, and there were riots, for example, at Tule Lake.

The U.S. government actively attempted to recruit Nisei men into an all–Japanese combat unit, the 442nd. Twenty percent of Nisei men responded "No" to questions 27 and 28 (loyalty questions) on the infamous Selective Service Form 304A also known as the "Statement of United States Citizen of Japanese Ancestry" or loyalty survey. Designed with the assistance of the Office of Naval Intelligence to determine whether the Nisei could be counted on being loyal to the United States in military service, the survey was a formal extension of racist policies of the U.S. Navy, which since the 1920s had refused Japanese Americans the opportunity to serve because of fears about their loyalty to the United States. The majority of questions in the survey (there were twenty-eight) focused on family members, past residence, educational levels, language skills, religion, recreational activities, and affiliations with associations. Respondents were scored on their degree of "Americanness" or "Japaneseness." Ironically, the *Densho Encyclopedia*, created for the purpose of exposing racist bigotry on the part of the white establishment and the U.S. government toward Japanese Americans, discusses the resistance of some Nisei to serve in the armed forces of the United States during World War II, not as an act of disloyalty, but resistance to perceived racist, unconstitutional affronts against Japanese Americans.[16]

Resistance to the "loyalty" questionnaire took the form of refusal to respond to questions 27 and 28 in the affirmative or at all. People who refused to signify their loyalty to the United States and to reject ties to Japan were referred to as the No-No Boys. The questionnaire was initially administered to all Japanese internees in 1943 and to Japanese already serving in the U.S. military, and later an attempt was made to give it to all resident Japanese in the United States between 1943 and 1944. Issei (first-generation Japanese in the United States) successfully lobbied for the War Relocation Authority (WRA) to change the form's name from "Application for Leave Clearance," implying that the form had been voluntarily requested, to "Questionnaire," as well as an alternative question that avoided respondents' renunciation of Japanese citizenship. The new version of the question, implemented on February 12, 1942, read: "Will you swear to abide by the laws of the United States and take no action which would in any way interfere with the war effort of the United States?"

All Nisei males were required to complete the form. Failure to do so could result in their prosecution under the Espionage Act. But some Nisei remained disturbed about the tenor of the questionnaire and the formation of a segregated all–Japanese combat unit, the 442nd. Twenty percent of the Nisei responded "No" to questions 27 and 28. Only 1,208 Japanese volunteered from the camps to join the 442nd (6 percent of eligible males, out of nearly 20,000).[17] In fact, by 1943, more than 9,000 Japanese had requested the WRA to be repatriated to Japan, and that figure reached 20,000 the following year, obviously as a result of their being threatened by the status of statelessness.

However, a film about the courageous Japanese Americans who composed the 442nd Regimental Combat Team took the opposite approach and touted the number of Nisei who volunteered to serve in the U.S. military while their relatives remained incarcerated in relocation camps.[18] According to the film, there was initial tension between Hawaiian and mainland Japanese volunteers and conscripts, but this enmity disappeared when the Hawaiians learned about the incarceration of mainlanders' families in the relocation camps. As one interviewee in the film concluded, "These mainlanders were better people than us."

Animosity between the groups faded, but the free-spirited Hawaiians' attitudes and penchant for risk-taking and gambling resulted in the unit's sobriquet "Go For Broke." That spirt would delineate their destiny from the time they trained under all white officers at Camp Shelby, Mississippi, when the unit was founded in 1943 under the command of Charles W. Pence. Joining the 10,000 Hawaiian volunteers of Japanese ancestry were 12,000 Nisei from the mainland. To this day, the unit holds the distinction of being the most decorated military unit in the history of the United States.

The white commanders realized the fight the young Nisei men had to wage against distrust and racism and respected their courage in the face of adversity. The unit was not allowed to serve in the Pacific theater of operations and was confined to the European front—France, Germany, and Italy. There they distinguished themselves by their indomitable will to prove their loyalty to the United States, and despite what may have seemed official indifference to their humanity and safety, they earned recognition and respect for their bravery and accomplishments.

The nickname for the 442nd was the "Purple Heart Brigade"

because of the high rate of casualties it sustained. More than 4,000 Nisei received purple hearts for injuries they received in various campaigns, such as breaking through the German encirclement of the "Lost Battalion" (a Texas National Guard group of 211 men from the 141st Infantry) in the Vosges Mountains after a five-day fight in October 1944 that left more than 800 Japanese American men killed or wounded. I–Company entered the fray with 185 men and only eight came out unscathed. Prior to that engagement, the 442nd had been involved in the liberation of the German-occupied towns of Bruyere and Biffontaine, where they also sustained numerous casualties.

Among the many accolades received by the Japanese American soldiers of the 442nd were 4,000 Bronze stars, 588 Silver Stars, fifty-two Distinguished Service Crosses, and seventeen Medals of Honor (many of them upgraded from Distinguished Service Crosses under the Clinton Administration). The 442nd received seven Presidential Citations for its efforts, and in 2010 Congress awarded the unit the Congressional Gold Medal. In all, men of the 422nd earned more than 18,000 awards for their service and bravery during World War II, at a time when many of their family members were interred in isolated and inhospitable regions of the country.

One illustrious member of the 442nd became a famous U.S. Senator, Daniel Inouye from Hawaii. Born in Honolulu, he received his bachelor's degree from the University of Hawaii and law degree from George Washington University in Washington, D.C. He lost his right arm fighting for this country, but was turned away from a barber shop because, as the owner averred, "We don't serve people like you here." Racial animosity against the Japanese ran high in those days, and even though Inouye received the Congressional Medal of Honor, a Distinguished Service Cross, the Bronze Star, and a Purple Heart with cluster, ignorance and fear fed into the irrational behavior of the public. Inouye later became the first U.S. Representative from the new state of Hawaii and served in the U.S. Senate from 1963 until his death in 2012. He was posthumously awarded the Presidential Medal of Freedom in 2013 and remains the only U.S. Senator to have received both the Medal of Freedom and the Medal of Honor.

In hindsight, the hysteria that gripped the country after the attack on Pearl Harbor was blatantly racist and deplorable. To this day, treatises are published about the abject failure of our social system to prevent and correct the injustices that were perpetrated against the Japanese living in America, a majority of them U.S. citizens. Although many of the Nisei fought bravely against the Axis powers, perhaps in an attempt to prove their loyalty to this country, there are lessons to be learned from this sordid episode that culminated in the abrogation of the laws and Constitution established to guide us. While we study events like the Holocaust and the illegal internment of Japanese Americans in World War II, our collective memory of them seems ephemeral, or perhaps uncomfortable. As recently as 2019, the Obama and Trump Administrations used Fort Sill, in Oklahoma, to detain unaccompanied immigrant children—the same place that housed 700 Japanese Americans during World War II. The treatment of the children was eerily similar to the treatment of their predecessors and should serve as an illustration of the likelihood that racism may produce a repetition of hysterical, jingoistic behavior.[19]

Our discussion of this event would not be complete without reviewing some of the most significant legal challenges to the constitutionality of the relocation and incarceration of the Japanese. Four cases heard by the U.S. Supreme Court in the early 1940s are reviewed here, beginning with a young Nisei lawyer, Minori Yasui, who was born in the United States, graduated from the University of Oregon's law school in 1939, and then worked for the Japanese consulate in Chicago. He returned to Oregon following the Japanese attack on Pearl Harbor, but was incensed

Japanese camp survivors protesting placement of immigrant children in Ft. Sill, Oklahoma (courtesy John Ota/Tsuru for Solidarity).

4. The Treatment of Japanese Americans in World War II

by President Roosevelt's Executive Order 9066 and General De Witt's imposition of a curfew from 8 p.m. to 6 a.m. for "enemy aliens." Intentionally defying the curfew to create a test case, Yasui was arrested in March 1942 and tried before Judge James Alger Fee (he waived his right to a jury trial) in a District Court in Oregon, where he was found guilty. Judge Fee ruled that Yasui had forfeited his U.S. citizenship because he had worked for the Japanese government in the Chicago consulate and was therefore an "enemy alien." He was fined $5,000 and sentenced to a year in prison.

Another pivotal case involving the implementation of the curfew was that of Gordon Hirabashi. He, too, was prosecuted for refusing to abide by the curfew. A member of the Quakers (Society of Friends), he also refused induction into the U.S. Armed Forces. He served ninety days in prison for the curfew violation and one year in the federal penitentiary on McNeil Island in the state of Washington for refusing to serve in the U.S. military.

The Supreme Court of the United States heard the Yasui and Hirabashi cases together and unanimously ruled against them on June 21, 1943, upholding their convictions and the legality of the curfews. However, in the case of Yasui, the Court ruled that Judge Fee was wrong in lifting his U.S. citizenship for working at the Japanese consulate in Chicago, but sided with the U.S. government's position that the military should retain discretion in determining the necessity for implementing a curfew and, according to Solicitor General Charles Fahy, "racial characteristics" made it reasonable for the Japanese to be excluded. Judge Fee then lowered Yasui's jail sentence to time served (9 months) and removed the $5,000 fine. He was then sent to the Minidoka Detention Center.

But animosity toward Japanese Americans still held sway in the courts, as the infamous case of Fred Korematsu revealed in July 1944. The case revolved around the right of the government to relocate Japanese, in line with Executive Order 9066. Korematsu, born in 1919 in Oakland, California, was living with his girlfriend at the time of the order, having been rejected for service in the U.S. Navy. He ignored the order to evacuate. He even resorted to plastic surgery on his eyes to avoid authorities. He was found posing as a Spanish Hawaiian when he was apprehended by the FBI in 1942 and was initially sent to the assembly center in Tanforan, California (a racetrack), and then, with his family, to the relocation camp in Topaz, Utah.

The Supreme Court voted six to three to uphold the legality of Executive Order 9066, making Korematsu a criminal, and legalizing the evacuation of Japanese and their removal to relocation camps, based on the justices' belief in the military necessity of separating them to avoid acts of espionage and sabotage.

Believing in the unconstitutionality of the order and his innocence, Korematsu subsequently filed briefs asking for rehearings of his case. When documents pertaining to the loyalty of Japanese Americans were found by political scientist Peter Irons and researcher Aiko Herzig-Yoshinaga in 1983, Korematsu's case was overturned by a federal court in San Francisco. He was awarded the Presidential Medal of Freedom in 1998 by President Bill Clinton for his lifelong work to promote equal treatment for minorities, and in 2010 the state of California passed the Fred Korematsu Bill, which officially named January 30 as Fred Korematsu Day, the first such designation for an Asian American.

Numerous other Japanese Americans sought redress of their situation through the courts, but without success until the positive outcome to the war with Japan seemed assured. In 1944, Mitsuye Endo (323 US 283) asked the Supreme Court to void the exclusion order, and the Court ruled unanimously that the U.S. government could not continue to detain a citizen who was "concededly loyal" to the United States. "The War Relocation Authority ... was without authority, express or implied, to subject to its leave procedure a concededly loyal and law-abiding citizen of the United States. ... Executive Orders Nos. 9066 and 9102 afford no basis for keeping loyal evacuees of Japanese ancestry in custody on the grounds of community hostility."[20] This case authorized the release of Japanese from the camps, but it was rendered near the end of the war, and it applied to Japanese who had signed the loyalty oath affirmatively.

On December 12, 1944, U.S. Supreme Court Justice William O. Douglas read the court's opinion. He noted that General DeWitt's concern about the threat posed by the Japanese to U.S. security and Executive Order 9102, which gave the War Relocation Authority the right to remove Japanese pursuant to Executive Order 9066, might have been a "military necessity [but] required only that the Japanese population be removed from the coastal area and dispersed in the interior, where the danger of action in concert during any attempted enemy raids along the coast, or in advance thereof as preparation for a full scale attack would be eliminated. That the evacuation program necessarily and ultimately developed into one of complete Federal supervision, was due primarily to the fact that the interior states would not accept an uncontrolled Japanese migration." Further, "A citizen who is concededly loyal presents no problem of espionage or sabotage. Loyalty is a matter of the heart and mind, not of race, creed, or color. He who is loyal is, by

4. The Treatment of Japanese Americans in World War II

definition, not a spy or a saboteur. When the power to detain is derived from the power to protect the war effort against espionage and sabotage, detention which has no relationship to that objective is unauthorized. Mitsuye Endo is entitled to an unconditional release by the War Relocation Authority."[21]

In his concurrence, Justice Francis (Frank) Murphy, appointed by President Roosevelt, noted, "I am of the view that detention in Relocation Centers of persons of Japanese ancestry regardless of loyalty is not only unauthorized by Congress or the Executive but is another example of the unconstitutional resort to racism inherent in the nature of the entire evacuation program. ... Racial discrimination of this nature bears no reasonable relation to military necessity and is utterly foreign to the ideals and relations of the American people."[22]

Clearly, the monolithic climate surrounding the war and the racist perception of Japanese Americans was changing. In 1976, President Gerald R. Ford issued a proclamation formally terminating Executive 9066, noting that "this kind of error shall never be made again."[23] In 1978 the Japanese American Citizens League began to campaign for monetary redress and a congressional apology. In 1980 President Jimmy Carter helped establish the Commission on the Wartime Relocation and Internment of Civilians, which in 1983 concluded that the promulgation of Executive Order 9066 was not based on analysis or military conditions. "The broad historical causes which shaped these decisions were race prejudice, war hysteria and a failure of political leadership. Widespread ignorance of Japanese Americans contributed to a policy conceived in haste and executed in an atmosphere of fear and anger at Japan. A grave injustice was done to American citizens and resident aliens of Japanese ancestry who, without any individual review or probative evidence against them, were excluded, removed, and detained by the United States during World War II."[24]

In the mid–1980s, an archival researcher found the last remaining copy of a report prepared for the Office of Naval Intelligence (the Ringle Report) in January 1942 that provided evidence that Japanese Americans and persons of Japanese ancestry in the United States were, indeed, loyal to this country.[25] The existence of this report, as well as another corroborating report by Curtis Munson,[26] did not deter General John DeWitt, the head of the relocation plan for removing Japanese from the West Coast of the United States, from casting aspersions on the loyalty of Japanese in his public proclamation No. 1 (7 Fed. 2320) that specified the entire Pacific Coast of the United States was to be evacuated of Japanese because "by its geographical location [it] is particularly subject to attack, to attempted invasion by the armed forces of nations with which the United States is now at war, and, in connection therewith, is subject to espionage and acts of sabotage, thereby requiring the adoption of military measures necessary to establish safeguards against such enemy operations."

During the war, racism ran high, as evidenced by the comments of then governor of Oregon Walter Pierce: "We should never be satisfied until every last Jap has been run out of the United States and our Constitution changed so they can never go back."[27] In fact, postwar Japanese Americans in Oregon were only able to regain 25 percent of the land they owned prior to the war.

In 1987, the U.S. Court of Appeals for the 9th Circuit granted a writ of *coram nobis* overturning Gordon Hirabashi's prior criminal conviction, when it was disclosed that documents relevant to his alleged misconduct had been withheld from the U.S. Supreme Court. When he learned that evidence was improperly withheld from the U.S. Supreme Court by Solicitor General of the United States Charles Fahy, acting Solicitor General of the United States Neal Katyal apologized, noting that hiding the truth from the Supreme Court harmed 120,000 Japanese Americans. "It harmed our reputation as lawyers and as human beings, and it harmed our commitment to those words on the court's building, 'Equal Justice Under the Law.'"[28]

In 1988 President Ronald Reagan signed H.R. 442, the Civil Liberties Act of 1988, which provided restitution to Japanese American survivors of the camps. He remarked that the wartime internment of Japanese Americans was without trial and jury, and it was "a mistake." Reagan said that the bill, which provided $20,000 to every survivor (82,219 people estimated to be $1.6 billion), had less to do with property than with honor. "For here we admit wrong; here we reaffirm our commitment as a nation to equal justice under the law."[29] The payments began in 1990, and President George H.W. Bush sent a signed apology to all surviving former detainees.

Atom Bombs, Politics, and Racism

Much speculation has surrounded the use of atomic weapons by the United States in World War II. The famed Manhattan Project brought together some of the greatest minds in the world to create weapons of mass destruction on a scale heretofore unknown, but the social and psychological implications surrounding the use and utility of nuclear weapons were, and still are, the subject of debate. In their incisive analysis of this issue, psychologist Robert Jay Lifton and journalist

4. The Treatment of Japanese Americans in World War II

Greg Mitchell summarized the military and political machinations that permeated decisions pertaining to the use of atomic weapons on Japan and the subsequent explanation and justification of them.[30]

Although many scientists working on the project harbored reservations about the use of such weapons, these objections were generally overridden by the belief that the war would be shortened by their implementation and, concomitantly, human suffering would, with the hastened conclusion of the war, be limited. This perspective was generally propounded by the military and political leaders of the time, and was enforced through carefully crafted press releases, articles, and photographs that extolled the benefits and virtues of such weapons, as well as through tight censorship of the press, which limited information about the bombing of Hiroshima and Nagasaki. The result, according to Lifton and Mitchell, was a lopsided emphasis on the physical property devastation wreaked by the blasts and a minimization of the catastrophic effects, particularly radiation sickness and death, on the Japanese people.

I have often wondered about the utilitarian justification of utilizing weapons of mass destruction for the good of the commonweal. The military claimed that a million American lives were saved through them, but that figure was later disputed, and a more realistic figure of approximately 46,000 was later advanced. Nevertheless, President Truman persisted using the higher figure: "I lost plenty of sleep—but not over saving Japanese lives. I lost sleep worrying about our boys ... and it broke my heart when just one of our soldiers, sailors or marines died."[31] In a 1953 interview Truman noted, "The Japs were much more vicious fighters hand-to-hand than the people we had been standing up against [in Europe]. I thought that wiping out completely cities with the bomb would be better."[32] Ironically, President Truman placed blame for the two cities' devastating bombing on the Japanese because they ostensibly rejected the Allies' peace terms derived from the Potsdam Conference with Truman, Stalin, and Churchill (and later Attlee), but one of the key sticking points, allowing the Japanese to keep their emperor, was eventually acceded to by the Allies.

Even high-ranking military personnel doubted the bombing. For example, General Dwight Eisenhower, the Supreme Allied Commander and our last five-star general (who would soon become the 34th president of the United States), believed the bombing was unnecessary because the Japanese were about to surrender.

Controversy surrounding these events and their portrayal led to the cancellation of a controversial Smithsonian Institution exhibit in 1995 that was attacked by some "true believers," especially World War II veterans and politicians. The initial Smithsonian version was denounced by some as "historical cleansing" and "political correctness."[33] In place of the original exhibit, a sanitized version was displayed at the Smithsonian Museum of Air and Space, one minus controversy, that omitted references to the human suffering and consequences in the aftermath of the bombings.

Physicist Ralph Lapp noted, "If the memory of things is to deter, where is that memory? Hiroshima has been taken out of the American conscience, eviscerated, extirpated."[34] Indeed, as Lifton and Mitchell noted more than a quarter century ago, "There remains today a reluctance to face squarely what America did, or excuse it, perhaps even wish it away."[35] But their painstaking research into the events surrounding the bombings paints a picture of the masterful use of propaganda by the military and government that initially cloaked the events in nationalism and secrecy to the exclusion of depictions and information about the depredations of the Japanese victims. Early announcements of the events of August 6 and 8, 1945, extolled the technological achievement of American science, which purportedly foreshadowed the coming evolutionary wave of beneficial advances in the production of energy and an enriched quality of life. Absent were descriptions of the human devastation caused by the blasts and, more importantly, the lingering and long-lasting effects of nuclear radiation that poisoned the environment and caused a continuing legacy of human pain and suffering.

The official justification for bombing Hiroshima was that it was the site of a large military base with over 40,000 soldiers, but the bomb was detonated over the center of the city (population at the time was 255,000) and approximately 69,000 people were killed instantly. "Little Boy," the name for the device that was dropped from the B-29 bomber called the *Enola Gay*, was equal in power to 15,000 tons of TNT; the device known as Fat Man, detonated above Nagasaki two days later, contained plutonium, unlike the uranium bomb used on Hiroshima, and was equal in power to 20,000 tons of TNT. Thirty-nine thousand people were initially killed by this blast. These pale in comparison to modern thermonuclear weapons, for which the power is measured in megatons (one megaton is equal to one million tons of TNT). Modern weapons far exceed the "low yield" bombs used on the Japanese, ranging as high as 50 megatons in payload (equal in power to 50 million tons of TNT).

Another official justification for bombing the Japanese was revenge for their attack on Pearl Harbor and the vicious "Death March" on Bataan (9,000 Filipino and 1,000 American soldiers perished on that), but saturation bombing of Japanese cities had already left the country in ruins and seriously interrupted its ability to continue to produce war material. The Allies were, prior to the bombing, aware of the possibility of a Japanese surrender because of the B-29 bombardment and a naval blockade that severely limited the ability of the Japanese to conduct the war. Hence, one primary reason for using the weapons was for political gain—to demonstrate American scientific capability to the Soviet Union and promote the notion of American technological prowess to the world. Saying and implying that the use of the weapons was morally justified by preventing their use by the Axis powers was a necessary moral justification, but hardly sufficient considering the devastation they caused. The Strategic Bombing Survey, appointed by President Truman and composed of one thousand members, including John Kenneth Galbraith and Paul Nitze, concluded that Japan would have surrendered without the United States dropping the bombs, even if Russia hadn't entered the war, and even without an invasion.[36] Lifton and Mitchell further pointed out that Emperor Hirohito and his staff had concluded by May 1945 that the war should be ended, even if it meant acceptance of defeat on allied terms.[37]

If the intent of the blasts at these sites was military, then they were not entirely successful. A damage survey by the U.S. government revealed that less than 10 percent of Hiroshima's manufacturing, transport, and storage facilities were damaged by the bomb, but fully 60 percent of the city was destroyed. A more decisive but troubling justification for the bombing was the racist perception among the predominantly white American public that held the Japanese to be an inferior species of human. Negative attitudes and behavior about Asians, especially Japanese and Chinese, were, as we have seen, widespread in California and other Western states in the late 19th and early 20th centuries, and resulted in discriminatory policies that prevented them from owning land or living in certain areas, and ultimately restricted their immigration to the United States and becoming citizens, as with the Chinese Exclusion Act of 1882 and the Immigration Act (Johnson–Reed Act) of 1924.[38]

There was reluctance of some scientists to use the weapon on humans: Frank Oppenheimer, a nuclear scientist and the brother of J. Robert Oppenheimer, who was the wartime head of the Los Alamos laboratory and who became known as "the father of the atomic bomb," once said, "We had somehow always thought it would not be dropped on people."[39] Leo Szilard, one of the architects of the atomic bomb, called dropping it "one of the greatest blunders in history."[40] According to Lifton and Mitchell, scientists working on the Manhattan Project were "horrified." J. Robert Oppenheimer wondered whether the living would envy the dead. Henry Wallace, Secretary of Commerce under Franklin Delano Roosevelt, noted, "The guilt consciousness of the atomic bomb scientists is one of the most astounding things I have ever seen."[41]

Lifton and Mitchell noted that "joy over the end of the war overwhelmed moral qualms," and a Roper poll taken then revealed that 50 percent of Americans supported President Truman's decision and 23 percent of the respondents thought we should have used more atomic bombs before the Japanese surrendered. A Gallup Poll later in August 1945 found that 85 percent of Americans endorsed the use of the atomic bomb, only 10 percent disapproved, and there was no difference in respondents' age, sex, or education. Lifton and Mitchell regretfully concluded, "It would be years until Americans saw—or were allowed to see—any Hiroshima images that put a human face on the consequences of the bombing."[42] But Oppenheimer's quote from the Bhagavad Gita at the first detonation of a nuclear device (test codename Trinity) in Alamogordo, New Mexico, "Now I am become Death, the destroyer of worlds," revealed his premonition about the possible future of mankind.[43]

Clearly, racism made the situation and casualties easier for Americans to accept, especially when the Japanese were referred to in the media as fanatics, savages, and beasts. Cartoon depictions of bucktoothed Japanese permeated the media. Even the esteemed progenitor of diversity and inclusion, Theodor Seuss Geisel (Dr. Seuss), published derogatory images of them—although it should be noted that he later apologized for his racist cartoons and dedicated one of his books, *Horton Hears a Who* (1954, an allegorical child's book about the postwar occupation of Japan), to "My Great Friend, Mitsugi Nakamura of Kyoto, Japan."[44]

Obviously, patriotic pronouncements abounded in the aftermath of the attack on Pearl Harbor and revelations about Nazi atrocities inflamed feelings against the Japanese abroad and home, culminating in

Hiroshima after atom bombing (National Archives).

4. The Treatment of Japanese Americans in World War II 91

the wholesale evacuation of Japanese Americans from the West Coast to the relocation camps.

But some social critics and philosophers were appalled by the use of atomic weapons against the Japanese. For example, James Agee of *Time Magazine* said, "The demonstration of power against living creatures instead of dead matter created a bottomless wound in the living conscience of the race."[45] Through secrecy, suppression, and distortion of the events and aftermath, the American public was manipulated into believing that the bombings were justified. Believing in the natural biological superiority of whites over Asians, General Leslie R. Groves, Jr., who led the Manhattan Project from the military side, even questioned the assumption whether Japanese and white American blood was biologically different.[46] This was another indication of the white racist ideology that still pervades the thoughts of some people here and around the world.

It was not until a young reporter, thirty-two-year-old John Hersey, wrote a four-part series for the *New Yorker* magazine in 1946, describing the human suffering in the aftermath of the bombing of Hiroshima, that the American public began to consider the implications of the events of August 6 and 8, 1945.[47] Still, racist attitudes and behavior toward the Japanese flowed freely in American society as chroniclers of the incarceration of Japanese attest. A common denominator among the accounts demonstrated the theme that Japanese were subhuman and undeserving of U.S. citizenship and equal treatment.[48] Signs painted in the windows and prejudicial treatment such as restrictive covenants and local policies that prevented Japanese from owning and renting property and fully participating in society were reminiscent of 19th- and early

Dr. Seuss cartoon (Dr. Seuss Collection, Special Collection and Archives, UC San Diego).

20th-century discriminatory actions.[49] The recent spate of anti–Asian and Pacific Islander hate crimes and the behavior of land speculators after the devastating wild fires on Maui, Hawaii, testify to the fact that Asians are still discriminated against in the United States.

5

Contemporary Struggles: How Asian Discrimination Looks Today

> "These days, I only travel above ground. I carry a flashlight with me at all times, and I wear only shoes and clothing that I can run in, or dropkick someone in, if attacked."
> —Ava Chin, *Mott Street: A Chinese American Family's Story of Exclusion and Homecoming*, New York: Penguin Press, 2023, p. 96.

An elderly Asian woman was pushing a shopping cart and wearing a surgical mask to shield her from Covid-19 germs as she entered the vestibule that led to her apartment in a maze of high rises in Yonkers, New York. As she struggled through the heavy glass door, she was accosted from behind by a burly middle-aged man who punched her in the back of the head. She fell over and slumped in a heap on the floor as he continued to pummel her, landing 125 punches to her face and body. The security camera revealed that he stopped when he was fatigued—out of breath, but sufficiently able to muster enough strength to stomp on her limp body seven times—and he finished the attack by spitting on the semiconscious sixty-seven-year-old before he left the building. The dazed woman received care at a nearby hospital trauma center for her multiple injuries, including lacerations and contusions. She was in stable condition despite her ordeal. Her assailant, a forty-two-year-old man, was taken into custody by the Yonkers police and charged with one count of attempted murder and one count of assault as a hate crime.

Hate crimes against Asian Americans have escalated since the onset of the Covid-19 pandemic, but they have been part of the American social fabric for over a century. One of the most notorious hate crimes perpetrated against Asian Americans was the murder of twenty-seven-year-old Vincent Chin in 1982. He was a draftsman at an automobile plant in Detroit. Chin had been out celebrating his forthcoming marriage with friends when he got into a dispute with Ronald Ebers, a supervisor at a Detroit Chrysler plant, and Ebers's stepson, Michael Nitz, a laid-off auto worker. They beat Chin mercilessly with a baseball bat. He died in a hospital four days later. Fueled by anger over the loss of American jobs because of increasing Japanese imports, the misguided attack was not only illegal and inhumane, it was misdirected. Chin was Chinese. But despite abundant evidence against the men, Wayne County Circuit Court Judge Charles Kaufman sentenced the pair to three years of probation and a fine of $3,000 with no jail time.[1]

Outraged, the Detroit Chinese Welfare Council called the judgment a "$3,000 license to kill." Although a civil court judgment held the men liable for compensating Chin's mother, Lilly, they were remiss on the payments and never served time in jail.

Anti-Asian Hate Crimes in Historical Perspective

Hate crimes have always plagued Asian Americans, from the time of the arrival of the first waves of immigrants on the shores of this country in the mid–1800s to today. Unfortunately, there have been numerous instances of their abuse and persecution, such as the massacre of nineteen Chinese in Los Angeles on October 21, 1871, when a mob of 500 enraged white and Hispanic workers ransacked the Chinese community in retaliation for a fight by rival tongs that left a policeman and a rancher dead. Although eight of the suspects were charged with manslaughter, and despite overwhelming evidence against them, all were released a year later, on a technicality.

Since Chinese, blacks, and Native Americans were barred from testifying in court against whites in those days, members of these groups were frequently victimized without recourse. Historian Ken Waite found more than a dozen attacks on Chinese workers between 1868 and 1870 by the Ku Klux Klan in California. Houses of worship and businesses that aided the Chinese were also victimized by the Klan.[2] The results were similar when a mob of white workers drove Chinese laborers from their work site in San Francisco in 1867, injuring twelve and killing one—all ten attackers were exonerated.

Fear of labor competition was the primary impetus for these early transgressions against Asians in the United States, fear that led to the implementation of the now infamous Chinese Exclusion Act of 1882 and its successors. But contemporary hostility against Asians in the United States may be traced to white supremacy. When Wade Michael Page, a forty-year-old Army veteran, killed five Sikh men and one Sikh woman and wounded four others at a Sikh temple or *gurdwara* on August 5, 2012, including a policeman who was shot fifteen times, his motive died with him when he shot himself in the head after a policeman wounded him in the stomach. But his affiliation with white supremacist causes was undeniable, as evidenced by the white supremacist tattoos that adorned his body and his associations with white supremacist music organizations.

Contemporary Hate Crimes Against Asian Americans

Although Asian Americans have made and continue to make significant contributions to American scientific, business, and creative culture,[3] some of the animosity directed against them has been linked to the pandemic that had its origin in Wuhan, China. Antipathy toward Asians was heightened by the continual reference to the disease as "the Chinese virus" or "the Kung flu" by Donald Trump. Although he was advised against using these terms, and the exact origin of the disease hasn't been established, that is, whether it was a pathogen that escaped from a laboratory or jumped to humans from animals (zoonotic), Asians have borne the brunt of discriminatory behavior from non–Asians over the last few years.[4]

Research by Hswen et al. conclusively demonstrated the effect of Trump's pejorative labels on anti–Asian sentiment in the United States. Writing in the *American Journal of Public Health,* they found that the number of anti–Asian hashtags on the social media platform Twitter (now X) rose by 17,400 percent following his use of the term to designate the disease. It was not uncommon to find tweets like: "F__k the ding dongs. F__k the Ching Chongs. And most definitely, F__k the goddamn chinks," "China lied people died," and "F__k China" and "#Nukechina."[5]

The coalition of organizations known as Stop AAPI Hate found a dramatic increase in hate crimes and incidents of discrimination directed against Asians following Trump's use of the term "Chinese virus." Stop AAPI Hate received reports of 11,500 incidents pertaining to Asians between March 2020 and March 2022. Seventeen percent of these incidents involved physical assaults and 10 percent occurred on public transit. In fact, 40 percent occurred in public spaces, such as on a street or in a public park. More than a quarter of the offenses (27 percent) took place in businesses, such as grocery stores and pharmacies. An additional 10 percent occurred online. The online phenomenon is vexing in light of the anonymity of the offender, which may induce that person to make audacious comments.

These affronts had a chilling effect on victims' safety. Only half of them reported that they felt safe going outside of their lodgings. Ninety-five percent of the victims viewed the United States as more dangerous for them today than prepandemic, and nearly all of the elderly respondents (people 60+ years of age) felt this way. Sixty percent of the victims were female, and nearly half (43 percent) of the victims were Chinese, followed by 16 percent Koreans, 9 percent Filipino, and 8 percent Japanese and Vietnamese.[6]

From these statistics there is little doubt that a dramatic increase in anti–Asian discrimination has occurred since the onset of the pandemic, no doubt fueled by the callous and irresponsible remarks of Trump and other so-called leaders. Yet the report candidly noted that most of the incidents did not meet formal definitions of crimes, even though 20 percent of Asian Americans and Pacific Islanders experienced a hate incident within this time period. Though a common complaint of the victims (two-thirds of them) was verbal or written hate speech or gestures, a distinction exists between hate speech and hate crimes. The former, though despicable, is protected under the First Amendment to our Constitution (the right to free speech) unless it rises to the level of harassment or actions intended to harm people for some particular characteristic they possess, such as ethnicity, skin color, age, disability, gender, body shape or size, religion, or sexual orientation.

The contemporary emphasis on the prosecution of hate crimes emanates from an initiative of the ADL (Anti-Defamation League), a Jewish organization that was founded in 1913 by Chicago attorney Sigmund Livingston for the purpose of stopping "defamation of the Jewish people and to secure justice and fair treatment to all."[7] He realized that all forms of prejudice must be targeted, not just antisemitism, for the struggle to create an inclusive society to be successful. After many years of working to combat hate and prejudice in the United States, I realized the wisdom in this objective. Bigots have one thing in common—they don't feel good about themselves, and they blame others for their misfortune, alienation, and lack of recognition. They don't love themselves. If you scratch an antisemite, you will uncover a homophobe, a misogynist, and a racist. These feelings are frequently fed by a bit of paranoia—some rabid racists are certain that sinister, unseen forces are nurturing and mustering minorities against them.[8] The current bogeyman, said to be responsible for all manner of leftist attacks on American society, is ninety-four-year-old George Soros (Gyorgy Schwartz), a Hungarian-born secular Jew worth nearly $9 billion. He survived the Nazi occupation of his native Hungary and became a successful investor (he currently controls the Quantum Fund, worth about $25 billion). Soros also created the Open Society Funds, which provide funds to independent groups working for justice, democratic governance, and human rights around the world. The Open Society Funds currently fund projects in 120 countries around the world. Soros has given away more than $32 billion, earning him the sobriquet "the most generous giver" from *Forbes Magazine*. His name has become associated with antisemitic rants in his native Hungary. There, dictator Viktor Orban, once his disciple, now eschews him. Also, Donald Trump and other right-wing politicians frequently disparage Soros as a result of his support for progressive and liberal causes.

What's Wrong with the Concept of Hate Crimes?

Despite the clamor about the increase in hate crimes in the United States, several problems are intertwined with the concept. Although forty-five states and the federal government have hate crime legislation that usually increases (accelerates) the penalty when it can be established that a perpetrator was motivated to commit a crime of bias against someone or property, it is difficult to establish motivation, unless the perpetrator provides authorities and/or witnesses with evidence of malice during the commission of the crime, such as uttering racist or antisemitic epithets or leaving hateful slurs in writing at the scene of the crime. Without a demonstrable indication of the perpetrator's intent, authorities and the courts are left to conjecture, interpret, guess, and assume malicious bigoted intent. Although the Anti-Defamation League created a model law that provided states and the federal government with a framework for drafting hate crime legislation, the ground upon which hate crimes statutes rests is spongy and porous.

Not until 2009 did the federal government pass national hate crime legislation, the Matthew Shepard and James Byrd, Jr., Hate Crimes Prevention Act, following the violent tortured deaths of Shepard, who was gay, and Byrd, an African American. Although there was a sordid history of lynchings, and a torrent of hate crimes committed against people in the decades before and after the Civil War, federal action to prevent and prosecute offenders for committing hate crimes was hampered by politically expedient decisions that ultimately forestalled federal intervention in this area. Despite a formal apology by the U.S. Senate on June 13, 2005, for federal inaction about lynching and after an estimated 4,743 lynchings from 1882 to 1968 according to the NAACP,[9] the federal government did not take action in the 20th century.

The grisly murders of Byrd and Shepard provided impetus for the legislation. Both crimes occurred in 1998 when the victims were given rides in pickup trucks by the perpetrators. James Byrd, Jr., was a forty-nine-year-old vacuum salesman when he was given a ride by Shawn Berry, Lawrence Brewer, and John King. Byrd was known to the men and became an unwitting victim when they drove to an isolated area outside of Jaspar, Texas, where they severely beat him, then urinated and defecated upon him. They then tied him to their truck and dragged him for three miles. He was conscious for much of the assault and was not killed until his body hit a culvert half-way through the ordeal, knocking off his right arm and head. While attending a meeting of the National Conference of Christians and Jews, I viewed the police tape of the heinous crime scene, which was dotted with Byrd's blood and eighty-one pieces of his remains.

The three men were unrepentant white supremacists sporting racist tattoos on their bodies. In a jailhouse letter seized by their custodians, King wrote Brewer expressing pride for the crime, showing no remorse, and concluding, "Regardless of the outcome of this, we have made history. Death before dishonor. *Sieg Heil*." Brewer and King were executed by lethal injections and Berry was sentenced to life in prison. He will be eligible for parole in 2038.

Matthew Wayne Shepard was only twenty-one years old when he accepted a ride from Aaron McKinney and Russell Henderson after a night of drinking and drug use at a bar in Wyoming. Ostensibly offended when Shepard touched his leg during the ride, McKinney proceeded to pistol whip Shepard so severely that his skull was fractured. After robbing and torturing Shepard, the pair tied him to a barbed wire fence on the outskirts of Laramie, Wyoming, where he was found eighteen hours later. His face was covered in blood except for an area where tears washed it away. He died from his wounds after lingering for six days in a Ft. Collins, Colorado, hospital.

Both assailants were twenty-one years old. They claimed the violence was related to their inebriation and use of methamphetamine. Henderson pleaded guilty and was sentenced to two consecutive life terms. McKinney went to trial and was convicted of felony murder, aggravated robbery, and kidnapping. He also received a double life sentence for the crime.

5. Contemporary Struggles 99

These heinous hate crimes undoubtedly influenced Congress in its passage of federal hate crime legislation that bears the victims' names. The act, signed by President Barack Obama on October 28, 2009, provides jurisdictions with funds to help them investigate and prosecute hate crimes. It also creates a federal law that criminalizes willfully causing bodily injury, or attempting to do so with a firearm, fire, or dangerous weapon, such as explosive, when the crime was committed because of actual or perceived race, color, religion, national origin, gender identity, sexual orientation, or disability. It must be associated with interstate or foreign commerce or have occurred within a special maritime or territorial jurisdiction. This last point is problematic, since under this act, the federal government can only become involved if the offense was associated with interstate or foreign commerce, essentially barring the federal government from interceding in local and state offenses unrelated to these forms of commerce. Threats of violence, it should be noted, are not criminalized under this act (or for that matter under local and state hate crime statutes); however, threats to inflict physical injury may be prosecutable under other federal hate crime statutes, for example, 42 USC 3631 or 18 USC 245. In essence, this federal law cannot apply to many of the petty insults that Asian Americans and other minorities routinely experience. That is another problem related to the concept of hate crimes, namely, people's perceptions of malicious intent.

There is a vast difference between actual and perceived hate crimes in the United States. The FBI publishes an annual index about the type and volume of these offenses. The total number of offenses hovers around 7,000–8,000 per year. Data for 2021 revealed an 11.6 percent increase in reported hate crimes (from 8,120 in 2020 to 9,065 in 2021). This may be indicative of an uptick in hate crimes committed, and certainly the 12,411 people who were victims of these offenses were distraught enough to report them. However, the FBI noted in a supplemental press release that its data covered 87,239,467 people. On the surface, this seems like a huge number, but it is only about a quarter of our population (332 million in 2021).[10] While the FBI data represented nearly 12,000 law enforcement agencies reporting hate crimes, 6,000 did not report such crimes. Furthermore, there is some reluctance on the part of victims to report hate crimes, whether to shield their privacy or protect themselves and their families from embarrassment or further victimization, so we can assume that hate crime statistics are underreported. For example, when a Holocaust memorial was desecrated outside a synagogue in Clearwater, Florida, I spoke with the president of the organization (herself the daughter of a Holocaust survivor) about publicizing the incident and she declined, stating that the congregation did not want publicity because they feared that might trigger further incidents. (Nevertheless, the media learned of the crime and featured it on the evening television news.)

Some jurisdictions are also reluctant to publicize hate crimes because it is bad publicity and might dissuade visitors. Many years ago, I was given a letter from a former mayor of Tampa, Florida, that she received from an angry Jewish couple who were contemplating moving to the area. Lost, they pulled into a service station to get directions and wound up being barraged with antisemitic insults by one of the attendants. Needless, to say, they decided against moving there, to the consternation of the mayor. While such incidents may be despicable, they do not rise to the level of hate crimes, and Stop AAPI Hate wisely observed that many of the 11,500 hate incidents reported to the organization between March 2020 and March 2022 do not meet the formal definition of hate crimes. Yet they noted that 20 percent of Asian Americans reported a hate incident in this time period, with two-thirds falling into the category of verbal harassment or written hate speech and gestures. Perhaps more ominously, 17 percent of reported incidents involved physical assaults, much of it related to blame for the Covid-19 pandemic and rhetoric of our leaders, and 40 percent occurred in public spaces. These incidents had a chilling effect on Asian Americans and Pacific Islanders—only half of them felt safe when they ventured outside their residences.

Although the FBI endeavors to collate valid information about the prevalence of hate crimes, we have seen that the data are suspect. No one really knows the extent of hateful incidents in the United States. For example, the Anti-Defamation League contends that there has been a dramatic increase in antisemitic incidents in recent years, reporting 3,697 in 2022, a 36 percent increase over 2021 and the most incidents since the organization began tracking antisemitic incidents in 1979. Included in this enumeration were 2,298 antisemitic incidents of harassment (up 29 percent from the previous year); 1,288 incidents of vandalism (an increase of 51 percent from the previous year); and a 26 percent increase in assaults (up 111 percent from the previous year).[11]

The questions remain, do these reported incidents reflect the actual number of antisemitic incidents, and, more importantly for our discussion, to what extent do these incidents rise to the level of crimes and, specifically, hate crimes? Because of problems in ascertaining actual data, we will never know, but a fascinating glimpse of the perceived number of hate crimes and incidents in the United States was generated through surveys conducted by the U.S. Department of Justice's Bureau of Justice Statistics.

5. Contemporary Struggles

Unlike data collected by the FBI on hate crimes through voluntary submissions of law enforcement agencies around the United States, the Bureau of Justice Statistics has conducted in-home surveys of tens of thousands of Americans through the U.S. Census Bureau, and these are referred to as National Crime Victimization Surveys (NCVS). For example, in 2011, 79,000 households containing 143,120 people were questioned about hate crime victimization by the U.S. Bureau of the Census as part of the survey. The Bureau of Justice Statistics, which is part of the U.S. Department of Justice, reported that from 2005 to 2019 the rate of hate crimes reported by victims remained fairly stable, ranging between 0.6 and 1.1 per thousand, or averaging 246,900 hate crime victimizations per year. More than half of the incidents were thought to be motivated by bias against race, ethnicity, or national origin. (Forty-nine percent were directed against blacks.)[12]

Obviously, there is a significant difference between the reported incidents of hate crimes proffered by the FBI and the Bureau of Justice Statistics' in-home surveys of nonfatal hate crime victimization. I do not believe that the difference may be solely attributable to the different methods of data collection. Indeed, as we have discussed, the odds are that both data collection techniques are undercounts because of the reluctance of victims to reveal their victimization to strangers. However, the in-home survey results reveal two important elements about the epidemiology of hate crimes in the United States. FBI data are based on actual law enforcement records of hate crime incidents, whereas the in-home surveys are based on the victims' perceptions of the motivation of offenders. The NCVS conducted for the Bureau of Justice Statistics are based upon nonfatal hate crimes reported to police as being bias-motivated according to victims, or that are perceived to be bias-motivated by the victim because perpetrators used hate language during the commission of the offense, or because, according to the victim, the offender left behind hate symbols. The categories of affected individuals are distinguished by race, ethnic background, national origin, religion, disability, gender, sexual orientation, or association with people who have certain characteristics or religious beliefs, or the perception of a victim's characteristics or religious beliefs.

We are not going to dismiss the validity of the Uniform Crime Report of the FBI, but the disparity between data collected through voluntary submission of hate crime incidents by reporting jurisdictions is dwarfed by the reports of victimization supplied through the in-home surveys conducted by the Bureau of Justice Statistics. No doubt some underreporting of hate crime incidents by law enforcement agencies is because of varying definitions of such offenses, and certainly some locations may be reluctant to self-identify as being inhospitable to certain groups, such as blacks, Jews, and Asians. But the enormity of the disparity between the two types of reports reveals that in addition to undercounts, a great many people in this country believe they have been victimized because of some particularized criterion they possess, such as their skin color or religion, and perception is akin to reality. We base our decisions and actions on what we believe to be true, even when outward indices may point in a different direction. The tragic events of January 6, 2021, are an indication of the false beliefs thousands of people had and their misguided actions based on their belief about the supposed theft of the presidential election by members of a so-called Deep State.

The previous discussion is not designed to dissuade readers from believing that Asian Americans and Pacific Islanders have been subjected to a recent torrent of hate incidents. As we have seen, Stop AAPI Hate's informative report substantiates this assertion, just as the data from the Bureau of Justice Statistics confirm that a sizeable proportion of people in this society believe that they have been the victims of hate incidents. While the nature of the offense may not rise, as the authors of the Stop AAPI Hate report note, to the level of actual hate crimes, the aggregated effects of these incidents, be they crimes or harassment, can have a lingering negative effect, similar to what Sniderman and Piazza described in *The Scar of Race*.[13] Once a person has been, or perceives she has been, victimized through a hate incident, she is likely to blame her misfortune on presumed similar discriminatory behavior. But the data are incontrovertible—Asian Americans and Pacific Islanders have been increasingly targets of hate crimes in recent years, and Asian women have been disproportionately victimized by assailants since the onset of the Covid-19 pandemic.

Publicity surrounding the victimization of Asian Americans can have a negative impact on other members of these ethnic groups, leading to fear of being harassed in public places and causing circumscribed lifestyles to forestall possible untoward advances. A recent analysis of Boston Public Schools' climate surveys revealed that while Asian American students surpassed whites, blacks, and Latinos in academic performance and graduating on time, they scored lower than the other groups in nine of sixteen school climate categories, including feeling less safe at school and feeling their studies were less relevant. Although Asian American students in the Boston Public School system comprise about 9 percent of the students (4,000 out of 46,000), less than 7 percent of the teachers are Asian. Asian American students reported feeling stereotyped and exoticized by teaches and peers, like an "afterthought" according to one Asian American teacher.[14]

As Sniderman and Piazza's work indicates, past experiences may be a prelude to present and even future behavior. Based on the increase in hate incidents directed toward Asian Americans since the Covid-19 pandemic, and the increasing tension with China, students' fear and suspicion may be well placed.

Sinophobia Again

The youthful chief executive of TikTok, one of the largest and most successful social media applications in the world, pleaded his case before the Congressional Committee on House Energy and Commerce. Shou Zi Chew denied that the Chinese Communist Party controlled the popular app (more than 150 million Americans use it), but he acknowledged that it had the ability to manipulate data. The committee's chief concern was the security issue, but members, like the committee chair (Congresswoman Cathy Morris Rodgers, Republican from Washington State), also expressed dismay over TikTok's algorithm that may promote eating disorders, drugs, and suicide among impressionable teenagers, especially girls. "We do not trust TikTok will ever embrace American values," she said as she challenged Chew while he sat stolidly before the committee.

Committee members appeared unmoved by Chew's assertions that TikTok has not shared and never will share sensitive information with the Chinese Communist Party. But a recent report that the Chinese Communists are pursuing mainland Chinese citizens who commit fraudulent acts abroad, especially in Western Europe and the United States, by conducting policing operations and monitoring the activities of Chinese immigrants raised some eyebrows.[15] Even more sinister is the worldwide fear of TikTok's possible subservience to demands the Chinese Communist Party may make upon it to provide sensitive information. Article 7 of the Chinese National Intelligence Law compels companies to provide to the Chinese Communist government data they have or can collect.[16] Although Chew contended that TikTok had never been asked for such information, and a proposed Texas Project proffered by him would invest all data in U.S. control, committee member Anna Eshoo (Democrat, California) responded, "I find that preposterous." With committee members commenting that "Everything is seen in China," "TikTok is a grave threat to American life," and "We must prevent any app from ever spying on Americans again," the prognosis for the company's continued prominence in social media looked bleak.

One should not underestimate the support that TikTok has among the American public. Donald Trump considered banning the app in July 2020. He changed his position, but banned Chinese telecommunications giant Huawei in 2019 when it was avidly pursuing contracts in the United States to manufacture hardware for the 5G telecommunications network, even though the company's founder, Ron Zhengfei, declared that the company would not build a "back door" to allow gathering of information that could surreptitiously be given to the Chinese government.[17] In view of fears about possible Chinese Communist Party access to sensitive data, the Biden Administration banned the company from U.S. government phones in November 2022 because of its potential national security risk.

A recent contretemps of ByteDance (the parent company of Tik-Tok) surrounding the release of data on users did not reassure detractors. An internal investigation of the company found that employees inappropriately obtained data on TikTok users, including two reporters. This information included internal conversations and business documents and the use of IP addresses, all purportedly in pursuit of identifying the source of leaked information (which was not found). ByteDance said it restructured its internal audit and risk team and removed access to all U.S. data, and four employees involved in the transgression were fired (two in China and two in the United States).[18]

Banning TikTok not only would disappoint the company's millions of users, but many people rely on the app for income from products like beauty items, books, and music. With more than a billion users worldwide, TikTok hosts can charge as much as $500,000 for a post on the site, with normal costs ranging between $150,000 and $200,000. All of the top earners in 2021 were under twenty-five years old. They have legions of followers and earn enormous sums from promoting their wares. Half their income is generated from paid advertising, much of it from corporations. The top-grossing TikTok celebrity in 2021 was Charli D'Amelio. She has 133 million subscribers and earned an estimated $17.5 million. With sponsors ranging from Invisalign to Dunkin' (formerly Dunkin' Donuts), the aspiring singer is poised to launch a new career as a performer. Her sister Dixie reportedly has 57 million followers and earned $10 million in 2021, largely from sponsorships with sources including Hollister, Hulu, and Snap. She is an aspiring singer like her younger sister, and one of her songs, "Psycho," hit number 25 on the U.S. Billboard pop chart in 2021.

Addison Rae, with 2021 estimated income of $8.5 million and 86 million followers, also earned money from producing videos on Netflix and has corralled sponsorships from American Eagle and Item Beauty, while the fourth most popular TikTok personality, Bella Poarch, a

Filipina, has 87 million subscribers and has done ads for Google, Prada, and Tinder. She earned $5 million in 2021, and her single "Build a Bitch" hit number 56 on Billboard's Pop Chart.

Josh Richards earned $5 million in 2021 largely through sponsorships from Amazon, Cash App, and Sportscaster, as well as hawking energy drinks and pursuing venture capital deals. Although Richards has 26 million followers, Kris Collins's total of 42 million adherents dwarfs his retinue. Her 2021 earnings, estimated at $4.75 million, lagged behind those of Richards, but her comedy show, where she plays a number of characters, also appears on YouTube and is sponsored by Hershey, Lionsgate, and Pantene.

Avani Gregg, with an estimated income in 2021 of $4.75 million, rounds out the top TikTok earners. With 39 million followers, her income is derived in part from the makeup tutorials she teaches, as well as her Simon & Schuster book *Backstory: My Life So Far*.[19]

Aside from the fact that ByteDance has some influential friends in Congress and has spent over $13 million lobbying to promote its interests in the United States,[20] the existence and import of Article 7 from the Chinese National Intelligence Law may preclude its future in the present form and condemn it to the same fate as Huawei. As Julian Ku, professor of law and faculty director of international programs at Hofstra University, noted, "The problem is that no matter what they [ByteDance, TikTok] offer, there's no way to completely shield the data from the Chinese government … as long as there continues to be a shared entity."[21] Also, a recent study by the Rutgers Network Contagion Research Institute revealed that TikTok systematically promoted and demoted content on the basis of whether it was aligned with the interests of the Chinese Communist Government.[22]

Subtle Reminders of Hate

The murders of six Asian women[23] by twenty-two-year-old Robert Aaron Long at spas in Georgia on March 16, 2021, may be an extreme example of hate crimes perpetrated against Asians in America. The mass shooting of Asian and Hispanic farm workers, killing five men and two women in Half Moon Bay, California, preceded by the murders of eleven Asians a few days before in Monterey Park, California, may not be a hate crime. These may reflect the availability of and access to deadly weapons by disturbed individuals. Although the struggle to counteract gun violence in the United States has become prescient in recent years, racist policies against Asians have been around since the mid–1800s, and recent overtures to prohibit land ownership by Asians, in particular Chinese, are caustic reminders of a racist past that threatened the livelihood and well-being of Asians in America.

Earlier we noted the attempt of local politicians and state legislatures to curb and even prevent land ownership by Asians, particularly Chinese and Japanese, who became successful farmers in California and other western states. These so-called "alien land laws" were fueled by labor strife and union agitation that reflected white workers' anxieties about competition for jobs and agricultural property ownership. Following violent anti–Asian outbreaks in California and other western locales, the Chinese Exclusion Act was passed by the federal government in 1882, legally preventing Chinese from immigrating to the United States. Though the act was formally repealed in 1943, when China was an ally of the United States in World War II, the U.S. Supreme Court did not rule on the constitutionality of so-called "alien land laws." While many states, especially those in the western region of the country, had prohibitions against Asians, particularly Chinese and Japanese purchasing or bequeathing land to parents and children, it was not until 1952 that California attorney Sei Fujii scored a crucial victory that nullified the alien land prohibition in California,[24] when the California Supreme Court held that the law was in violation of the United Nations Charter to which the United States was a signatory.

The current trend prohibiting or limiting the acquisition of land by foreign governments, notably China, Russia, North Korea, and Iran,[25] is reminiscent of obsolete state laws that disappeared in the 1950s. Many state courts ruled that they were prima facie discriminatory and declared them unconstitutional. Yet currently eleven states, mostly in the western part of the country, are reinvigorating statutes that preclude foreign governments from purchasing large tracts of land, especially agricultural land. The rash of bills introduced in state legislatures stems from the fear that China main gain control of and destabilize the food system in the United States. However, Agri Pulse, an organization that monitors agricultural activities, found no evidence of a spike in Chinese land sales based on an analysis of U.S. Department of Agriculture data. In fact, Chinese landholdings pale in comparison to those of other countries, as can be seen from the chart here, with fifteen countries surpassing China, including Canada, with the largest landholdings, followed by the Netherlands, Italy, Portugal, and Germany, respectively.

Chinese investors' purchase of land has remained constant since 2013. The Chinese held about one half of a percent of the overall 35.8 million acres of U.S. farmland and forests in 2019, while total foreign ownership of farmland and forests is equal to 2.7 percent of the total

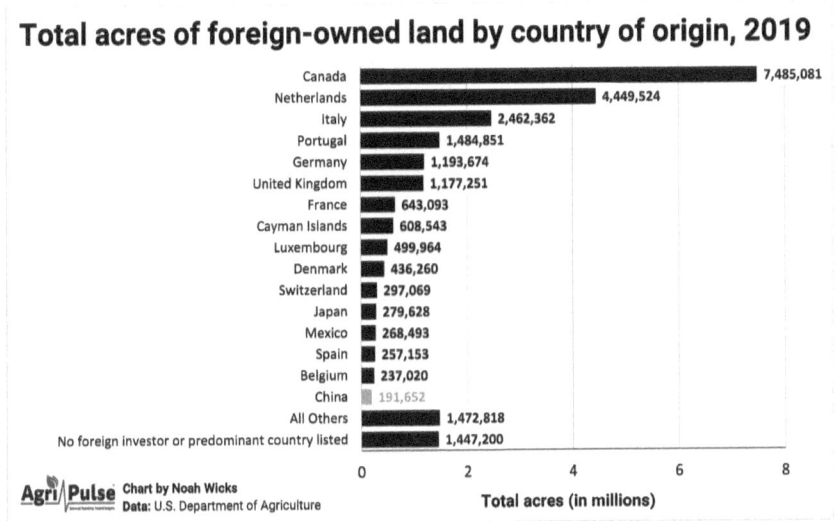

Table Comparing Chinese- and Foreign-Owned Land in the United States (reprinted with permission from www.Agri-Pulse.com).

acreage. Most Chinese land acquisitions have been in Southeast Asia, Russia, and Africa, but that has not deterred some politicians from introducing restrictive land acquisition bills in state legislatures.[26] Some legislators, such as Congressman Dan Newhouse (R–Washington), have expressed a fear of China controlling United States food production. "We know that there is a stated goal of the Chinese Communist government to accomplish the control of not just agricultural assets, but many different kinds of assets around the globe."[27] A provision to restrict Chinese acquisition of farmland passed the U.S. House of Representatives in August 2021 as part of the appropriations bill for the U.S. Department of Agriculture. Sanford Bishop (D–Georgia), then Chair of the House Committee on Agriculture, said he supported the "concept" and called Chinese ownership of land in the United States a "national security issue," while Congressman Jeff Fortenberry (R–Nebraska) viewed the initiative as a measure of "fairness" because China does not allow the United States to purchase land on the mainland.[28]

A sheaf of bills has been introduced at the state level, all with the intent of reining in China's supposed aggressive acquisition of farmland. This unfounded hysteria may be attributed to the acquisition of Smithfield Foods (pork products), with holdings in Georgia, North Carolina, and Virginia, in 2013 by a Chinese firm. That sale concerned 146,537 acres and caught the attention of many politicians. For example, North Dakota House Bill 1135 became law in 2024 after it passed the House

93–0 and Senate 47–0 in that state. In part, this was a reaction by the legislature to the overture by the Fufeng Group's purchase of 370 acres to build a wet corn milling plant just 12 miles from the Grand Forks Air Force Base, which the legislature contends will pose a "significant threat to national security." The city of Grand Forks has gone on record stating it will deny building permits for the project.[29] HB 1355, backed by Governor Ron DeSantis of Florida, was introduced along with a companion bill SB 264 in the Florida legislature in April 2023 and passed that legislature, becoming effective on July 1, 2023. The bills restrict ownership of land within twenty miles of a military installation or critical infrastructure by people or corporations from China, Cuba, Venezuela, Russia, Iran, North Korea, or Syria if they are not U.S. citizens or permanent residents. Only foreigners from China were singled out by being prohibited from owning any property statewide, including homes.

In the final analysis, prohibitions against the purchase of land by China, Russia, North Korea, and Iran may be based on valid fears about the intentions of these governments, but the line between barring countries from purchasing property and prohibiting foreign or even ethnic nationals from owning land can become blurred in these Sinophobic times. The recent downing of a Chinese "weather" balloon that was actually acquiring and transmitting data to China about sensitive military sites in the United States and the heightened tensions between the United States and China over hegemony in Asia and Africa have helped build an adversarial wall between the two countries and complicated the existence of Asian Americans. Limitations on land acquisition and fears of incursions by foreign powers are recurrent themes in the history of Asians in America, most notably marked by the relocation and incarceration of Japanese in World War II. The surfeit of hate incidents perpetrated against Asians in America, as well as the mass shootings of Asians, should never be accepted or tolerated, despite the fact that such actions appear to have become normalized in our society.

Inter-Ethnic Antagonism

Finally, we must consider the issue of inter-ethnic hostility between Asian Americans and African Americans. Some of the animosity between these groups emanated from the early years of the Civil Rights movement in the United States, which began following the murder of Emmett Till.[30] Strife between these groups grew as Asians assumed greater roles in the ownership of properties and businesses in inner cities.[31] As white property owners were displaced by Asians, some

African Americans perceived the locus of control shifted from one ethnic group to another, and turned their animosity toward their perceived new exploiters. Nowhere was this situation more pronounced than in Los Angeles. The facts that beaches and parks were segregated and that there was an ongoing feud between the African American mayor of Los Angeles, Tom Bradley, and the white chief of police, Daryl Gates, complicated the situation. A review of television coverage showed an initial lack of police presence in Koreatown in response to the outbreak of hostilities discussed next.

Conflict between these two groups erupted in Koreatown in Los Angeles, on April 29, 1992 (called Sa I Gu, for the numbers four-two-nine), following the acquittal of four Los Angeles policemen who beat African American Rodney King. Writer Jay Caspian Kang's recapitulation of the event is a stark portrayal of the conflict, and journalist John Lee (then reporting for the *Los Angeles Times*), provided an iconic description of the looting and arson in the area of South Central Los Angeles known as Koreatown.[32]

Speculation about the cause of the rioting has raged for decades, but the wrath of African Americans was projected onto Asians, especially Koreans, who owned many of the small stores in the area. Some of the rage of African Americans was linked to the murder of Latasha Harlins, a fifteen-year-old African American girl who was shot in the head by Soon Ja Du, a forty-nine-year-old Korean convenience-store owner, a month prior to the riots during a dispute over whether Harlins was attempting to steal a $1.79 bottle of orange juice. Security cameras showed that Harlins was not trying to steal the juice, and that after a skirmish between them, Du grabbed a revolver and shot Harlins in the back of the head.

Although Du, the co-owner with her husband of the Empire Liquor Store, where the killing occurred, was convicted of voluntary manslaughter and sentenced to ten years in prison, the judge suspended the sentence and placed her on five years of probation and 400 hours of community service. She was also required to pay $500 in restitution and funeral expenses. A California Court of Appeals unanimously upheld the sentence in July 1992.[33]

This event occurred thirteen days after the release of the tape of the beating of Rodney King by Los Angeles police officers. It heightened the tension between the two ethnic groups and contributed to the frustration of the African Americans about their apparent powerlessness. The adverse economic situation of African Americans in the area was exacerbated by the worst recession since 1938, which may have contributed to the feeling of alienation among some residents of the inner city.

Over the next six days, rioters and looters, primarily but not exclusively African Americans, set fires, looted, and vandalized stores in the South Central section of Los Angeles. Sixty-five percent of all businesses vandalized were Korean owned, among them Du's store, which was looted and burned and never reopened.

Korean shop owners were accused by the black community of undercutting the prices of other shop owners in the area. Koreans bought stores in that area because they were less expensive than elsewhere, but some African Americans resented them. An editorial in a black community newspaper in 1984 urged blacks to boycott Korean stores, calling patrons "traitors." During the six days of rioting, sixty-four people (two Asians, twenty-eight African Americans, nineteen Latinos, and fifteen whites) lost their lives. Nine were shot by law enforcement or the military, but no law enforcement personnel were killed. Nearly three thousand people were injured and about three thousand fires were set, contributing to nearly a billion dollars in property losses, two-thirds of them incurred by Korean owners.

The threat of black violence against Koreans loomed large, and is reflected in Ice Cube's lyrics from *Black Korea:*

> So pay respect to the black fist
> Or we'll burn your store right down to a crisp
> And then we'll see ya
> Cause you can't turn the ghetto into black Korea.[34]

Korean Americans (and other Asians) got a stern lesson from the way they were treated by various governmental authorities. Mayor Bradley did not extend himself in assisting the recovery of Korean American businesses, nor did Governor Pete Wilson. Many Korean Americans felt forsaken by the white-dominated establishment when the Los Angeles City Council denied them the opportunity to reopen their stores by because the shops were defined as liquor stores and their licenses were not renewed.

Subsequently, President George H.W. Bush visited the area and 100,000 Korean Americans peacefully demonstrated for racial and economic justice. The Korean Americans were attempting to show their solidarity with the African American community and lobbying the Bush Administration for economic compensation in light of their losses—many shop owners were uninsured, and some insurance companies refused to compensate claimants, asserting that the riot was "an act of God."

Animosity between Asian Americans and blacks surfaced again when African American Michael Brown was killed by a white

5. Contemporary Struggles

policeman, Darren Wilson, in Ferguson, Missouri, on August 9, 2014, after a dispute with an Asian shop owner. In the days following Brown's death, rioters vandalized twenty stores, half of them owned by Koreans, even though the Asian population in Ferguson is only .05 percent. Although this situation did not become a national incident, it reflects the underlying rocky relationship between the black and Asian communities.

Nevertheless, Asians have been trying to improve relationships with African Americans. Koreans and other Asians demonstrated solidarity with African Americans in Black Lives Matter demonstrations in the aftermath of the murder of George Floyd. As Yi and Hoston note, the highly visible and successful Korean pop group BTS donated a million dollars to the Black Lives Matter movement after the death of George Floyd, and this was matched by their followers, the BTS A.R.M.Y., who also launched a campaign against racist hashtags such as #whitelivesmatter and #alllivesmatter.[35]

Given the overwhelming social and economic pressure exerted on minority groups in the United States, we may assume that similar enmity between blacks and Asians may erupt in the future. That sentiment is reflected in Jay Kang's incisive discussion of this topic. He recalled the disappointment of Vicci Wong, a seventeen-year-old University of California at Berkeley freshman who, upon trying to join the Black Panther Party in Oakland, California, was spurned and told to "form your own group." She joined the Asian American Political Alliance. Although this happened almost fifty years ago, and Asian Americans and African Americans have reached a rapprochement of sorts, there is still tension between them as they compete for political and economic pieces of the capitalist pie that continues to divide and conquer the disparate ethnic groups that comprise the majority of people in the United States.[36]

Kang's perspicacity about the superficiality of white, black, and Asian relationships in the United States is striking and finds expression in his statement about being Asian in America:

> Modern Asian American identity is built out of the assumption that because we aren't white, we must be "people of color." But this is all greatly complicated by class: the upwardly mobile Asian Americans hang in a suspended state outside the Black–white binary, while the millions of Asian working poor have been made entirely invisible.[37]

Kang raises a cogent point by quoting a Korean American shopkeeper whose business was destroyed in the conflagration:

"I've lived in the United States for twenty-nine years. I went to college here, and grad school, and got my doctorate here. But now none of my experiences here seem meaningful. I wonder whether I should leave here?"[38]

His rhetorical questions deserve to be considered:

White liberals talk about ending racism, but they don't mean us. In fact, they actually deny us justice to protect Black assailants. If the roles were reversed and Asian men were randomly attacking and even killing old Black people, there would be nationwide protests. All summer during the George Floyd protests, we were lectured by rich, educated Asians to examine anti–Blackness in the Asian community. But what about anti–Asianness in the Black community? If we have to examine why our parents follow them around in stores, shouldn't they have to examine why they shove helpless elders and kill them?[39]

At bottom, we are motivated by the stereotypes that hold sway over our emotions. Fear, suspicion, anxiety, and envy shape our beliefs and behavior. In the next chapter we analyze some of the prevalent stereotypical misconceptions about Asian Americans.

6

Persistent Stereotypes About Asian Americans

> "We need to look in that reflecting pool called America, where, as long as our eyes remain open, the images of ourselves will never cease."
> —Yunte Huang, *Charlie Chan*, p. 288.

In *The Loneliest Americans,* Jay Caspian Kang, a Korean American, recalled his reaction at first seeing his infant daughter, born with a "full head of dark hair and almond-shaped eyes." Knowing firsthand about whites' prejudice toward people of color and their racism, he had hoped that she might have some of her mother's WASP (white Anglo-Saxon Protestant) type of looks. But that was not to be, and he wondered if she would be able to "hide from whatever Trump had planned for us."[1] Kang, an author and writer for the *New Yorker,* evinced the same fear and trepidation many Asian Americans have about the stereotypical views that the dominant white society has about them.

Like the old stereotype printing presses that stamped out identical sheets of information, social psychological stereotypes are implanted in our consciousness shortly after birth—they assist us by simplifying our decision making, but they can be discriminatory and racist, too, by perpetuating myths and inaccurate information about individuals and groups. Some people learn to withhold judgment about an individual until they supplement their first impression with credible information to avoid oversimplifying and generalizing, making erroneous assumptions, and drawing spurious conclusions about someone or group. While our brains use stereotypes to simplify decision making, we must be cognizant of the fact that decisions predicated upon stereotypes may seem logical but be incorrect. Nevertheless, stereotypes about people and ethnic groups are ubiquitous in our society, and many of the memes pertaining to Asian Americans are not only persistent but pernicious.

We now turn the discussion to some of the prevalent stereotypes about Asian Americans.

Movies Make a Difference: The Inscrutable Asian

Among the long list of stereotypes about Asian Americans, the stereotype that depicts them as cold and calculating has endured. Certainly, colleges and universities have decided to capitalize on these traits, with, for example, Harvard College admitting more Asian American students in 2023 than ever before. (The school, along with the University of North Carolina, was under scrutiny by the U.S. Supreme Court, which rendered a decision that effectively scuttled affirmative action in colleges, although major Asian American organizations such as the Committee of 100 and Stop AAPI Hate were in favor of preserving affirmative action for Asian Americans.)

Some of the most enduring stereotypes about Asians were purveyed through motion pictures about a brilliant and enigmatic Chinese man, Detective Charlie Chan. Based upon the Hawaiian-born Honolulu detective Chang Apana, a diminutive five-foot tall Chinese policeman renowned for his fearless pursuit of "bad guys" in the islands, writer Earl Derr Biggers, born in Warren, Ohio, and a graduate of Harvard College, created the aphoristic-speaking inscrutable Chan in six novels that morphed into forty-seven films spanning two decades. Sadly, Biggers died from a heart attack at the age of fifty-five in 1933, before most of the films were made and the cult of Charlie Chan blossomed into the American psyche. However, motion pictures reach far more people than books and articles, and television extended the image of Charlie Chan to millions more viewers, cementing images of Asians that lingered on the pages of Biggers's novels.

Frank Chin, an acerbic American author and playwright, contended that the Chan (and Dr. Fu Manchu, discussed later) movies were parables of the racial order in the United States. Casting white men in the leads of these films was "visual proof of our [Chinese] acceptance and assimilation by whites."[2] From Chin's perspective, these movies perpetuated stereotypes of Asians as passive, submissive, accommodating, and feminine—the white male's "dream minority."[3] We return to this line of discussion in the next chapter as we consider the concept of the "model minority." We must first address the impression that the phenomenon of Charlie Chan had on the American public.

The role of Charlie Chan, an enigmatic, quasi-effeminate, mysterious Chinese detective, was made famous by the white Swedish actor Warner Oland, who starred in sixteen Charlie Chan films from 1931 to 1937, until he died of pneumonia at the age of fifty-seven. He was replaced by another white actor, Sidney Toler, who starred in twenty-one Charlie Chan movies from 1938 to 1946. When Toler succumbed to cancer in 1947, he was replaced by a third white actor, Roland Winters, who starred in six Chan films from 1947 to 1949. The character of Charlie Chan, the enigmatic, cagey, Chinese sleuth, was resurrected in comic books and strips, radio dramas, children's books, and board games, and was brought to life in the Hanna-Barbera 1972–3 production of *The Amazing Chan and the Chan Clan* that aired on Saturday mornings for children. The voice of Charlie Chan was that of the man who played Charlie Chan's Number One Son, Keye Luke, and who also played the blind Master Po in the *Kung Fu* series (1972–5), a program starring David Carradine on ABC television. J. Carrol Naish played Chan in a thirty-nine-episode (one season) television series in 1957–58, and Ross Martin also assumed the role in a television pilot that wasn't made into a series in 1973. Peter Ustinov played Chan in *Charlie Chan and the Curse of the Dragon Queen* (1981), and the following year, Wayne Wang produced *Chan Is Missing*, a screen spoof that did not reignite interest in the phenomenon.

Biggers introduced Charlie Chan in his first novel, *The House Without a Key* (1925), which was set, like most of his novels, in Hawaii. Throughout his books he established the Chan character as portly, with beady black eyes: "the expression in his eyes, a look of keen brightness that made the pupils gleam like black buttons in the yellow light."[4] Although Biggers frequently referred to Chan as heavy and past his physical prime, the detective was cast as a dapper figure who was fastidious about his appearance, highly ethical, and industrious. Throughout his exploits, which at times created a conflict with mainland police, as in his interactions with law enforcement in *The Chinese Parrot*, Detective Chan managed to solve conundrums that would have perplexed ordinary humans.

Biggers was not averse to perpetuating negative stereotypes about Asians, and throughout his novels Charlie Chan is presented as obsequious, frequently bowing to whites and uttering comments designed to assuage their hostility. Chan's self-deprecating comments are suffused throughout Biggers's writing, as when he addresses Sheriff Holt, in *Keeper of the Keys*: "You will perceive that your new assistant [Chan] has sinking spells of stupidity."[5] A bit later, he said "Large empty place makes good storehouse" as he tapped his forehead.[6] Another example is in *Charlie Chan Carries On* (1930), when he not so subtly implies his supposed incompetence: "a stupid substitute for Duff [a Scotland Yard detective] has been pushed into position for which he has not the brains, the wit, the reputation. Notably—myself."[7]

The reader should not mistake Biggers's penchant for dramatic stylistic descriptions of the detective, namely, his incessant use of pidgin English. The novels also contain antiracist barbs that reveal his sentiment for equitable treatment of Asians, such as an exasperated white British aristocrat's comment in *The Black Camel* concerning Chan's slow progress in investigating the murder of Ms. Fine: "Good lord! What kind of place is this? Why don't they send a white man out here?," to which Chan meekly responded, "The man who is about to cross a stream should not revile the crocodile's mother."[8] In *Charlie Chan Carries On*, Biggers deftly inserted the comment that the Chinese were an admirable race who succeeded around the world.[9]

Despite habitually referring to the Chinese as psychic and nocturnal, Biggers was aware of white racism against them, and he made Detective Chan, with his obsequious mannerisms, witty aphorisms, and unflappable personality, the poster boy for wise, contemplative American sleuths. Biggers summed up his admiration for the Chinese in his final novel (1932), *Keeper of the Keys*, referring to them as "a race that minds its own business. An admirable race."[10]

Nevertheless, times change, and some of the vituperation directed toward the novels and Biggers may have been justified. The frequent references to Chinese as psychic, nocturnal, inscrutable, and English-averse were complemented by his not infrequent negative references to women, as the retired septuagenarian sheriff Sam Holt mutters: "They're hard, women are—since they took to runnin' the world."[11]

Perhaps the key to comprehending the source of derision for the Charlie Chan phenomenon lies in the Civil Rights Movement that gathered strength among African Americans, Latinx, Native Americans, and Asians during the 1960s and 1970s. The drive for black, brown, red, and yellow power that emanated from this movement had a demonstrable impact on the visibility and volubility of its adherents. From lunch-counter and bus sit-ins and demonstrations, to riots in over 120 cities following the assassination of the Rev. Dr. Martin Luther King, Jr., to the occupation of the Bureau of Indian Affairs building in Washington, D.C., and the former Alcatraz prison by Native Americans, as well as the Lakota reservation at Wounded Knee, and the demand for comprehensive ethnic studies programs and courses in colleges and schools, the spirit of enthusiasm for self-recognition, individuality, and ethnic identity was catapulted into the consciousness of the American people and, most of all, members of traditionally oppressed minorities, who became more aware of their self-worth and rightful place in American society.

As ethnic consciousness was elevated, scorn was heaped upon cultural artifacts that were deemed stereotypical and racist. The Charlie Chan movies were a visible, easy target for such derision, especially when other reviled ethnic actors such as Stepin Fetchit and Mantan Moreland appeared in the films. As Asian author Yunte Huang noted, in more than two thousand films and stage productions, no Chinese actor played the role of Charlie Chan.[12] In fact, however, the roles in the first two Charlie Chan films were played by Asians. George Kuwa played Chan in *The House Without a Key*, and Kamiyama Sojin played Chan in *The Chinese Parrot*. Both men were Japanese. However, the three men primarily responsible for developing the role of Charlie Chan in motion pictures were white, and, as in other ethnic-oriented films in the early years of the motion picture industry, such as those involving African Americans and Native Americans, principal roles were played by whites. Aside from criticisms that Oland, Toler, and Winters's depictions of Chan perpetuated stereotypical images of Asians, the fact that white actors performed in "yellowface" reinforced critics' concerns about the inculcation of racist images in the general white public through movies and television. Asian playwright Frank Chin likened the Chan image to a white Christian crusade to convert and assimilate Asians into the United States and Western society.[13]

As the anti–Chan movement gained momentum, the films were withdrawn from television. The Fox Movie Channel removed them in 2003, and the Organization of Chinese Americans stated:

> Charlie Chan is a painful reminder of Hollywood's racist refusal to hire minorities to play roles that were designed for them and a further reminder of the miscegenation laws that prevented interracial interaction even on screen. Instead, they were inaccurately depicted by Caucasian actors, who wore face paint to act out stereotypical images of Asians as slanted eye, buck toothed, subservient, and non–English speaking.[14]

Law professor Lan Cao and feminist Himilce Novas presented a lurid description of Chan as an archetypical Asian stereotype that promoted bigotry and misunderstanding of Asians, bolstering white racism, leading to the devastating development of the "model minority" stereotype.[15] But there is some question about Biggers's conception of the Chinese detective. Biggers's first Chan novel, *The House Without a Key*, described the Hawaiian detective as "very fat indeed, yet he walked with the light dainty steps of a woman. His cheeks were chubby as a baby's, his skin ivory tinted, his black hair close-cropped, his amber eyes slanting."[16] Although most of the first Chan novel is devoid of racist stereotypes about Asians, he referred to Japanese characters pejoratively as "Japs" seventeen times, and frequently referred to detective Chan as a Chinaman (a pejorative term). Looking from historical and sociological lenses at such references may help understand Biggers's social myopia, and a careful reading of the text reveals occasional references to the Chinese detective in pejorative terms, such as "the slanted eyes blinked with pleasure."[17] Another example is when Miss Minerva admonished her nephew, John Quincy, that the subtle and perceived erudite stereotype about Chinese wasn't true: "You don't mean to say that you've fallen for all that bunk. They seem clever because they're so different."[18]

Perhaps more notable than the occasional allusion to stereotypical physical characteristics imputed to Asians was the persistence of Chan's use of pidgin English, which leaves the white reader with a feeling of Asian inferiority—Asians' purported inability to master the English language, as when detective Chan congratulates John Quincy for solving the murder of his uncle Dan: "One thought tantalizing me. At simultaneous moment you arrive at same conclusion we do. To reach there you must have leaped across considerable cavity."[19] Another is when he compliments Miss Minerva at the end of the novel: "From that compliment it glows rosy red. At this moment of parting, my heart droops. My final wish—the snowy chilling days of winter and the scorching windless days of summer—may they all be the springtime for you."[20] While the Charlie Chan novels themselves were not overwhelmingly infused with pernicious Asian stereotypes, the numerous motion pictures based on them certainly contributed to Biggers's (and society's) portrayals of Asians as mysterious, subtle, clever, inscrutable, and maladept with English.

Still, as Huang noted, some positive outcomes were associated with the Charlie Chan phenomenon. Charlie Chan became a genuine American hero "without whom American literature would be penurious."[21] Summing up the controversy, Huang noted that "All these characters [Nigger Jim, Huck Finn, and Charlie Chan] are indeed rooted in the toxic soil of racism, but racism has made their tongues only sharper, their art more lethally potent. Whether it's a jazzy tune coming from the lips of a blackface Jew [Al Jolson] or a yellow lie told by a ventriloquist Swede [Edgar Bergen], the resilient artistic flower has blossomed *in spite of* as well as *because of* racism. This undeniable fact, insulting and sobering, has uniquely defined America."[22]

Keye Luke, who played Chan's Number One Son, contended that working on the Chan films was a labor of love: "They [the motion picture studios: Twentieth Century–Fox and later Monogram, which became Allied Artists] spared no pains to turn out good Chan pictures.

6. Persistent Stereotypes About Asian Americans 119

Chang Apana (left) and Warner Oland (courtesy Everett Collection).

Sidney Toler (courtesy Everett Collection).

We thought we were making the best damn murder mysteries in Hollywood at the time. We were very proud of them. They were, oh, such fine entertainment."[23] Luke defended the films and their treatment of Asians and disparaged critics of them as naive. "They [Chinese activists] think it demeans the race. I said 'Demeans! My God! You've got a Chinese hero!'"[24] Film critic Ken Hanke observed, "Charlie's greatest sin perhaps is not himself, but in the fact that he was virtually the only positive depiction of an Oriental in film at the time. Much like the situation that later developed on television with *Amos 'n' Andy*, it is less a problem with the series than it is with the circumstances of no balancing material to compensate, making the single image seem to some more caricature than characterization."[25]

Roland Winters (courtesy Everett Collection).

In a nostalgic tribute to the Chan movies, film critic Ken Hanke concluded, "Thankfully, the indomitable Charlie Chan of Messrs. Oland, Toler, and Winters will be with us for many years to come, preserved on film and held in our hearts, forever, ready to take a case, reunite spatting lovers, patiently listen to an offspring pose the ubiquitous 'Gosh, is he dead Pop?' question and sum the whole thing up with a placid 'Thank you so much.' There is something inherently comforting and indefinably 'right' that this should be so—and for it, we should be the ones to be politely grateful. Thank you so much, Charlie."[26]

The Sinister Side of Asian Stereotypes

When Sax Rohmer penned his first novel about the sinister, manipulative, and depraved Dr. Fu Manchu, Sinophobia was prevalent in the United States. It would be three decades until the cessation of the draconian Chinese Exclusion Act. From its inception in 1882, the federal law reinforced negative stereotypes about Chinese immigrants to rationalize its existence. Labor unions and white workers were principal antagonists of Asian immigrants in their quest for jobs. The unions enjoyed some success in generating allies among obsequious and unscrupulous civil servants who supported their cause, which deprived Asian men of the opportunity to raise families like non–Asians in the promised land. When Asian men pursued white women, they were often stigmatized and worse. The Page Law of 1875 restricted the importation of Chinese women for immoral purposes, the notorious "sing song girls," forcing aspiring Chinese women immigrants to produce certificates testifying to their good character. As Cao and Novas indicated, this resulted in a third fewer Chinese women immigrating to the United States between 1875 and 1882.[27] The white majority established the laws and created the prevailing social climate that denied Chinese men the opportunity of forming stable families with Asian women who were prevented from emigrating to this country. One cannot conceive of a more appropriate illustration of a self-fulfilling prophesy than the predicament faced by Asian men in the United States prior to the repeal of the Chinese Exclusion Act.

As we previously noted, much of the vitriol directed toward Asians, especially Asian men (although the relative few Asian women in this country were also defamed and labeled as social misfits), emanated principally from a sense of competition for jobs and, ultimately, income. Since, like most immigrants, Asians were seldom involved in negative interactions with the legal system, stereotypical memes were spread about their purported sinister intentions. Nowhere is the theme about the evil, enigmatic, and sinister Asian more palpable than in the works of Englishman Sax Rohmer, who penned a series of novels that promulgated derogatory stereotypes about Asians, beginning with *The Mysterious Dr. Fu Manchu*, in 1913.

Rohmer was born in Birmingham, England, in 1883, as Arthur Henry Ward, of Irish immigrant parents. They moved to London, where he attended school three years later. Ward took the *nom de plume* when he embarked upon a literary career that followed contretemps in civil service, banking, and working as a clerk for a gas company. His literary career started when he composed ditties for comedy sketches of music hall performers. Although he had some measure of success as a poet, songwriter, and comedy author, it was not until he penned his first novel, *The Mystery of Dr. Fu Manchu*, which was serialized from 1912 to 1913, that he generated enthusiasm for his work. In it and his subsequent works (Rohmer wrote thirteen Fu Manchu books), he purveyed stereotypes that emphasized the evil, sinister, and megalomaniacal Dr. Fu Manchu and the threat to Western civilization of the "yellow peril." In his novels, Fu Manchu is presented as the leader of the secret Si-Fan society bent on world hegemony. (The similarities to Dr. No in the first James Bond movie [1962], and the earlier Ming the Merciless in the *Flash Gordon* series [1936] are striking and perhaps not altogether accidental.) Fu Manchu was portrayed as the yellow peril incarnate, a depraved manager of human events with homosexual tendencies, bent on world domination. Although Rohmer's choice of a Chinese villain was based partly on external events (the Chinese revolution had just occurred on the mainland [1911]), he perceptively sensed that conditions were right for launching a Chinese villain on the market.

Unlike his first novel, *Pause!*, which was an anonymous collection of sketches ghost-written for the English comedian, singer, and actor George Robey, Rohmer's Dr. Fu Manchu series generated enormous attention, making him one of the most financially successful writers in the 1920s and 1930s. Rohmer authored numerous other novels and short stories, but none garnered him as much attention as the Fu Manchu series. His promulgation of negative stereotypes about Asians, and Chinese in particular, resulted in condemnation by the mainland Chinese government and the Chinese community in the United States. Although some of his earlier works were set in the Chinese section of London known as Limehouse (and he was criticized for denigrating its residents and disparaging its surroundings), the infamous doctor was not averse to traveling around the world in his criminal quest for ascendancy.

In contrast to Charlie Chan being depicted as a cherubic amiable character by Earl Biggers, Rohmer invested Fu Manchu with the most sinister and diabolical qualities known to mankind. His descriptions of him are suffused with innuendos about the "yellow peril" and the purported goal of world domination by the Chinese. Fu Manchu is presented as an evil monster, "unquestionably, the most malign and formidable personality existing in the known world to-day."[28] Manchu is described many times as "the emissary of an Eastern power"[29] (China) bent on world domination. The doctor is said to be "the advanced agent of a movement so epoch-making that not one Britisher, and not one American in fifty thousand has even dreamed of it."[30]

Rohmer's rants against the Chinese included copious references to their purported cruelty, manifested in their supposed penchant for female infanticide by using scorpions to kill female babies and by throwing them over cliffs. A particularly unique characteristic of Fu's malevolence was his knowledge and use of exotic creatures like the venom of poisonous snakes, toxic plants, and even stealthy henchmen, *dacoits*, from Burma who possessed near superhuman physical abilities and who assisted him in the conduct of his nefarious activities. Rohmer was incessantly imbuing Fu Manchu with extraordinary intellectual abilities that provided him with advantages over his Western antagonists, Dr. Petrie (the narrator of the tales) and Denis Nayland Smith, Manchu's archrival. Much of the action in his novels is conducted at night, highlighting the sinister, creepy aura that suffused the life-and-death struggles between the principal characters. Although the Chinese are continuously disparaged in these novels, the intellect of the maniacal Manchu and therefore of the Chinese is held in high regard, as the character Dr. Petrie noted in *The Return of Fu Manchu*: "I would gladly had given my income for a year, to have gained possession of the books [of Fu Manchu] alone, for beyond all shadow of doubt, I know them to contain formulae calculated to revolutionize the science of medicine."[31]

Make no mistake about it, Rohmer painted a picture of Asians, especially Chinese, as opium-addicted, criminally disposed, cruel, and anti–West. As Nayland Smith remarked, "The entire white race and its survival depends largely upon the success of my mission"[32] because Fu Manchu and the Chinese were the enemies of the white race, and "No white man, I honestly believe, appreciates the unemotional cruelty of the Chinese."[33]

Dr. Fu Manchu is described as having a formidable intellect, "a person tall, lean and feline, high-shouldered, with a brow like Shakespeare and a face like Satan, a close-shaven skull and long, magnetic eyes of the true cat-green."[34] He is invested "with all the cruel cunning of an entire Eastern race, accumulated in one giant intellect, with all the resources of science past and present, with all the resources, if you will of a wealthy government—which, however, already has denied all knowledge of his existence."[35] This is a mental picture of the man Rohmer depicted as a villain bent on bringing the West under control of China, "the yellow peril incarnate in one man."[36] As Rohmer described it through Dr. Petrie, "We knew the reality of the danger that a veritable octopus has fastened upon England—a yellow octopus, whose head was that of Dr. Fu Manchu, whose tentacles were dacoits, thuggee, modes of death secret and swift, which in the darkness plucked men from life and left no clue behind."[37]

Rohmer published his first three Fu Manchu books from 1913 to 1917 and waited fourteen years before resurrecting the genre in *Daughter of Fu Manchu* in 1931. He wrote fourteen Fu Manchu novels and died in 1959 of, ironically, complications from the Asian flu. Along the way, he befriended the famous magician and illusionist Harry Houdini, and even based one of his later characters on him.[38] By my reckoning, thirty-five Fu Manchu motion pictures have been made, including the first two that were nontalking ventures (*The Mystery of Dr. Fu Manchu* [1923] and *The Further Mysteries of Dr. Fu Manchu* [1924]) made by Stoll Picture Productions, starring H. Agar Lyons. In addition, two television serials were aired, one of them a fifteen-part series titled *Drums of Fu*

Manchu produced by Republic Pictures in 1940 and subsequently made into a feature film by that name in 1943, and one in 1956 by Republic Pictures' Hollywood Television Service—a syndicated thirteen-episode piece. It's ironic, but not surprising, that Dr. Fu Manchu was always portrayed by white actors in "yellowface." The first three talking films of Fu Manchu starred Warner Oland, the Swedish actor who became famous as the hospitable Charlie Chan. Over the years, the role of Fu Manchu was played by many notable Hollywood actors, including Boris Karloff and Christopher Lee (who starred in five Fu Manchu films, ending in 1969).[39]

Although his books were banned by the Nazis, Rohmer's Fu Manchu works were widely regarded as racist against the Chinese. As critic Jack Adrian noted, "Rohmer's own racism was careless and casual, a mere symptom of his times."[40] But there can be little doubt that the Fu Manchu books, comics, movies, radio programs, and television broadcasts had an impact on the perceptions of Rohmer's countless fans. The stereotypes promoted in his works have endured to this day, depicting Asians, especially Chinese, as nefarious, criminal, opium-addicted, lecherous, and poverty-stricken. Rohmer made a fortune from the series and similar works that he penned after moving to the United States in 1947. He also published the sexually oriented Sumuru series featuring a female protagonist played by Shirley Eaton in two movies based upon it. However, literary critics have not been kind to him.

Writing in the *Oxford Dictionary of National Biography*, Robert Bickers concluded that Rohmer "was never considered to be more than a writer of lurid lowbrow shockers by his contemporaries. His reputation today rests on his creation of Fu Manchu, but largely because it has become a byword for racist stereotyping of Chinese people."

Christopher Lee as Dr. Fu Manchu (courtesy Alamy).

Further, "As a thriller writer Ward is of little importance. His prose is pompous and ponderous, and his plotting thin, predictable, and repetitious. However, Ward [Rohmer] was an entrepreneur with an instinctive knowledge of his market in the face of rapid developments in popular fiction in the twentieth century."

Martial Arts Mania

Perhaps one of the residual stereotypical casualties of Rohmer's Fu Manchu books is the lasting impression that Asian men are dexterous and universally gifted in the martial arts. A number of other factors have contributed to this belief. Perhaps underlying the Western fascination with Asian martial arts such as karate, jujitsu, judo, taekwondo, and mixed martial arts (MMA) is a recurrent trope that rationalizes the judicial use of force for good over evil in the pursuit of righteousness. Some writers have likened the ancient Samurai code of *bushido* to that of Western knights and their code of chivalry. While it is true that both groups sought a balance between violence, peace and wisdom, research indicates that there were numerous forms of *bushido* in Japan. While honor, obedience, duty, and self-sacrifice were cornerstones of *bushido* and the samurai way, *bushido* codes frequently mirrored the economic and political era of their time.[41]

The tradition of noble samurai warriors has had a dramatic impact on Western thought, especially that of young men and boys. Indeed, the mixed martial arts industry, which includes many of the Asian martial arts (as well as Brazilian capoeira), is one of the most rapidly growing businesses in the United States, growing at an annual rate of 18.7 percent since 2012. In 2022, there were 50,490 martial arts businesses in the United States, and more than one million people participated in mixed martial arts competition. Nearly 73,000 people were employed in martial arts schools, with average earnings per school of $114,657.

The domination of the television market by the UFC (Ultimate Fighting Championship) has had a tremendous influence on audiences in the United States and around the world. Fifty percent of people ages 18–44 years indicate that they are fans of the sport in the United States, which features a variety of kicks, punches, and submission holds.[42] Combined revenue from MMA activities in 2022 was over $9 billion.

There is a long and illustrious tradition among Asian nations that led to the contemporary recognition and inclusion of martial arts in the modern Olympic Games, commencing with judo (Japanese) in the 1964 Tokyo Olympic Games, and taekwondo (Korean) in the 1988

Olympic Games in Seoul. One of the earliest manifestations of martial arts among Asians was the practice of kung fu among Chinese Shaolin monks in 527 Common Era (CE); this was a hallmark of Chan Buddhism as taught by a visiting ascetic, Bodhidharma, from India. The residents of the Shaolin Temple, at the foot of Wuru Peak in the Songshan mountains of China's Henan Province (now a UNESCO World Heritage site), refined Chan Buddhism with its emphasis on meditation and centering the mind and self.

With their practice later evolving into Zen Buddhism, the ascetic monks focused on developing their martial arts kung fu skills while studying Chinese literature and medicine. Perhaps the little-known temple would have escaped the consciousness of Westerners, but the Shaolin phenomenon was catapulted into the awareness of Americans by an ABC television network series known as *Kung Fu*, which ran from 1972 to 1975. The star of the show was David Carradine (1936–2009), who played Kwai Chang Caine (with a Chinese mother and American father), in search of his lost half-brother, Danny. Trained as a Shaolin monk, Caine was involved in endless struggles between good and evil that weekly tested his Kung Fu martial arts skills that he used judiciously, having been trained by Master Kan (Philip Ahn) and Master Po (Keye Luke, who also played Charlie Chan's Number One Son).[43]

Warner Brothers gave the show new life in *Kung Fu: The Legend Continues* when it produced a new series, set in contemporary times, based on the original one. This ran for three years, 2020–2023, on the CW network. A unique feature of the program was the predominantly Asian cast.

Prior to the Western enthrallment with *Kung Fu*, a young Chinese American actor captured the imagination of American theatergoers in a series of high-energy films that demonstrated his lightning reflexes and martial arts skills. Bruce Lee (1940–1973; his Chinese name was Li Jun Fan) rarely spoke in his films, but his fists and kicks demonstrated proficiency in the martial arts as he portrayed minorities struggling against prejudice, inequality, and racism.

Born in San Francisco, Lee was raised in Hong Kong when his parents moved there; his Chinese father (his mother was Eurasian) was an opera singer and part-time actor. Bruce Lee was athletically gifted and learned kung fu to protect himself in brawls in the crowded streets of his adopted city. In 1958 he even won Hong Kong's cha-cha dance contest, but his parents were alarmed by his misadventures and sent him to live in Seattle, where he attended the University of Washington. He later opened a martial arts school there and another one in Oakland, California, where he taught his own style of kung fu that he called jeet kune do, combining kung fu, fencing, boxing, and philosophy.

He found his way in Hollywood after playing Cato in the television *Green Hornet* series (1966–1967). Lee starred in *Fists of Fury* (1971), followed by *The Chinese Connection* (1972) and *Return of the Dragon* (1972), a Hong Kong film that he also wrote, co-produced, and directed. His last film, made in 1973, was *Enter the Dragon*. These films made him a worldwide super star, but his career was cut short by his untimely death from swelling of the brain because of an allergic reaction to headache medication. He was only thirty-two years old. Tragedy struck the family again in 1993, when his son Brandon, an upcoming actor, was accidentally shot and killed while filming *The Crow*.[44]

The kung fu genre morphed into a series of motion pictures that perpetuated the stereotype of Asian dominance of martial arts. Jet Li, a Hong Kong celebrity, assumed the mantle of martial arts master and film star, for example, in *Once Upon a Time in China II*, and Jackie Chan became a star by combining martial arts, dexterity, and comedy in a number of films that drew enormous audiences and solidified his status while perpetuating the stereotype of Asians as martial arts aficionados. The enthrallment of the American television audience with mixed martial arts and the prevalence of martial arts schools and symbolism perpetuate the stereotype of Asians as martial arts experts in our society.

Bruce Lee (courtesy Alamy).

Another important development in the stereotypical depiction of Asian proficiency in martial arts can be traced to the 1984 comic book *Teenage Mutant Ninja Turtles* (TMNT) by Kevin Eastman and Peter Laird. The comic book sparked an American media franchise that led to a series of motion pictures, television shows, toys, books, comic books, video games, and associated items that produced annual sales in the billions of dollars during the decades of the 1980s and 1990s. The four Ninja turtles were anthropomorphic and named after Renaissance figures: Leonardo, Michelangelo, Donatello, and Raphael. They were trained in the ancient tradition of *ninjutsu*, a Japanese tradition based upon unconventional guerrilla warfare, also known as *ninpo*. This feudal constellation of techniques using stealth and deception was designed for the assassination of opponents in the Genpei War in Japan from 1180 to 1185 CE.

The modern comic book derivation of the ancient tradition was toned down and suffused with levity to facilitate its marketing to children. The first issue of the franchise comic book was published in 1984 by Mirage Studios. There followed a surfeit of associated marketing ploys designed to ensnare children around the world. Playmates Toys figures appeared in the early 1980s and raked in more than $1 billion between 1980 and 1992. By 1987 more than 400 TMNT figures had been produced, and they were the third best selling toys behind *Star Wars* and *GI Joe* figures.

Over the years there have been at least five live-action and animated series based upon TMNT, and several have run for many years; for example, TMNT series aired on television from the early 1990s until 2023. Video games (Xbox, Nintendo, Konami, iPhone, iPad, Android, Kindle Fire), are still appearing, in addition to the seven feature films released between 1987 and 2023, and Paramount and Seth Rogen have current projects. Two hundred and fifty newspapers carried Dan Berger's TMNT comic strip from 1990 to 1996, in addition to comic books published by Image and Archie Comics from 1985 to 1999. If one adds the TMNT concert tour of 1990 and all the appendages surrounding the TMNT phenomenon (even amusement rides were created on the TMNT theme), one can assume that millions of children in the United States and around the world were exposed to the stereotypical theme linking Asians to martial arts. Although the TMNT phenomenon peaked in the 1990s, it has been periodically resurrected, with all of its childish stereotypes, conditioning and misinforming subsequent generations.[45]

The reach of the martial arts stereotype about Asians extends beyond the TMNT franchise. It can also be found on the NBC

Television Network show *American Ninja Warrior*, which at this writing has run sixteen seasons. With a million-dollar grand prize, nimble contestants weave their way through obstacle courses in a competition that rewards the finest athletes for their strength, endurance, and dexterity, all the while promoting stereotypes about the supposed stealth and nimbleness of Asian adversaries.[46]

The major thrust of stereotypical intrusions about Asian martial arts into our culture has clearly been through influencing children. Another prime example of this has been the proliferation of the *Mighty Morphin Power Rangers* series, which debuted in 1993 and evolved into a megafranchise, even rivaling TMNT. By 2001, it was estimated that more than $6 billion had been spent on Power Rangers toys. As of 2022, the Power Rangers had completed twenty-nine television seasons, with the release of three feature films. In 2018 the franchise was sold to Saban Brands and Hasbro for $522 million, after making its mark on *Fox Kids* and putting in a stint with Disney. Not bad for its originator, Haim Saban, who came across the concept during a visit to Japan in the 1980s when he observed the Sentai Series produced by the Toei Company. Although there are many mystical sci-fi elements to the Power Rangers phenomenon, there is an unmistakable similarity between the martial arts maneuvers of the Power Rangers and other Asian manifestations of self-defense styles.[47]

Our discussion of stereotypes about Asian Americans would not be complete without a note about two important contributions that Asia has made to our culture: manga and anime. Both have their roots in Japanese graphic art. Together they account for a large and growing reading and viewing audience. Manga are themed graphic novels, rich in artistic (and often romantic and heroic) symbolism. Anime is hand-drawn and computer-generated animation and is of Japanese origin, also steeped in heroism and romanticism. In recent years manga and anime have emerged from diverse Asian and American markets. They are widely enjoyed and popular. Manga graphic novels have frequently been made into anime computer-generated animated films. Three manga graphic books of Japanese origin led the best-sellers of *The New York Times* graphic novels list for most of 2021: *My Hero Academia*, *Jujutsu Kaisen*, and *Chainsaw Man*. Again, the distinction between the two is that you read manga and view anime.

The graphic novel of Gene Luen Yang, *American Born Chinese*, has had a tremendous impact on the millions of people who have read it. Soon to be released as a live-action Disney+ streaming series featuring Michelle Yeoh and Jimmy Liu, the book won numerous awards after being published in 2006, but its author was ambivalent about the possibility of negative stereotypes being represented by some of his characters, especially Chin-Kee. Yang's reluctance about mass producing the messages in the book was overcome by careful script management and a sensitive portrayal of the characters.[48] His graphic novel was created in the genre of manga.

Most anime began as manga. There was a 43 percent increase in manga sales in the United States in 2020, and it totaled 25 percent of the U.S. book market by 2021. There are more than a million users of the manga subreddit r/MangaCollectors. Yen Press is a principal publisher of manga in the United States, and Kodansha in Japan.

In the United States, Tokyopop (formerly Mixx Entertainment and founded by Stuart J. Levy in 1997) is a principal American distributor, licensor, and publisher of manga and anime. Its parent company is in Japan and its sister company is in Hamburg, Germany.

The market for anime is exploding. It is estimated that 63.5 percent of Americans enjoy viewing it. In 2019, the North American anime market was reported to be $3.56 billion, with the age cohort eighteen to twenty-four years old accounting for 39 percent of the viewers. In 2020 there were 3.17 million legal digital downloads of anime in the United States, equaling 5 percent of the total streaming content. Seventy-four percent of Netflix subscribers watched an anime series in 2020, and the market grew by 150 percent between 2016 and 2019.

Though manga and anime are becoming increasingly diverse, there can be little doubt that these media are of Asian origin, reflecting common stereotypical depictions and presentations of that culture, and reinforcing stereotypes about that part of the world.[49]

We would be remiss if we did not mention the enormous impact that video games have had on billions of people around the world. Two of the largest manufacturers of game consoles (Sony's PlayStation and Nintendo), as well as many of the creators of the most popular video games, have their origin in Asia, particularly Japan. An estimated 3 billion people play video games (many people are now using their smartphones and computers), but the Asian influence on people, especially children and young adults, is almost unfathomable. Global sales of video games are projected to top $23 billion by 2028.[50]

There's No Accounting for Tastes

One of the most prevalent and persistent stereotypes about Asians concerns their dietary habits. There is a common belief that "they eat cats and dogs." Looking at this from a sociological perspective, we know that the consumption of food, including the choice as to what to eat as well as the preparation and serving of the food, is closely linked to one's culture. Since most Asians in the United States have been born here, it is logical to conclude that they have been reared in the predominant cultural climate of our society with its emphasis on junk food, beer, wine, and deserts. Nevertheless, many contemporary Asian American writers painfully recalled their fears of being ostracized at school because of the non–American lunches their immigrant mothers packed for them.[51]

The stereotype that Asian Americans, and Asians in general, are fond of consuming dogs and cats is a recurrent meme that surfaced when I did diversity training and conflict resolution among middle and high school students.[52] In fact, many Asian countries have banned the sale and human consumption of cats and dogs, often because of the work of the Humane Society International. For example, Taiwan was the first Asian country to establish protections for domestic animals like dogs and cats. Its Animal Protection Act, revised in April 2017, strengthened animal cruelty penalties. Those found guilty of animal cruelty can face fines up to 52,000 pounds (roughly $100,000 U.S.) and two years in jail. The law is also intended to counter cultural beliefs about the supposed benefits of eating dogs and cats—for example, some people believe that eating black dogs in the winter will keep you warm.

Cultural beliefs and practices are resistant to change. The International Humane Society estimates that about 30 million dogs and 10 million cats are annually consumed by humans in China alone. Many of these animals are obtained illegally (by theft of pets) and undergo brutal conditions before being slaughtered. However, human consumption of dogs and cats is not widespread in China—most Chinese citizens have never eaten them, and of the 20 percent who reportedly have, they have done so only once or twice.[53]

Research indicates that China's dog meat consumption is found primarily in South, Central, and Northeast China, but dogs are stolen and transported around the country. VSHINE is the Humane Society International's partner in China. Together the organizations are working to reduce animal cruelty and human consumption of domestic animals like cats and dogs. The groups have focused their efforts on the annual festival in Yulin in the Guangxi Zhuang Autonomous Region, where large quantities of dog meat are consumed. Their efforts have met with some success, and it should be noted that 72 percent of the population there does not regularly consume dog meat.

Dog meat has been banned in Thailand, the Philippines, Singapore, Hong Kong, and many cities in Indonesia, making China the only major industrially developed country in the world that doesn't have an anti-animal cruelty law, but VSHINE and the Humane Society International are working to remedy that. In 2020, the cities of Shenzhen and Zhuhai banned human consumption of dog and cat meat, and China's Ministry of Agriculture declared that dogs are considered companions, not livestock. The goal is to get the National People's Congress to institute a ban on their consumption.[54]

South Koreans consume dog meat in a dish commonly called gaegogi. Seventeen thousand dog farms dot the country, but the dog meat market in Seongnam was closed prior to the Winter Olympics in 2018. A South Korean municipal court ruled that it was illegal to consume dog meat that year, but it was not illegal to raise dogs for human consumption. Nevertheless, market pressures have nearly ended the legal farming, slaughter, and sale of dog meat in South Korea. The largest dog meat market, Moran, closed in 2018. Changing tastes and pressure from animal rights groups have nearly ended the dog meat trade in that country. The dog meat market in Daegu closed in 2021, and a recent survey found that 84 percent of South Koreans had never eaten dog meat, nor did they intend to.[55]

Another problematic country is Vietnam, where approximately five million dogs are eaten each year by humans. However, a 2021 report by the Four Paws organization, an animal rights group, found that the distribution of dog meat in the country was basically informal. Their survey of 600 people from North and South Vietnam (Hanoi and Ho Chi Minh City) revealed that the custom of eating dog meat was more common in the northern part of the country than the southern. Only 38 percent of all the respondents claimed that they had ever eaten dog meat.

Again, cultural factors influenced the consumption of dog and cat meat. Some respondents believed that the bones of black cats had a medicinal benefit, and that these meats conferred good luck on consumers. Some consumers noted that they preferred the taste of these meats. While it is still legal to sell such meat in Vietnam, the authors of the report concluded that eradicating the practice would be difficult because the habit of consuming such meat is difficult to break.[56]

Obviously, the prevailing social and cultural environment has an influence on the rate of consumption of domesticated animals such as dogs and cats, which is why the phenomenon is relatively rare in the United States. More importantly, the influence of one's home life, especially during childhood, has a dramatic effect on Asian Americans' diet, which can be likened to the vaunted Mediterranean diet. The focus of Asian American diets is to create wellness through healthy eating, and Asian Americans do have lower incidence of some types of cancers than the white population.[57] Cold drinks are limited during meals,

6. Persistent Stereotypes About Asian Americans   133

which facilitates digestion, and soup is frequently consumed, providing important vitamins and minerals. Unlike some American diets, which feature mammoth portions and meat, vegetables are a mainstay of many Asian diets, and meat and dairy products are minimized with parsimonious portions. Rice, preferably brown, black, red, or purple (not white), is served with most meals, and seafood (a source of consternation among some Asian children bent on assimilating into the larger American culture) is regularly consumed, along with nuts, seaweed, dried fruit, and seeds. Asians also prefer to match their meals to the prevailing climate, serving cold foods in warm weather and hot foods in the winter.[58]

Just as the category of Asian Americans is diverse, so too are the diets and differences in food consumption among them. For example, while most Asian Americans incorporate fresh food, especially fruits and vegetables, in their diets, Thai food is hot and spicy, while Koreans consume kimchi (cabbage marinated in saltwater, peppers, and spices—the longer the better); Indians, Bangladeshis, Pakistanis, and Sri Lankans often use spices such as ginger, garlic, cumin, and fenugreek, and many of them are vegetarians, and fond of eating at Taco Bell because its Mexican pizza can be served that way and other items on the menu provide meatless dishes.[59]

Americans are fascinated with Asian food. Between 1999 and 2015 sales of Asian food grew 135 percent, faster than sales of Latin and Middle Eastern food. The growth in Asian food sales parallels the growth in the Asian American population, but Americans' interest in and willingness to experiment with different foods has contributed to the explosion in sales of Asian food. From Thai food to Asian fusion, East Indian lassis to Taiwanese bobas, chow mein to Szechuan, kimchi to pad thai, the seasonings and presentations are as varied as the more than 40,000 Asian restaurants that are found in the United States, including the $2 billion annual sales of the Asian fast food chain Panda Express, which has more than 2,200 locations and employs more than 39,000 people.[60] It is no coincidence that immigrants have traditionally sought upward mobility by feeding America, thereby exposing the general population to diverse ways of preparing food and teaching cultural diversity as a by-product.

It's ironic that Americans have a fondness for eating pork, despite the fact that pigs are the most intelligent barnyard animal. Some European countries have an affinity for consuming horse—a species of animal that is anathema for human consumption and seldom on the menu of most Americans. Still, the 15.2 million licensed hunters in the United States manage to kill 6 million white-tailed deer annually, despite reminiscences about Bambi. The nation's 40 million anglers catch nearly a billion fish a year, landing around 350 million of them. So there's no accounting for tastes and techniques of harvesting food worldwide. Perhaps even more ironic is the fact that it was not until 2018 that the United States, under President Donald Trump, signed a farm bill making the slaughter, trade, importation, and exportation of dog and cat meat illegal.[61]

Mean Moms

Another persistent stereotype about Asian Americans is that they are obsessed with inculcating their children with the desire to overachieve. In the beginning of her best-selling book *Battle Hymn of the Tiger Mother*, Amy Chua states that her two daughters were never allowed to attend a sleepover, have a playdate with other children, be in a school play, watch television or play computer games, choose their own extracurricular activities, get any grade less than an A, or not be the number one student in every subject in their school except gym and drama, and they could only play the piano or violin.[62]

While Chua's children grew to be successful in terms of graduating from Harvard and Yale law schools and becoming attorneys, one wonders whether they paid a price for this success. Still, her oldest daughter, Sophia, at one time a concert pianist, noted in a 2016 interview that "It was always unequivocally clear in my mind that my parents were on my side, no matter what. They did have high expectations of me, but because they had the confidence that I could do amazing things." For the record, the sisters planned to raise their own children the same way.[63]

Chua continuously disparaged the "Western" parenting style, which she contended was laissez-faire and too accommodating to the desires of American adolescents. In contrast, "the Chinese parenting style" was based on "tough love," frequently relying on threats, shaming, and harsh discipline. Her daughters had to practice seven days a week for up to six hours a day on musical instruments (Sophia the piano and Louisa [Loulou] the violin).

Chua remarked that she didn't have time to improvise about parenting; the primary consideration was to make her parents proud of her and carry on the tradition of reverence for the family name. The emphasis was always on excellence and achievement. "What Chinese parents understand is that nothing is fun until you are good at it," and to get good at something you have to sacrifice and work at it.[64] She stated that

6. Persistent Stereotypes About Asian Americans 135

the "solution to substandard performance is always to excoriate, punish and shame the child."⁶⁵ But one wonders whether her own personal preferences became more important than her children's interests. Later in the book, Chua even speculated about whether she should allow them to make more decisions, but she didn't refrain from criticizing the prevailing "Western" predilection of affording children more options in decisions affecting their social, emotional, and intellectual endeavors.

The antithesis of this model was the Summerhill School, founded by A.S. Neill in Leiston, England, in 1921. Without a formal curriculum and mandatory courses, students were reared in a laissez-faire environment where they had the right and responsibility of democratically running the institution.⁶⁶ Summerhill was designed to promote the development of creative expression among the fifty-nine boys and girls originally enrolled. (There are fewer than seventy students enrolled there today.) Unlike the Chinese parenting model espoused by Chua, the Summerhill School allows students to choose what, when, and how they want to study. Though Chua affirmed her belief that "Western children are definitely no happier than Chinese ones,"⁶⁷ a look at the general level of satisfaction among Summerhill students seems to belie her assertion.⁶⁸

I am reminded of a discussion I had with a graduate of Summerhill. He told me about a friend "who didn't speak the Queen's English" but wanted to become an auto mechanic. He never learned to read or write well, nor did he enroll in math classes until he reached a level of auto mechanics that required him to take more advanced classes and learn how to read blueprints. "He seems to be well-adjusted. We write one another from time to time," he said. "You know, I did a study of about 600 graduates of Summerhill to find out what they were doing," said this professor of management at the State University of New York at Buffalo (who later became a high-level manager at the National Science Foundation). He received his doctor of philosophy in sociology from the University of California at Berkeley. "What did you find?" I asked. "Can't say definitively. I never finished the study."

Judging from her narrative, Chua spent an enormous amount of time and money coaching, teaching, and shepherding her children around the planet. Her commitment to making her children excel took them to distant countries such as Russia, Austria, and Hungary, as well as a variety of locations in the United States where they entertained the public and celebrities with their musical skills. It does appear that her efforts met with success to a point, and the diffusion of Asian Americans in the legal, political, educational, and scientific professions supports the assumption that the Chinese parenting model works. (See

Chapter 2 for examples of Asian American achievements and Yang, Yu, and Wang, *Rise*,[69] for a summary of their contributions in popular culture.) But one is left with the timeless conundrum: Were her children genetically superior to their peers or was their seeming success the result of the harsh "tough love" environment in which they were reared? It's the old nature versus nurture argument.

I conducted a forum in Tampa, Florida, more than thirty years ago. Funded by the Hillsborough Humanities Council, the series of four two-hour symposia was designed to inform the public about the struggles the Asian community was having with racism and their fight for social equality. At the first public forum, after an hour presentation by a panel composed of academicians and business leaders, during a question and answer exchange an Asian American man rose from the audience and remarked: "I grew up in a family that pushed me to work harder and achieve the highest grades I could in my schools. I was admitted to the University of Chicago and became a successful engineer. But I never had any life outside of my studies, and I think I lost something from that. I think I lost my childhood, and I'm not sure that it was worth it."

One cannot escape the numerous references Chua made throughout her book that convey the feeling that she (and perhaps other Asian Americans utilizing similar parenting models) was vicariously living through the experiences of her children, just as many American fathers push their sons (and daughters, in the case of Richard Williams and his tennis-playing daughters Venus and Serena) into sports. Despite her protestations to the opposite, "everything I do is unequivocally 100% for my daughters,"[70] her narrative frequently belied her feigned denunciations. Here is an example: "Everything seemed to be going exactly to the plan."[71]

On reading the tome, one asks, whose plan? Her children certainly had minimal input into it. Her daughters, once teenagers, gained a sense of independence and began to disagree with her, claiming that she was pressuring them because she derived satisfaction from their accomplishments.[72] While the pursuit of success through academic and musical accomplishments may be commendable, and even noteworthy, as in the case of Sophia and Lulu (and in hindsight they said that they did not resent the onerous schedules forced upon them), one wonders about the success, utility, and applicability of the Chinese parenting model to the United States and the world. At the risk of sounding chauvinistic, the United States is still revered for its scientific and technological accomplishments, so much so that other countries, including Russia and China, devote considerable resources to gathering information about such developments—at times surreptitiously. For a leader in artificial intelligence, medicine, and science (the United States is still the only nation to have landed people on the moon), one wonders whether such a stringent parenting model contains within it the creative seeds that can grow into scientific and technological mastery, and whether the sacrifices and hard work are worth it, especially in light of evidence presented later in this volume about the "bamboo ceiling" of prejudice that has limited many Asian Americans' upward mobility. Of course, if one doesn't try to succeed and pursue aspirations, then the prospect for achieving distinction, which many Asian Americans have attained, would never have happened.

One thing must be made very clear about this discussion: Differences in achievement, accomplishments, and success are the result of cultural/environmental stimuli, not genetics. There are no significant differences in the physical or intellectual ability of different ethnic groups, despite periodic attempts to demonstrate this—for example, in the early 20th century eugenics movement, the Nazi infatuation with the Aryan myth, Arthur Jensen's essay to demonstrate the inferiority of Africans and African Americans, and Herrnstein and Murray's analysis and conclusion about creating a utopian society.[73] Research consistently demonstrates that environmental influences, such as childrearing techniques, are causally related to the accomplishments of children and adults.[74]

The Asian Wealth Gap

Contrary to the stereotypical image of Asians depicted in Kevin Kwan's novel *Crazy Rich Asians*,[75] not all Asian Americans are wealthy (or crazy). In fact, while some Asian American groups have managed to accumulate wealth as measured by financial assets, other Asian American ethnic groups are barely managing to survive. These disjunctures were boldly illustrated in an article by Patraporn, Ong, and Pech,[76] social scientists who analyzed U.S. Census data on wealth and found glaring disparities among different Asian American ethnic groups in wealth. Overall, Asian Americans were near parity with non–Hispanic whites in wealth holdings in the United States, especially in terms of income, home ownership, and entrepreneurship, but there were significant differences in these areas among the diverse Asian American ethnic groups they studied. Reviewing the financial status of approximately 222,000 Asian Americans up to 2012, they concluded that there was greater wealth inequality among Asian Americans than between them and non–Hispanic whites, especially since 2008 following the Great Recession and housing bust.[77]

The authors found that Asian Americans were worse off than their non–Hispanic white counterparts, with white total net worth more than double that of Asians in the bottom quarter bracket (whites' wealth was $37,000, compared to $15,000 for Asian Americans). Even more illuminating was their finding of wealth variations between Asian American groups; for example, Chinese and Asian Indians were found to have wealth status similar to that of non–Hispanic whites, but Hmong and Laotians had only half the average wealth of all Asian Americans, except regarding home ownership. The most financially successful group of Asian Americans was the Japanese, who were more than six times more likely to hold wealth than Vietnamese Americans. (Chinese Americans were five times more likely to hold key financial assets than Vietnamese Americans.) Overall, the Japanese, Chinese, and Southeast Asian Indians were deemed to be the most prosperous groups of Asian Americans, while the Cambodians, Hmong, and Laotians were found to be the least wealthy.

Being male, having more education, and residing in the United States longer were factors that had a favorable effect on wealth assets, while having limited English proficiency decreased them. The authors noted that discrimination also affected the wealth status of the subjects under investigation, with darker-skin immigrants treated differently than lighter-skin immigrants, a phenomenon reported on earlier by Painter, Holmes, and Bateman.[78] After analyzing data based on 4,592 legal permanent residents in the United States from the New Immigrant Survey of 2003, they concluded that darker-skinned individuals were hindered in acquiring assets and that they also had lower wealth than lighter-skinned immigrants based on their lower acquisition of stocks, mortgages, and cash accounts. They reported that this finding was especially relevant to skin tone differences among Asians and concluded that "darker-skinned Asian and black immigrants may encounter a double disadvantage that affects their ability to acquire certain assets and improve their life chances: one layer of disadvantage due to their skin tone and another layer of disadvantage due to their racial minority status."[79]

Television and Stereotypes

The profusion of television in our society has presaged wider acceptance of Asian Americans. With their increasing exposure in advertisements and "stars," Asian Americans are achieving recognition for their thespian talents, and the exposure has a cascading effect on the white American psyche, leading, perhaps, to the diminution of the adage that Asian Americans are "perpetual foreigners." Certainly, there was much hype surrounding the nine seasons Chinese American actress Lisa Ling headed up her CNN series *This Is Life with Lisa Ling*, which began in 2014 and was canceled for budgetary reasons in November 2022 (but she landed a position with CBS News thereafter). Her series presented topics ranging from opioid addiction to racism against Asians and sexual encounters at a swinger convention. And who can dispute the stardom of Korean actress Sandra Oh, born in Canada, who became a stalwart of the popular television show *Grey's Anatomy*, where she played Dr. Christina Yang, among numerous other credits in her illustrious career?

Perhaps the pinnacle of thespian stardom belongs to Chinese American actress Michelle Yeoh, who won an Academy Award for Best Actress in the 2023 film *Everything Everywhere All at Once* at the 95th Academy Awards. But to diehard Marvel fans, that honor may go to Simu Liu, Canadian born Chinese actor, the first Asian Marvel hero, who starred in *Shang-Chi and the Legend of the Ten Rings* (2021). The ongoing series about time travel, *Quantum Leap*, a reboot of the 1990s series of the same name that starred Scott Bakula, stars Korean American actor Raymond Lee, and he has turned the heads of many white American viewers as it enters its third season. Perhaps even more impressive in its attempt to deprecate stereotypes about Asian Americans was the television series *Fresh Off the Boat*, derived from the

Actress Michelle Yeoh at Cannes (George Biard, Wikimedia Commons).

book of the same title written by Chinese American Eddie Huang. This ABC television series lasted six seasons (from 2015 to 2020) and featured an all–Asian cast playing the family of the author.

Set in Orlando, Florida, where Huang spent his formative youth, the series was designed to puncture racial stereotypes about Asians, just as his best-selling book did.[80] The book is named for a concept that depicts newly arrived Asian immigrants (as well as other new immigrants) as naive and unworldly. Yet there is a demonstrable sense of innocence and industriousness that pervades the characters that Huang deftly used to attack stereotypes that demeaned well-intentioned newcomers to this country. In his campaign to deflate white racism, Huang managed to dispel the image of the Asian model minority by recounting some of the counterculural antics that pitted him against law enforcement, for example, when he dealt drugs to other students at Rollins College, although he graduated with honors from Yeshiva Law School and became a successful chef and restaurateur in New York City after appearing on the Food Channel's "Ultimate Recipe Showdown."[81] The book is an insightful treatise about a Chinese American's struggle for independence and success, eschewing the traditional appendages that ostensibly necessitate achievement. In text laced with expletives and slang, Huang manages to skewer the racist stereotypes used to prevent Asians from becoming full-fledged members of our society while showing the futility of striving for success in a society rigged against them.

Huang narrated the series for the first season but relinquished that job as the show took other turns. Nevertheless, *Fresh Off the Boat* was filled with repartee among the cast that humorously detoxified white American racism by demonstrating its foolishness. From eating to dating and his mother's infatuation with status and money, the series poked fun at and holes in conventional stereotypes about Asians and American white supremacy.

This discussion helps us understand the prevalence and persistence of racial stereotypes that operate in the United States to penalize people of color and prevent them from fully engaging in our society. Whites have been able to infuse our culture with negative conceptions about people of color and ethnic groups who are viewed as foreigners because they do not approximate the ideal type of white Christians who ostensibly settled here, that is, stole this land from Native Americans. Although dark-skinned people generated wealth and status for whites through chattel slavery, their contributions to establishing wealth in our society have been ignored or minimized (witness the pro-slavery argument inherent in the anti–Advanced Placement Black History course in Florida). It's just a simple matter of cultural legerdemain—the manipulation of attitudes and values to put people of color at a permanent social and economic disadvantage. Worse, some members of these targeted groups have bought into these memes and actively discriminate against members of their own ethnic group.[82]

Me So Horny!

What a subheading! I remember hearing it in a video I used to show my classes on racism in society. An Asian woman sex worker was trying to solicit American GIs. She was standing on a street in Saigon (now called Ho Chi Minh City) and calling out alluringly to the young men, advertising her merchandise. It doesn't take a rocket scientist to figure out why the stereotype about sexy, aggressive Asian women emerged, and why it persists to the detriment of Asian American women in the United States.

The phenomenon that launched this stereotype was similar to the effect of anti-miscegenation laws that emanated from the Page and Geary Acts, Chinese Exclusion Act, and subsequent laws of the 19th and 20th centuries in the United States that made it nearly impossible for Chinese and other Asian men to connect with Asian women as sexual partners and wives. Like U.S. servicemen deployed to the Philippines, Korea, and Vietnam, the principle of propinquity, that is, nearness, helped determine the likelihood of sexual encounters with women from different ethnic backgrounds.

One of the saddest chapters in the transient relationships between the United States and a foreign country derives from our involvement in the Korean War—a conflict that ended in an armistice in 1953. Some 5.7 million American men and women served in Korea during this conflict. Young men away from their homes often availed themselves of the sexual opportunities presented by the ubiquitous camptowns near military bases. These offered female companionship and liquor.

It is estimated that between 20,000 and 40,000 children were fathered by American servicemen during the American participation in the conflict, ranging from some men who had little or no interest in marrying and raising their offspring, to others who desperately tried to marry their Korean girlfriends and bring them to the United States.[83] As many as 100,000 Amerasian (American father and Korean mother) children were "rescued" from Korean orphanages following cessation of hostilities between North and South Korea in 1953. Children born from these mixed-race relationships were frequently reared by their Korean mothers who lived in poverty. Korean society roundly rejected these children, and they were often unable to receive state medical care, social services, and education. Since the 1950s, more than 100,000 of these children have been adopted by people in the United States. Until 1998, South Korea conferred Korean citizenship only on a child whose father was a Korean citizen, often leading single Korean mothers to abandon their children and put them up for adoption in the belief that their offspring would qualify as Korean citizens and be eligible to receive health and social service benefits.[84]

A similar situation occurred following the Vietnam War, when American servicemen were thought to have fathered over 100,000 Vietnamese Amerasian children (American father and Vietnamese mother). They, too, were discriminated against by the Vietnamese population, which referred to them as "children of the dust" and "half breeds," but unlike for the Korean situation, legislation was passed in Congress in 1987 (the Amerasian Homecoming Act) that allowed children of American fathers and Vietnamese mothers to immigrate to the United States. Although the act originally projected that 20,000 to 30,000 Amerasian children and their families would seek refuge in the United States, by 2018 more than 75,000 Vietnamese had resettled here, even though 80–90 percent of applications were rejected.[85]

Despite efforts to resettle Amerasian children, they are still stigmatized in their homelands, and the perception of their Asian mothers as collaborators and/or indecent resonates with many people in their native land. The stereotypical depiction of Asian women as hypersexed endures and surfaced recently in the brutal killing of six Asian women (five Koreans and one Chinese) who worked in massage spas in the Atlanta, Georgia, area in March 2021. Just a short time before that, in January 2019, Robert Kraft, the widowed owner of the New England Patriots, and twenty-four other men were arrested for soliciting sex acts with Asian women at the Orchid of Asia Day Spa and Massage. Charges against the men were dropped in December 2020, but the women paid thousands of dollars in fines. Thus, stereotypes about hypersexualized Asian women not only persist in our society—they are reinforced through legal institutions that promote them.

7

The Model Minority Myth

"To be yellow in America. A special guest star, forever the guest."
—Charles Yu, *Interior Chinatown* (New York: Vintage, 2020), p. 119.

"In our efforts to belong in America, we act grateful, as if we've been given a second chance at life. But our shared root is not the opportunity this nation has given us but how the capitalist accumulation of white supremacy has enriched itself off the blood of our countries. We cannot forget this."
—Cathy Park Hong, *Minor Feelings* (New York: One World, 2020), p. 90.

In the Beginning

When sociologist William Pettersen used the term "model minority" in his *New York Times Magazine* article more than fifty years ago,[1] few people initially realized that the concept would be used to stigmatize and denigrate other people of color, especially African Americans and Latinos. But Petersen's concept, which attributed economic, educational, and cultural success to the Japanese in the face of the adverse situations they faced, such as incarceration during World War II, could not presage the divisive connotation of the term. Nor could Petersen foresee the beneficial effect that the Hart–Celler Immigration and Nationality Act of 1965 would have on the cultural and financial success of Asian Americans. One cannot think of a more divisive way of separating ethnic minorities than linking success to supposedly random social attributes of Asian Americans while ascribing failure to blacks and Latinx for purportedly lacking these same virtues. Of course, hard work and individual initiative play an important role in the success of some Asian Americans, but lumping all Asian Americans into the melting pot of American life overlooks the economic, political, and social differences among these diverse groups.

Earlier, we described the vast social and economic differences among Asian Americans, disparities in educational, income, and occupational attainment that belie facile comparisons of people who represent a broad spectrum of human needs, wants, and cultures. Even more alarming is the way an artificial barrier is constructed between Asian Americans and blacks and Latinos. Holding less privileged Americans hostage to institutionalized racist evaluations establishes a "wall of indifference" that has found expression in popular stereotypical assumptions that presume deficits in the motivation of disadvantaged minorities and simultaneously bestow enormous pressure on Asian families and their children to succeed. The Asian Pacific American Center at the Smithsonian Institution recognized the insidious nature inherent in the use of the term "model minority" and, fifty years after the term's inception, launched a social media campaign to encourage discussion about deficits inherent in it.[2]

Contemporary literature is replete with acerbic comments about the pernicious effects that the term "model minority" has on Asian Americans. Some Asian American writers exhibit a sense of self-loathing from being socialized into their parents' belief in the myth of the American meritocracy. They regret their naivety, having believed they would be accepted by the dominant white society if they imitated whiteness. As Cathy Park Hong put it, "I've been raised and educated to please white people and this desire to please has become ingrained into my consciousness."[3] These feelings are compounded by their realization that Asian Americans are often invisible to whites. As Jay Kang noted, "The loneliness comes from the realization that nobody, whether white or Black, really cares if we succeed in creating any of these identities. At best, our white suburban neighbors regard us with conditional acceptance. Our fellow minorities look upon our race work with a mixture of bemusement and suspicion. It's hard to blame anyone for not caring enough about Asian Americans, because nobody—most of all Asian Americans—really believes that Asian America actually exists."[4]

Following the Los Angeles riots that destroyed more than two thousand Korean-owned businesses, the *Los Angeles Times* interviewed a despondent Korean shop owner whose business was destroyed: "I've lived in the United States for twenty-nine years. I wonder if I am not really welcome in American society?"[5]

Which racial/ethnic category do they fit into: white, black, other? Even worse, Hong contends, Asian Americans are unable to provide parental protection for their children because they are powerless to defend them. And despite the sometimes desperate, even frantic maneuvers of parents like Amy Chua, these social critics contend that Asian Americans will never be fully accepted by white society in the United States. "When I hear the phrase 'Asians are next in line to be white,' I replace the word 'white' with 'disappear.' Asians are next in line to disappear. We are reputed to be so accomplished, and so law-abiding, we will disappear into this country's amnesiac fog. We will not be the power but become absorbed by power, not share the power of whites but be stooges to a white ideology that exploited our ancestors."[6]

Many of these writers attribute white disdain for Asian Americans to the principles of white supremacy, which, though frequently unwritten, guide interethnic relationships in this country and preserve the preeminence of whites over people of color. By relegating black, brown, and yellow people to an inferior social status, the possibility of equality becomes a chimera in a social system predicated upon the domination and exploitation of people of color. For example, Yang insists such behaviors as white tokenism, bootstrap theory, cultural appropriation, the white savior complex, blaming the victim, denials of racism and white privilege, paternalism, racial profiling, racist mascots, unchallenged racist jokes, color blindness, English-only initiatives, the Eurocentric curriculum, believing that the United States is a postracial society, fearing people of color, defensive claims of reverse racism, not believing the experiences of people of color, and adhering to the "virtuous victim narrative" are indices of nascent white supremacy.[7] According to these authors, whites have pitted, and will continue to pit, one ethnic group of color against another in the strategy of divide and conquer. (We revisit this theme in the next chapter in the discussion of replacement theory.)

Is There a Bamboo Ceiling?

Vestiges of white racism toward Asians Americans are readily apparent. Although it is generally acknowledged that the U.S. economy greatly benefits from the work of Asian Americans through their endeavors in science and technology—for example, 26.3 percent of scientists in the United States are Asian Americans, and nearly two-thirds (63.5 percent or 107,018 people) of the workers in Silicon Valley tech firms are Asian Americans (out of 168,500)—the number of Asian

Americans in positions of influence (CEOs) in these and other firms doesn't match their participation rate. For example, 11 percent of associates in U.S. law firms are Asian Americans, but only 3 percent of partners are, and while 30 percent of the technology work force are Asian American, only 15 percent of the executives are.[8]

Since Jane Hyun coined the term "bamboo ceiling" in 2005,[9] there have been a multitude of studies and articles about the supposed racism and discrimination leveled against Asian Americans in the U.S. labor force. Although some of the leading tech companies in the United States (and around the world) have been founded by Asians, including the graphics designer and leader in artificial intelligence, Nvidia, co-founded by Jensen Huang, and Mastercard, founded by Ajaypal Singh Banga, and a number of Asians have headed or currently head dominant tech companies in the United States, like Sundar Pichai (CEO of Alphabet—parent company of Google), Tony Xu (CEO of DoorDash), and Eric Yuan (founder and CEO of Zoom), the vast majority of leading tech companies in the United States have been founded by non–Asian white Americans.

Numbers don't lie, and the facts about the relatively low numbers of Asian Americans in executive and high-level administrative positions in the corporate world reveal significant disparities in achievement levels between Asian Americans and white ones. Many Asian Americans believe differences in occupational attainment between them and whites are the result of prejudice and discrimination. This belief is supported by articles that rely on the experiences of Asians who contend that their lack of upward mobility was the result of discrimination. For example, Anand and Huet reported that their Asian American interviewees attributed their poor professional progress to prejudice, citing comments like "You're lucky to be Asian. White men will love to date you," and you were only promoted because "someone in leadership has an Asian fetish." As one young Asian American woman, formerly a product manager at Facebook, summarized it, "Being White is like having a skip pass at Disney World. I realized there is a bamboo ceiling, and I'd have to work 100 times harder."[10]

There can be little doubt about the obvious disparities between the levels of employment and achievement of Asian Americans and whites in the U.S. labor force. As of 2021, whites comprised 77 percent of the U.S. labor force, compared to 7 percent comprised by Asians. The largest group of Asian American workers was East Indians (25 percent), followed by Chinese (22 percent), Filipinos (15 percent), Vietnamese (10 percent), Koreans (7 percent), Japanese (4 percent), and all others (18 percent).[11] However, white males occupied 61.3 percent of executive positions nationally.

Whether from discrimination emanating from racism, bad timing, or plain bad luck, Asian Americans are consistently left out of higher level positions in our labor force. For example, although Asian Americans comprise 12.8 percent of college and university professors in the United States, compared to 10.2 percent Hispanic and 65 percent white,[12] a study by *Inside Higher Education* in 2022 revealed that while the number of non-white hires as college and university presidents increased by a third among the 336 presidents hired between 2020 and 2021, there was no change in the overall representation of Asians and Native Americans holding these jobs—the increase was primarily the result of hiring increases among black and Hispanic candidates.[13]

The diffusion of Asian Americans into the higher paying professional job categories such as scientists, engineers, physicians, and corporate managers has helped create an income, educational, and occupational gap among the diverse groups of Asian Americans in this country. Asian Americans are overrepresented in the scientific and engineering fields; approximately 36 million people are engaged in such work in the United States. Asian American students lead all ethnic groups, including whites, in educational test scores, and Asian Americans receive about 30 percent of National Merit Scholarships in the United States while constituting approximately 6 percent of the population. And while Asian Americans' income places them among the highest earners in the U.S. labor force, they are underrepresented in high-profile leadership and managerial positions.[14]

While much discussion addressing these disparities has focused on presumed prejudice and racism that has purportedly eventuated in the "bamboo ceiling" limiting the upward mobility of Asian Americans in the U.S. labor force, a fascinating article by Lu, Nisbett, and Morris[15] indicates that cultural differences among the diverse Asian ethnic groups may be responsible for differential workforce achievement. After analyzing nine studies encompassing over 11,000 Asian workers from diverse countries, they found that East Asians were less likely than South Asians to attain leadership positions, but South Asians still outperformed whites. Differences in occupational attainment were attributed to cultural differences, that is, assertiveness, not prejudice or motivation. The lack of assertiveness among some Asian Americans was determined to be the primary reason Asian Americans were regarded less seriously as managerial candidates by some employers. The authors concluded: "The Bamboo Ceiling is not an Asian issue, but an issue of cultural fit—a mismatch between East Asian norms of communication and American norms of leadership."[16]

However, looking at the data one cannot deny the existence of racial disparities. Clearly, Asian Americans are stuck in the meatgrinder of the American workforce, and that is exactly the conclusion of the Committee of 100, a predominantly Chinese-oriented organization that has been conducting numerous workshops to inform the public about these disparities and, hopefully, rectify the situation.[17] Whether from racism or cultural artifacts, there are significant differences in the occupational attainment and mobility of Asian Americans and whites. And that is the argument that Professor Margaret Chin made in her book *Stuck*, which focused on that issue.[18]

Professor Chin conducted interviews with 103 Asian Americans who had graduated college (most from highly selective elite schools) between 1980 and 2008. Virtually all of them held professional jobs and had worked in corporate America for more than twenty years. Although it is generally assumed that they pursued the formula, what she called "the playbook," that would yield financial and material success, she found that being a member of the "model minority" and industriousness were insufficient means to move up the organizational ladder and gain a C-suite. She concluded that the upper rungs of corporate leadership were frequently blocked to Asian Americans because they were "rife with racial, gender and class inequalities."[19] Her analysis of the career ladders of Asian Americans, many of whom were Chinese, confirmed the pitfalls inherent in a corporate system that was rigged against them, even though they initially perceived themselves as pathfinders, supposedly opening corporate leadership opportunities for Asian Americans behind them. Instead, they wondered why their own career progress had been so slow, despite affirmative action decisions that initially facilitated their entry into the rarefied atmosphere of the corporate elite. Although progress in hiring and promotions occurred, many of these Asian Americans recognized that they "were still not fully accepted."[20] But Chin concluded that affirmative action programs benefited Asian Americans by helping them gain admittance to elite educational institutions and the corporate sector of our economy.

Chin described the Asian American "playbook" that was composed of the accrued knowledge about methods Asian Americans used to advance and succeed, that is, move up the corporate ladder. Though unwritten, this knowledge was shared and passed on to succeeding generations of Asian Americans in the elite sectors of the labor force. A review of its components reveals a great deal of emphasis on hard work and diligence, and, perhaps most of all, getting along with co-workers but not being too assertive.[21] Corporate climates vary, and so, too, do leadership styles, although Chin concluded that improved communication skills and building trust among co-workers and superiors were indispensable for moving up the corporate ladder for her Asian American interviewees and for creating trust with subordinates and superiors.

One size fits all is as outmoded in shoes as it is in positing corporate leadership styles. There is no magical formula or panacea for solving the corporate myopia that has forestalled the careers of many Asian Americans when stereotypes and racism lie at the bottom of some decisions about the readiness and suitability of Asian Americans to fit in with images of corporate elitism. Chin ruefully noted that even though many competent Asian Americans followed the "playbook," they did not progress up the corporate ladder. "Fewer understood that moving ahead was often out of their control."[22]

The participants in the Committee of 100 Zoom broadcast on July 20, 2023, proposed that upwardly aspiring professors in colleges and universities should consider finding allies and mentors to assist them in their struggle for recognition. They should focus more on being good colleagues and institutional citizens, ready to stand up and speak out in defense of self and others when necessary to protect academic freedom. President Wu of Queens College encouraged young professors to get out of their cultural comfort zones and learn how to interact with strangers—"how to work a room." The group recognized the need for affirmative action to promote and protect Asian American students and professors, and, in light of a recent U.S. Supreme Court decision, *Students for Fair Admissions Inc. v. the University of North Carolina and the President and Fellows of Harvard College* (June 29, 2023), they remain committed to pursuing the goal of equal educational opportunities for all students.

The Affirmative Action Trap

Federal data link earnings to education.[23] Generally, the higher the education attainment, the higher are the lifetime earnings. Perhaps that is why some Asian American parents, like Amy Chua tiger moms, place such an extraordinary emphasis on educational attainment. Data on college admissions seem to support the emphasis Asian Americans place on obtaining admission to elite colleges and universities in this country. For example, Asian American enrollment at the most selective colleges and universities in the United States rose steadily until it plateaued in the mid–1990s and then began to rise again after 2010. A Manhattan Institute report by Robert VerBruggen[24] hints that the slowdown in Asian American college admissions may have been the result of discrimination against them, but the number of Asian American students admitted to highly selective institutions rose at a rate corresponding to their increase in the U.S. population. By 2022, 52.1 percent of the admissions to select U.S. colleges and universities were Asian Americans, compared to 2.8 percent African American, 21.1 percent Latinx, and 1.8 percent Native American. Twenty-five percent of incoming students in the fall of 2023 at Harvard were Asian Americans, compared to 12 percent Latinx and 14 percent black. Since 2010, the proportion of Asian students at Harvard has grown by 27 percent. At the prestigious University of California Berkeley, nearly half (42 percent) of the freshmen class is Asian American.

Some members of the Asian American community are staunchly opposed to affirmative action policies, which, they believe, hamper the opportunities of Asian American students by placing admission quotas on them. However, the Chinese-dominated Committee of 100 and Stop AAPI Hate, dedicated to combatting prejudice and discrimination against Asian Americans in this country, opposed bans on affirmative action. And a survey of 1,570 Asian American voters conducted in 2020 revealed that 70 percent of Asian Americans supported the concept of affirmative action in college admissions.[25]

On June 29, 2023, the Supreme Court of the United States rendered its decision in two landmark cases, *Students for Fair Admissions Inc. v. the President and Fellows of Harvard College* and *Students for Fair Admissions Inc. [SFFA] v. the University of North Carolina.* Voting six to two in the Harvard case (with Justice Jackson recusing herself), and six to three in the University of North Carolina case, the Court ruled that race-based affirmative action in admission decisions was no longer allowable. Writing for the majority in both disputes, Chief Justice Roberts concluded that the criterion, notably the use of racial data pertaining to incoming students at Harvard College and the University of North Carolina, was a violation of the Equal Protection Clause of the Fourteenth Amendment to the United States Constitution. While race was taken into consideration at Harvard College by a forty-person admissions committee to insure there was no dramatic decline in minority admissions, and a similar process was in place at the University of North Carolina, the suits alleged the policies and practices used by the two schools also violated Title VI of the Civil Rights Act of 1964.

After establishing that Students for Fair Admissions (SFFA) had a legitimate right to bring the suits, the Court reiterated that "the law in the States shall be the same for the black as for the white; that all persons, whether colored or white, shall stand equal before the laws of the States." Summarizing pitfalls in the *Plessy v. Ferguson* (1896) case, the Court noted that the 1954 *Brown v. Board of Education of Topeka* decision

7. The Model Minority Myth

declared that the right to a public education "must be made accessible to all on equal terms," and a year later it affirmed that students must be admitted on "a racially nondiscriminatory basis." Citing other cases that dealt with eliminating racial biases, such as *Gayle v. Browder* (1956, concerning segregation in busing) and *Loving v. Virginia* (1967, concerning interracial marriage), the Court noted that the "core purpose" of the Equal Protection clause was "do[ing] away with all governmentally imposed discrimination based on race." Also, "Eliminating racial discrimination means eliminating all of it." Further, the Court noted that the Equal Protection clause applies "without regard to any differences of race, color, or nationality." It is "universal in [its] application."[26]

The Court reviewed previous affirmative action decisions in college admissions cases, *Regents of the University of California v. Bakke* (1978), *Grutter v. Bollinger* (2003), and *Fisher v. University of Texas at Austin* (2016), and concluded that though a narrow path was established for allowing differential selection of minority students in the tradition established by former Justice Lewis Powell for purposes of creating a diverse student body, Harvard and the University of North Carolina were not able to adequately demonstrate why this was necessary and how it was being achieved within the scope of the Equal Protection Clause of the Fourteenth Amendment. Furthermore, the *Grutter* decision hinted that the task of creating a diverse student body would be accomplished within twenty-five years, and despite the passage of time since its rendering, there was no indication that colleges and universities were inclined to remove what the Court had viewed as temporary programs for adjusting the racial balance on campuses. Indeed, Chief Justice Roberts reiterated that "outright racial balancing is patently unconstitutional,"[27] and he concluded that the admissions processes at the two institutions were inherently flawed (they were even unable to determine the effectiveness of their approach) and in violation of the Due Process Clause of the Constitution.

In a lengthy opinion supporting the majority decision, Justice Clarence Thomas cited numerous historical activities that indicated the rectitude of the Court's decision and concluded, "The Court [in its attempt to bar discrimination against Asian American students] made clear that the 14th Amendment's equality guarantees applied to all races, including Asian Americans, ensuring all citizens equal treatment under the law." Furthermore, "The Court today makes clear that in the future, universities wishing to discriminate based on race in admissions must articulate and justify a compelling and measurable state interest based on concrete evidence. Given the strictures set out by the Court, I highly doubt any will be able to do so."[28]

Justice Sonia Sotomayor provided a dissent (along with Justices Kagan and Jackson), which recognized the constitutional necessity for racially integrated schools—a trend begun with the *Brown* decision in 1954. She stipulated that allowing colleges and universities to consider race in a limited way helps promote diversity and equalizes educational opportunities. She accused the majority of the Court of impeding racial progress, a point made in the eloquent dissent of Justice Jackson as she highlighted disparities between whites and blacks in health, wealth, education, and general well-being. Without citing Cornell West, their arguments asserted that race matters.[29]

Justice Sotomayor contended that "Equal educational opportunity is a prerequisite to achieving racial equality in our Nation,"[30] a belief repeated in Justice Jackson's dissent. Citing historical facts about the subordination of blacks through slavery, Justice Sotomayor noted that "from this Nation's birth, the freedom to learn was neither colorblind nor equal."[31] The irony of her argument is contained in her conclusion that the Fourteenth Amendment to the U.S. Constitution, the very mechanism used to repudiate affirmative action admission decisions by the Court's majority, was passed to remedy abuses of blacks and protect previously enslaved persons. Furthermore, she contended that the Court's majority misread and misunderstood the intent of the *Brown* decision, which affirmatively served to promote educational opportunities. "The Court's recharacterization of *Brown* is nothing but revisionist history and is an affront to the legendary life of Justice [Thurgood] Marshall, a great jurist who was a champion of true equal opportunity, not rhetorical flourishes about colorblindness."[32]

Citing *Bakke* (1978), *Grutter* (2003), and *Fisher* (2016), she provided evidence demonstrating that the Court previously endorsed the use of race to promote diversity. The rejection of previous precedent by the majority (*stare decisis*) was a point of contention between the majority and minority, as in the prior year's *Dobbs v. Jackson Women's Health Organization*. Both Justice Sotomayor and Justice Jackson reiterated the importance of having a diverse student body, especially because it would provide opportunities for social, cultural, and financial improvement of minorities and break down negative stereotypes about them. As Justice Sotomayor put it: "It is thus an objective of the highest order, a compelling interest indeed, that universities pursue the benefits of racial diversity and ensure that the diffusion of knowledge and opportunity is available to students of all races."[33] And Justice Jackson concluded that putting off or ignoring the race-linked opportunity gap will widen instead of narrowing it.[34]

Ironically, the Students for Fair Admissions organization lost their case in a previous trial when they tried to prove that Asian Americans were discriminated against in relation to white students in Harvard's admission process. Serious reverberations occurred after California banned affirmative action in college admissions in 1996: There was a fifty percent decline in black enrollment at the University of California at Berkeley (already low, it went from 6.32 percent to 3.37 percent), and Latinx enrollment declined by a like amount, from 15.57 percent to 7.28 percent. Today, black freshmen at UC Berkeley comprise only 2.76 percent of the freshmen class. Asian American students were also adversely impacted by this action. I recall derogatory stereotypical comments at the time about Asian American students "destroying the curve" and white students dropping classes because Asian American students were in the room.[35]

John Yang, President and Executive Director of Asian Americans Advancing Justice, believes the "model minority"/affirmative action issue is a ploy used as a wedge to pit Asian Americans against blacks, Native Americans, and Latinx. Also, there is some indication that Edward Blum, the founder of Project Fair Representation and the conservative legal scholar who helped initiate the FSSA affirmative action suits on behalf of purportedly discriminated-against Asian American students, was, in reality, attempting to improve the admission of white students.[36] Still, members of the Supreme Court's majority, Thomas and Kavanaugh, believe that race-neutral factors might be used instead of race. Of note was their mention of socioeconomic factors such as generational inheritance and financial background for promoting diversity on campuses.

A study done for the National Bureau of Economic Research revealed that nearly half (43 percent) of the white students admitted to Harvard College were recruited athletes, legacy students (relatives had attended the school), and children of faculty and staff.[37] In fact, the researchers found that seventy-five percent of the white students admitted under these categories would have been rejected without them. ALDCs (athletes, legacies, those on the dean's interest list—people who have contributed or may contribute to Harvard—and children of faculty and staff) are predominantly white. Focusing on nonlegacy groups may help to democratize the admissions process and create a more diverse student body—although it could generate considerable institutional resistance. Still, the authors concluded: "Removing preferences for athletes and legacies would significantly alter the racial distribution of admitted students, with the share of white admits falling and all other groups rising or remaining unchanged."[38]

The struggle for autonomy and material success among Asian

Americans is closely linked to academic achievement. It is not unreasonable to assume that contemporary tiger moms are lurking in society, eager to push their children into the most prestigious colleges and universities because that is the generally acknowledged ticket to success. Future generations will increasingly be measured and rewarded for academic excellence and achievement. There will be a battle for brains, as brawn takes a back seat to a different kind of star power. The desire to fit in, to look like the majority, will become increasingly insatiable.

Fitting In

Being a minority in a majority culture that accentuates European values and appearance can have an inordinate influence on someone's perception of self. The desire to fit in with, be a part of, and look like the dominant majority can be a powerful force motivating members of an outgroup to mimic clothes, styles, and speech, as well as attitudes, values, and behavior, with the goal of approximating the group one wishes to be in—the ingroup. For some Asian Americans, people who may perceive themselves as outgroup, members of a perpetual minority or forever foreign, plastic surgery is viewed as the path to belonging.

Two of the most common forms of plastic surgery performed on Asians and Asian Americans are eyelid surgery (blepharoplasty) to minimize the perceived narrowness of the eyes, and surgery to refine the nose, especially the bridge, known as rhinoplasty. While Asian Americans utilize these procedures more often, South Korea leads the world in performing these procedures. In fact, South Korea is known as the plastic surgery capital of the world, and Gangnam Street is the most famous part of Seoul where physicians who practice this type of medicine proliferate. It is estimated that more than 600 plastic surgery clinics in Seoul performed more than 50,000 cosmetic procedures at a cost of more than $189 million in 2022.[39]

Some observers contend that the boom in plastic surgery among Koreans originated upon cessation of hostilities at the end of the Korean War in 1953. With nearly six million men and women from the United States serving there during the war, and a continued presence of about 30,000 soldiers, Western influence on South Koreans, including their looks and habits, made an indelible mark, so much so that many South Koreans opted to Westernize their appearance. It was no coincidence that some of the impetus for the ubiquitous use of plastic surgery mirrored the practice of United States military surgeons who "fixed" "oriental eyes" through reconstructive surgery after the war. In 1974, the

South Korean Supreme Court gave further impetus to the plastic surgery craze by recognizing plastic surgery as an approved medical practice.

South Korea has achieved worldwide status as a plastic surgery destination, and Seoul neighborhoods like Gangnam Street are lined with cosmetic surgery clinics.[40] It is estimated that about 20 percent of Korean women have some type of plastic surgery, and high school girls frequently receive as a graduation present "ulzzang" plastic surgery to increase the prominence of the nose tip, make the jaw less angular, and alter the eyelids. The so-called "natural look" is viewed as desirable and worthwhile by some Koreans, and it is featured in televised makeover shows with world-renowned South Korean plastic surgeons.

The efflorescence in plastic surgery has also been linked to the 1988 Olympic Games in Seoul, which precipitated an explosion in the Korean gross domestic product. In 1988 the GDP was about $200 billion, but because of a phenomenal growth rate in recent years, it is now much higher: $1.7 trillion. Part of the economic resurgence in South Korea has been intentional government initiatives to promote Western music and customs,[41] which, no doubt, helped to increase the predilection of many South Koreans for Western looks and behavior. Added to this is a popular Korean belief (and a sentiment echoed by some Asian Americans) that attractive (i.e., Western) looks have a beneficial effect on love and financial success. Photos are often requested from job applicants and looks may be considered in hiring in South Korea.

Double eyelid plastic surgery designed to make the eyes look bigger and rounder is the most popular form of plastic surgery in South Korea, and it's the second most frequently obtained cosmetic surgery among Asian Americans after rhinoplasty. Asian Americans received 1.2 million cosmetic procedures in the United States in 2020, amounting to 8 percent of the total of 15.6 million procedures. Eyelid and nose procedures among Asian Americans amounted to 11 percent of those procedures performed in 2020 in the United States. Although physicians reported that more plastic surgeries have been performed since the pandemic, cosmetic procedures in the United States declined by 5 percent from 2019 to 2020. Likewise, rhinoplasty surgery declined by 3 percent among Asian Americans and blepharoplasty among them decreased by 8 percent in that time frame.[42]

Nearly half (44 percent) of plastic surgery performed on Asian Americans is blepharoplasty (eyelid surgery), no doubt linked to the Western ingroup influence that promotes wider eye appearance. Some Asians and Asian Americans resort to this type of plastic surgery because of the real and perceived pressure on them to have that Western look—in their perception, to avoid looking dull or passive.[43] Although Asian men are less inclined to view plastic surgery positively, Asian women were found to view it as a means of self-improvement (nearly one-third of the respondents to the RealSelf poll), and a similar percentage (31 percent) felt that having plastic surgery empowered them and assisted them in building confidence (30 percent).[44]

Fair skin is also prized among most South Koreans. Tan skin is associated with laborers, and this biased stereotype is widespread in Asia and Africa, where light skin is desirable among some people. There is a connection between the white colonizers (most often British, French, and Belgian) and racist ideologies that evolved into the concept of colorism, which places a priority on light skin. This association led to the marketing of beauty products that denigrated dark skin and placed stigma on women who had it. The priority on light or "fair" skin led to an industry in Asia and Africa estimated at more than a billion dollars annually.[45]

The industry, dominated by multinational firms like Unilever, Procter & Gamble, L'Oréal, and Johnson & Johnson, has promoted skin whitening products, especially among young women, for decades through aggressive marketing strategies that reinforce the racist belief that the path to a successful marriage and material success lies in having lighter skin. With catchy names that emphasize "fair," "light," and "white," impressionable young women in search of mates and a better life are lured into believing in the dubious efficacy of such products. However, societal pressure to conform to this racist ideology is real and reinforced through the use of motion picture celebrities such as Priyanka Chopra Jonas, a Bollywood film star who, along with other Bollywood celebrities often having light skin tone, endorsed fair skin creams. The Indian–based Bollywood film industry, which produces 1,500 to 2,000 films a year and generates more than three and a half billion dollars annually, has long emphasized heroic actors with light skin tones and villains with dark skin.

Even more alarming is the trend in some African nations where unscrupulous individuals and firms are marketing skin whitening products that are detrimental to users' health. The World Health Organization estimated that half of all skin care products in India were lighteners ostensibly to whiten the user's skin color. While some of these products contain vitamins such as B3, others have bleach, mercury, and steroids and might damage the skin, or worse, harm fetuses or produce cancer.[46] Still, the desire to look like Westerners, that is, white, is embedded in the culture of India and other developing nations, precisely because whiteness signifies progress, privilege, and heightened economic and social status. In India, for example, matrimonial ads in newspapers reinforce colorism using such descriptors for skin color as "fair," "dusky," and "wheatish," soliciting matches based on the lightness of prospective mates. And Shaadi.com, one of the world's largest matrimonial sites, until recently used a skin tone filter, but removed it when protests developed following the murder of George Floyd. That incident also triggered numerous changes in the skin whitening industry, with manufacturers altering the names of their products but nevertheless still promoting them.[47]

The killing of George Floyd precipitated changes in an industry built on racist illusions. Many corporations changed the names of their skin whitening products, but the allure of mega millions in income dissuaded them from terminating their product lines, although Johnson & Johnson announced it would cease selling its Neutrogena Fine Fairness and Clean and Clear Fairness skin lighteners. Still, Unilever, though changing product names, will continue to sell its highly successful Fair and Lovely cosmetic line but removed its shade guides that were used to assess transformations by users.[48]

The chorus of opponents' objections to the demeaning impact of colorism has been boosted by the work of women like Kavitha Emmanuel from southern India, who started Women of Worth in India and spun off the "Dark is Beautiful" campaign. Closer to home, Nina Davuluri, the first East Indian American to be crowned Miss America (2014), vocally opposed colorism here and elsewhere and called on Procter & Gamble, Unilever, Johnson & Johnson, and L'Oréal to stop promoting and manufacturing products that support racism and colorism. A special edition of the journal *Asian Studies Review* contains articles that indicate that values appear to be changing about the efficacy of colorism and plastic surgery in many Asian countries.[49]

Also, there is a growing self-awareness in South Korea and other Asian countries as well as among Asian Americans—one that increasingly eschews ephemeral cosmetic "cures" that falsely promise recognition and acceptance into the dominant Western society. This movement emphasizes individual self-worth and creativity above simplistic cosmetic alterations. Led by the photographer Lina Bae, a backlash emerged in South Korea to the degrading stereotypical image of Asian women encapsulated by the prevalence of cosmetic surgery and its associated demeaning caricatures of them. Using the slogan "escape the corset," Bae and her followers are urging women to abandon denigrating stereotypical images about them by returning to authentic looks and avoiding social pressures to conform to unnatural body shapes and sizes. The movement seeks to ignite female opposition to male dominance, especially since a 2017 poll found that 40 percent of respondents stated that they had experienced discrimination based on their appearance when they applied for jobs,[50] and a YouTube video "I Am Not Pretty" aired in 2018. Such movements have ramifications and repercussions among Asian American men and women, and the "forever foreigners" label will be scrutinized and tested as the percentage of Asian Americans increases in the United States. However, their ascent to the pinnacles of the corporate world and our society will not be a smooth journey. As discussed in the next chapter, economic, political, and racial obstacles pose formidable obstacles to the recognition of Asian Americans as equals in a society established upon white supremacist ideology.

8

The Future of Asians in American Society

> "'Where are you from? No, where are you *really* from?'—is so unnerving, even threatening. It's an old, divisive sentiment questioning our right to be here, like anyone else, from the very soil upon which so many of us were born."
> —Ava Chin, *Mott Street*, p. 339.

Forever Foreign

The preceding pages have shown us that Asian Americans are comprised of diverse economic, political, attitudinal, and ethnic groups. It is impossible to encapsulate them under a single rubric. They are bound together, like other non-white minority groups in the United States, by pejorative stereotypes designed to render them powerless and portray them as foreign, unwanted, and deficient despite their formidable contributions to our society. Asian Americans' contributions to our nation across history, from constructing the trans–American railroad to discoveries in medicine and science, have been enormous, and they continue to share them despite their rejection by some segments of our population.

In this chapter we focus on the types of contemporary exclusionary policies used against Asian Americans (and other ethnic minorities). These techniques are designed to isolate and dominate Asian Americans, and to exclude them from mainstream society, because Asian Americans and other ethnic minorities create fear and anxiety among many in the dominant white population.

A recent faction of the Republican Party, the MAGA (Make

America Great Again) wing, adheres to the sentimental belief that the United States was exceptional in the past, when men were men, women knew their roles, rights, and responsibilities, and ethnic minorities were unseen and unheard. While the past (1950s) may have seemed to this group to be idyllic, the Civil Rights Era, stemming from that time through the 1970s, revealed gross inequities in our society—inequalities that not only pitted one ethnic group against another (still an issue), but often relegated (frequently de jure but often de facto) millions of non-whites to an inferior position in our labor force, education, housing, health care, and overall quality of life.[1]

While improvements have been made to rectify some of the inequities perpetrated against ethnic minorities in our contemporary social system, much work needs to be done before ethnic minorities, like Asian Americans, become fully accepted, integrated, and recognized in our society. Witness the "anti–Woke" legislation promulgated by Governor Ron DeSantis of Florida, as well as his steadfast refusal to expand Medicaid (health care for the medically indigent).[2] What is the rationale for the increase in and fascination with whiteness? Why do some whites long for a bygone era? We now turn to the prevailing ideology that has fueled the infatuation of white supremacists with the past.

The Origin of Replacement Theory

When the youthful young men brandishing torches strode defiantly through the streets of Charlottesville, Virginia, on August 11 and 12, 2017, in their "Unite the Right" rally, chanting "Blacks and Jews will not replace us!," they were expressing their fear of competition from Jews and non-white ethnic groups. Both economically in the labor force, and from competition for sexual partners, the antidemocratic sentiments they proffered were poignantly directed toward minorities that have been systematically discriminated against for decades in this country. Aside from immigration laws, such as the Chinese Exclusion Act that wasn't repealed until 1943, there were de facto and de jure practices such as Jim Crow laws in the South that impeded African American social mobility and "gentlemen's agreements"[3] based on antisemitism that impeded the ascendancy of Jews in our society.[4]

Underlying the bigotry among these white men and their compatriots, such as the Three Percenters, Proud Boys, Blood Tribe, and the Boogaloo movement, as well as other white supremacist organizations and movements, is their fear of being displaced by upwardly mobile ethnic minorities. Aside from the obvious visual and social reality that demonstrates the ubiquity of non-whites throughout our society, from medicine to law, science to business, and in private and public schools at all levels, many of these bigoted groups share a belief in an ideological framework created by Frenchman Renaud Camus in his novel *The Great Replacement*, published in 2011.[5]

The central thesis of his contemporary works (he began his career as a writer, philosopher, photographer, and artist and as a liberal socialist, but gradually moved to the right) is that Western, that is, white European, nations are being invaded (colonized) by hordes of immigrants, mostly Muslims and other people of color, and, because the invaders have higher fertility rates than whites, they are taking over cities, regions, and nations—replacing the morally, aesthetically, and racially superior white "indigenous" people. It is an old argument, one that has reoccurred many times in the last 150 years. The fear of social change hastened by technological development, scientific discoveries, and mobility (physical and social) has had a dramatic effect on human psychological development. Large-scale social movements threaten the status quo and the predilection of humans to maintain control over their environment. When people are displaced by war, pestilence, famine, and disease, they migrate in search of safer and more stable food supplies. This phenomenon has been tracked from humanity's inception to the Great Leap Forward when our ancestors left Africa in search of better lives.[6]

Nearly a century and a half ago, another Frenchman, Comte Joseph Arthur de Gobineau, delineated how the gene pool of indigenous people was being denigrated through the introduction of outside genetic material. Such reasoning has recurred in Western writing for more than a century. Houston Stewart Chamberlain, at one time the son-in-law of the famous but antisemitic musical composer Richard Wagner, published his seminal work, *The Foundations of the Nineteenth Century*,[7] which became a progenitor of similar works that followed it. For example, at the turn of the 20th century, the eugenics movement was gaining ground in the United States, fueled by the writing of Madison Grant in *The Passing of the Great Race*,[8] and Lothrop Stoddard's *The Rising Tide of Color Against White World-Supremacy*[9] and *The Revolt Against Civilization: The Menace of the Under-Man*.[10] These authors extolled the virtues of white civilization and lamented its supposed decline because of presumed pollution of the gene pool by immigrants from southern Europe, notably Italians, Greeks, and Jews.

If this argument sounds familiar, it is. Despite the dire warnings white supremacists have made about the denigration and despoliation of the fabric of Western (white) society through the introduction of ostensibly inferior genetic material from immigrants and people of color, our society has emerged from successive waves of immigrants who have made enormous cultural contributions to it by lending their ingenuity and industriousness to the larger social fabric; for example, scientific, medical, and technological innovations contributed by Asian Americans and other people of color have and continue to leave indelible influences on the way we communicate, treat and prevent diseases, and manage our working lives. Still, periodically, the ugly remnants of racial prejudice resurface.

After the defeat of Nazism, the eugenics movement and its popularizers were discredited. The purported Aryan "master race" was revealed to be led by a degenerate and deranged group of megalomaniacs consumed by their egos and obsessed by the depths to which their inhumanity and moral perversions led them in their quest for world hegemony. This did not prevent the periodic recrudescence of similar ideas in the West. Even before the World War II struggle between the American capitalist ideology and free expression and Nazism with its morbid obsession with racial purity and preoccupation with centralized state control over the economy, a strain of American populism suffused with fascist attitudes was paraded for the world when 20,000 rabid fascists filled Madison Square Garden on February 20, 1939, complete with a floor-to-ceiling rendering of George Washington, heralded by the assemblage as the "first fascist president of the United States."[11]

The eugenics movement was dealt a setback by the Nazis at home and abroad through revelations about its "scientific" attempt to demonstrate the inferiority of Jews and non-whites.[12] However, periodic trends occurred in the United States and European countries that espoused populist, simplistic attempts to "blame victims," especially dark- and brown-skinned immigrants, for the maladies of crime, overcrowding, deficient health status, educational attainment, and unemployment. Statistics consistently demonstrate there are more poor white people than people of color living in the United States. However, the image of people of color sucking the proverbial teats of the motherland, using and consuming the munificence generated by the capitalist system, is alluring to some, even though our social system is the only one of the thirty-eight countries of the Organization for Economic Cooperation and Development (OECD) that does not provide its citizens with low-cost or socialized medicine and paid family leave.

The eugenics movement of the early 1900s, which focused on improving the human species by curtailing the birth rate of poor and working-class women, especially women of color, spawned a movement that led to tens of thousands of women being forcibly sterilized or coerced into operations designed to limit their reproductive ability. A U.S. Supreme Court decision (*Buck v. Bell*, 1906) when Supreme Court Justice Oliver Wendell Holmes concluded that the state had the right to sterilize people deemed mentally deficient, saying "three generations of imbeciles is enough," eventuated in the sterilization of tens of thousands of men and women (mostly working-class women, especially blacks) in the early 1900s. The practice, though outlawed, continues with the coercion of prisoners, even though such behavior supposedly conflicts with the expressed values of our so-called "enlightened society."[13] Even famed civil rights activist Fannie Lou Hamer was forcibly sterilized in what she disparagingly referred to as a "Mississippi appendectomy."

Thus, the United States has been no stranger to enforced sexual brutality, and underpinning such behavior has been the recurrent theme of curtailing the reproductive freedom of minorities, especially people of color, to prevent, as de Gobineau, warned, the defiling of white racial purity. Compare these comments:

"There exists to-day a widespread and fatuous belief in the power of environment, as well as of education and opportunity to alter heredity, which arises from the dogma of the brotherhood of man, derived in its turn from the loose thinkers of the French Revolution and their American mimics. Such beliefs have done much damage in the past and if allowed to go uncontradicted, may do even more serious damage in the future."

"That culture, and the civilization that birthed it, and on which it wrested for centuries, are among the most precious, the highest, and once the most admired that the earth has ever borne and that mankind has witnessed in the course of its history. We must defend and promote them from the inside and from the outside, *a fortiori* against ready-made substitutes that are far from being as worthy, being in terms of gentleness, intelligence, dignity for man, freedom for women, spiritual elevation."[14]

The similarity of these statements, though written nearly a century apart (the first is Madison Grant), is representative of a recurrent ideological stream of thought exemplified by the Great Replacement position, advocated by the second writer, French philosopher and author Renaud Camus. Although these writers did not know one another, their predilection for focusing on what they considered to be the natural superiority of the white European race above all others, especially black and brown people, has been a persistent recurrent theme in Europe and the United States for centuries. It was important for the eugenicists of the early 1900s in this country, such as psychologist Carl Bingham of

Princeton University, who also created the SAT but later repudiated his eugenicist perspective. Nevertheless, Bingham and other prominent eugenicists evinced a nativistic disdain for immigrants, who, they assumed, were, degrading the American (white, Anglo, Aryan) gene pool.[15]

The Reincarnation of Racism

When William Bradford Shockley received the Nobel Prize in 1956 it was for physics. Working at New Jersey's Bell Laboratory, his team discovered the vital role that transistors could play in conducting electric signals. Shockley did not have the training for his avocation: touring the United States and denigrating the academic performance of African Americans. I can still remember Dr. Shockley in a bustling academic core with a smile on his face, wearing a sign that read "15 points lower"—a message that blacks, from his perspective, had lower test and IQ scores and were incapable of competing and making worthwhile contributions to our society. While he was discredited, this theme reoccurred in a 1969 screed in the *Harvard Educational Review* written by psychologist Arthur Jensen that purportedly demonstrated the innate intellectual deficiency of Africans and African Americans.[16] It unleashed a torrent of demurs that largely disputed his methodology and findings.[17]

Nevertheless, the theme again resurfaced in the 1994 treatise *The Bell Curve*, written by the late psychologist Richard Herrnstein, then of Harvard University, and the itinerant sociologist and public intellectual Charles Murray.[18] Despite evidence to the contrary, they tried to link individual creativity and accomplishment to genetic rather than environmental factors, and concluded that our country and the world would be better served if we allowed "the cognitive elite" to run things.

Even now, the desire to juxtapose heredity and genes with scholarly and intellectual achievement is being pursued by social and physical scientists like Harvard psychologist Steven Pinker, who is obsessed with linking overpopulation to the downfall of our civilization.[19] Some of these ideas have even found their way into the thinking of contemporary politicians. For example, Donald J. Trump, speaking to a group of U.S. Senators at the White House on January 11, 2018, referred to Haiti, African nations, and El Salvador as "shithole countries." In his remarks, which unfortunately occurred on the eighth anniversary of a devastating earthquake in Haiti, the former president launched into a white supremacist diatribe against chain migration, which allows relatives of citizens to move to the United States, and he lamented that we don't have more immigrants coming here from Norway. "Why do we need more Haitians? Take them out." Criticism of his remarks poured in from around the country and the world, including the United Nations Human Rights Office, which condemned the comments as racist.[20]

Trump's words were defended by White House aids who contended that "he will always fight for the American people" and that he is tough on immigration. However, his favorable comments about participants in the Unite the Right rally in Charlottesville, Virginia, on August 11–12, where a counterprotestor, thirty-two-year-old Heather Heyer, was killed by a white supremacist, James Alex Fields, Jr., when he drove his car into a crowd, also reflected animus toward multiculturalists, as did his ban on Muslim immigrants to the United States as of January 27, 2017, ostensibly designed to protect the country from foreign terrorists.

Trump's ethnocentric policies and code words designed to attract and placate white supremacists, such as his comment at a press conference on August 15, 2017, that "there were fine people on both sides" of the Unite the Right rally, or his remark during a presidential debate on September 29, 2020, that his purported allies, the Proud Boys, should "stand back and stand by," could have come right out of the comments made by Renaud Camus during an address in Lumel, France, on November 26, 2010. Camus denigrated immigrants,[21] especially people of color from Africa, and Muslims, who he believed were ghettoizing large French cities, destroying their white cultural heritage, and replacing it with alien, hostile, even violent minisocieties that did not conform to or assimilate into what he considered the exceptional French Western cultural tradition.

In recent times it has become fashionable for politicians to espouse retrograde conservative ideology similar to that advocated by Camus. Numerous "think tanks" openly advocate a conservative agenda that links individual achievement to freedom without considering the implications of promoting individuality over the necessity for collaboration and cooperation.[22]

As one of the ideological forebears of contemporary white supremacy, but nevertheless in a long tradition of white ethnocentric racist ideas as we have seen, dating back to de Gobineau, Camus's anti-immigrant rant appeals to contemporary white Christian nationalist sentiment in the United States, as well as in other countries in Europe where it has established roots. Examples of this, at times cited as a self-defense against supposed hordes of invading Africans and Muslims, are evident in the mistreatment of African immigrants by the Greeks, which has led to thousands of drownings in the Mediterranean Sea in recent years (since 2014, it is estimated that more than 19,000 migrants have drowned attempting to cross it),[23] the hostile treatment of immigrants of color by the Orban Administration in Hungary, and the Polish administration that welcomed white Ukrainian immigrants fleeing the war with Russia but sought to exclude students of color.[24]

The ethnocentric theories of men like Camus can have dire consequences. In addition to these theories giving aid and comfort to white supremacists and white Christian nationalists who desire to make their countries into safe homelands exclusively for white Christians,[25] people have lost their lives after being targeted by renegade white supremacists in violent outbursts. Take, for example, Anders Breivik, who killed 77 people in July 2011 (eight with a car bomb in Oslo and sixty-nine youth attending a multicultural retreat on Utoya Island nearby, through shooting), or white supremacist Brenton Tarrant, who murdered fifty-one Muslims attending two mosques in Christchurch, New Zealand, in March 2019. There have also been numerous attacks on minorities in the United States in recent years. We earlier described the dramatic increase in hate crimes perpetrated against Asian Americans and Pacific Islanders, which has led to one in five AAPI people in the United States experiencing a hate incident, and the killing of six Asian massage parlor workers in March 2021.

In these times, age-old bigotries have resurfaced. The Anti-Defamation League estimates there were 8,873 antisemitic incidents in the United States in 2023, the highest number ever recorded since the ADL began tracking antisemitic incidents in 1979; this is a 140 percent increase from the 3,698 incidents in 2022.[26] The rise is directly related to what has been going on in the Gaza war. Obviously, animus derived from such incidents fed into the largest mass killing of Jews in the history of this nation when, on October 27, 2018, Robert Bowers shot and killed eleven members of the Tree of Life Synagogue in Pittsburgh and wounded six others. Prior to that, on June 17, 2015, Dylan Roof, also a white supremacist, murdered nine African American congregants of the Emanuel A.M.E. Church in Charleston, South Carolina. Other ethnic groups have not been spared the wrath of white supremacists in the United States. On August 3, 2019, Patrick Crusius killed 23 Latinos and wounded 22 others in a Walmart shooting in El Paso, Texas. The assault by white supremacists against African Americans has been relentless, including the murder of ten people (all African Americans) and wounding of three others by eighteen-year-old Payton Gendron, an avowed believer in replacement theory. More recent was the killing of three African Americans at a Dollar General store in Jacksonville, Florida, by twenty-one-year-old Ryan Palmeter, also an adherent of neo–Nazi perceptions about white supremacy.

This string of hate crimes can be linked to the growing malaise and dissatisfaction among white people around the world. In the United States, about a third of the populace evince sentiments that approximate white supremacist concepts as expressed by Donald Trump. They believe that he actually won the 2020 presidential election and that whites in this country are being replaced by immigrants, especially people of color. Camus railed against the incivilities purportedly perpetrated by Muslim immigrants, expressing his revulsion for them: "one is French essentially by birth and by ancestors." "If they [immigrants, especially Muslim Arabs] are just as French as I am, I repeat, then French doesn't mean much." He lamented "the decay of these [white European] cultures, the extinctions of these ways of life, the massacre of the landscape."[27]

Camus even attacked what he termed "the media political complex," not unlike the vituperative assault waged by Trump against the free or "legacy" press, such as *The New York Times* and *The Washington Post*. These groups assume a clandestine, secretive motivation among liberals and progressives in our society.[28] Right-wing zealots, in their war against replacement and the "dark or deep state" (a common trope among QAnon devotees), single out people of color and Jews for having ulterior motives such as pedophilia, child trafficking, and a desire to remake America into a multicultural state. Many of them believe that the media try to influence public opinion to accept immigration and, with that, the replacement of white Christian values by allowing black and brown people into our society so they can vote to legitimize changes that will fundamentally alter the nature of society. Camus likened such attitudes to hypocritical statements of pro-immigrant anti-racists who purportedly embrace the moral law while actually destroying the fabric of French society.

Demographic Trends

Much of replacement theory, as well as the public sentiments of white supremacists, depends on the supposition that the white birth rate is declining in the United States and predominantly white Western European countries, while the birth rate among black and brown people is higher. Camus, as well as white supremacists around the world, believes that white culture and civilization will be overrun by this "colonization by the belly."[29] While this statement is technically correct, that the birth rate is higher in some developing countries than it is in many European nations and the United States, several important points must be made to clarify the demographic changes the world and the United States are undergoing.

As we previously noted, when Thomas Malthus wrote his famous essay on population in 1798, he warned of the negative effects of increasing population. "The superior power of population cannot be checked without producing misery or vice."[30] From his perspective, prior to the industrial revolution, human population growth was bound to outstrip our ability to provide for increasing population. Fortunately, for us, technological developments intervened and mitigated this phenomenon, and Malthus's predicted result has not occurred.[31]

Along the way to developing cities and concentrating humans in them (it is estimated that more than two-thirds of the earth's people will live in urban areas by 2050), agricultural production also benefited from technological innovations. Although the relationship between population growth and technological innovation is complex, such that the introduction of technology often spurs an initial increase in the food supply and a concomitant increase in the population, generally, nations with high levels of education and technological development also experience higher longevity through these and public health initiatives. This phenomenon, as we previously noted, is sometimes referred to as the "technological imperative" and is assumed to result in a decline in population growth. It is believed that as the levels of education and technological innovation are infused into a society, women and girls are more likely to seek and use contraception and, through public health initiatives, people will live longer and family size will decrease because the necessity for having heirs and helpers will diminish. Hence, Western (predominantly white) nations (Great Britain, Europe, Russia, and the United States), which have experienced a florescence of technological innovation in the last two hundred years, have also experienced increased longevity through the application of technological innovation to improved public health, and registered a decline in population growth. The population of Europe in 2023 declined by 0.17 percent from the previous year, which means that the continent is losing people, although there are still more than 740 million residents there. Simultaneously, the population increased by 2.37 percent on the continent of Africa in 2023, and increased by 0.64 percent in Asia that year. However, as the graphs here indicate, population growth has declined and will continue to decline in these areas until the year 2100, by which time, predicts the United Nations, the world's population will number around 10.4 billion people. Experts disagree about the actual size of the world's population in the future, depending on the availability of educational opportunities and access to birth control for women and girls. Nevertheless, data indicate that the decline in population, even among the previously most dynamic population growth countries, will continue.[32]

Looking at the graphs shows there has been a steady, nearly consistent, and significant decline in the population growth rates on all these

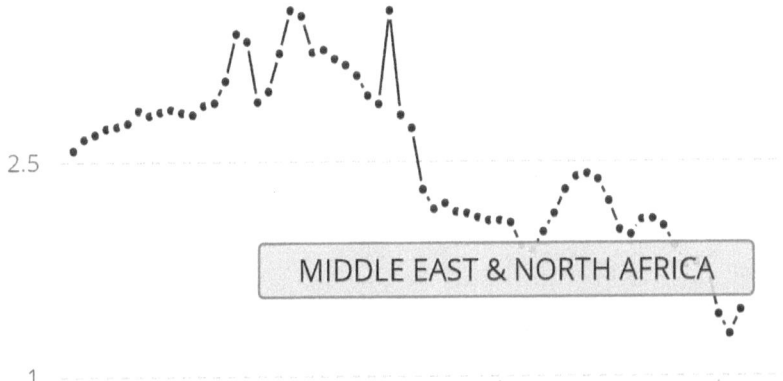

Table of Population Growth Rates in Africa, 1961–2022 (World Bank).

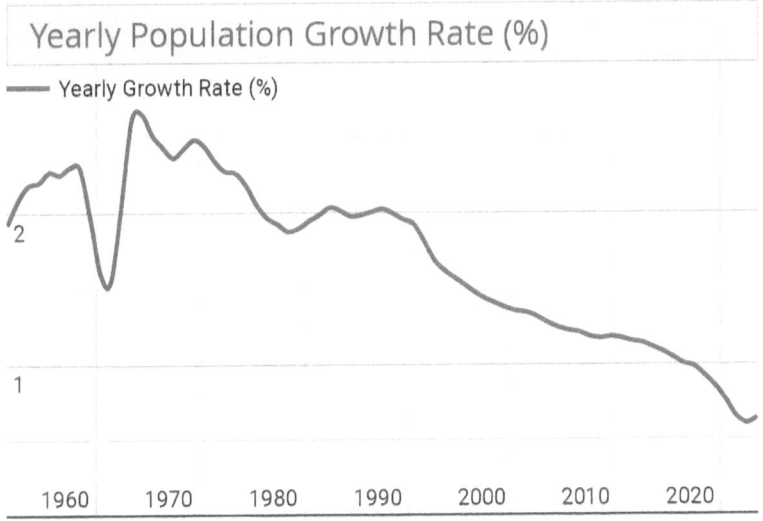

Table of Population Growth Rates in Asia, 1960–2022 (macrotrends.net/world-population/asia-population).

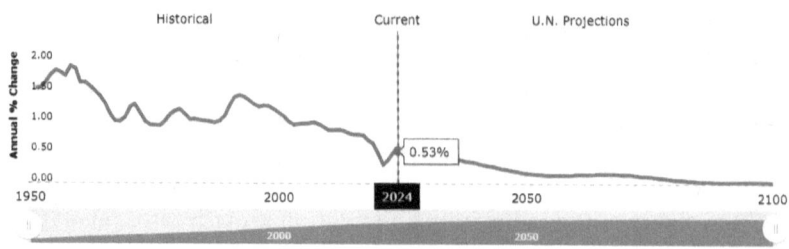

Table of Population Growth Rates in U.S., 1950–2024 (macrotrends.net/countries/USA/United-States/population-growth-rate).

continents since 1961. However, in the future, the pace of decline will be faster in developing countries, that is, those in Africa and the Middle East, than in the United States and Europe. However, according to United Nations estimates, by 2100 the world's population will level off and stabilize.[33]

Population Growth and Immigration

Another straw man that white supremacists like to posit in their delusional xenophobic screeds is focused on the immigration of "aliens" into predominantly white nations, namely France, Great Britain, and North America (especially the United States).[34] Before we take a closer look at the immigration phenomenon that has become an obsession and political football in the United States, it should be noted that the percentage of the U.S. population that is composed of immigrants is today almost exactly what it was at the height of the immigration stream in the 19th century—roughly 14 percent—but what irks white supremacists is the fact that immigrants will compose a quarter of the population increase in this country over the next decade.

Many immigrants coming to this country are from Central and South America. Mexican immigration has been drastically reduced (only 37 percent of encounters with people attempting to cross into the United States were Mexican in 2021), but it has dramatically increased in 2021 from countries in the so-called Northern Triangle—Honduras (up 19 percent), Ecuador (up 17 percent), and El Salvador (up 6 percent). It should be noted that more than a quarter of encounters at the U.S. southern borders are with repeat crossovers. Ecuador, Nicaragua, Brazil, Venezuela, Haiti, and Cuba have in recent years contributed increasing numbers of border crossers. While single adults continue to account for the majority of border crossers (60 percent), there was an eightfold

8. The Future of Asians in American Society

increase in the number of families attempting to cross (451,000) in 2021.[35]

With more than 45 million immigrants living in the United States, Asians comprise about 31 percent of them, with India, China, and the Philippines contributing the most people. The number of Asian immigrants to the United States has increased 29-fold since exclusionary laws and policies were changed following the passage of the Immigration and Nationality Act (Hart–Celler Act) of 1965, removing the national origins formula previously used to limit immigration from southern and eastern Europe and Asia. Putting this into perspective, in 2020, there were about 115 million migrants from Asia worldwide, but more than 60 percent of them went to other Asian countries, with 20 percent going to Europe and 15 percent to North America.[36] The situation becomes a bit clearer when we consider that Asians have the lowest birth rate, 48 (number of births per 1,000 women), of any ethnic group in the United States, with the exception of Native Hawaiians and Pacific Islanders, who account for only 14 percent of Asian Americans. Clearly, the fears of white supremacists and people like Camus are exaggerated, especially on a worldwide scale.

But there is some truth to their assumption that there may be changes in the composition of the people who comprise traditional white societies in the future, because the growth of the population base of the combined ethnic minorities is already in place. Even though the population of non-white ethnics in the United States and around the world is growing slowly, immigrants are younger and have higher birthrates, as found for Latinx and Asian Americans. The youthfulness of these groups and the older white population, which perforce registers fewer births and more deaths, mean that there will continue to be a decrease in the white population and an increase in non-whites in the United States. Noted demographer William Frey identified twenty-seven of the largest 100 metropolitan areas of the country that had minority white populations by 2019, including New York City, Los Angeles, Washington, D.C., Miami, Dallas, Atlanta, and Orlando. For the first time that year, more than half of the U.S. population under 16 identified as a racial or ethnic minority, and the decade from 2010 to 2020 was the first time since the first U.S. census in 1790 that the white population did not grow.[37] Today, whites compose about 60 percent of our population, compared to 19 percent for Latinx, 13 percent for blacks, 6 percent Asian Americans, less than 1 percent for Native Americans, and about 2 percent for all others. Although the population of the United States grew by about 20 million people from 2010 to 2020, most of the increase was due to the growth of Latinx and Asian populations.

Frey noted that "racial and ethnic diversity will be an essential ingredient in America's future. The demographic underpinnings for this have been set in place for a while."[38]

Given these trends, it is estimated that whites will become a minority group in the United States by around 2044. The thought of this may be behind the hysteria of the white supremacists and fellow travelers who sense that their world is turning upside down. Perhaps they are afraid of losing their privileged status in society. To many of them, privilege is a zero-sum game—sharing and collaboration with "undesirables," that is, people of color, means less for them. White privilege, as Professor Peggy McIntosh defined it, is "an invisible package of unearned assets which I can count on cashing each day, but about which I was 'meant' to remain oblivious. White privilege is like an invisible weightless knapsack of special provisions, maps, passports, codebooks, visas, clothes, tools and blank checks."[39] They choose not to recognize their privilege and blame others for their adverse situation. I am reminded of Lee Mun Wah's suggestion to David Christiansen (a white male who did not believe the comments of the men of color in their encounter group) in his classic documentary about racism, *The Color of Fear*. When Christiansen complained that his daughters were having difficulty getting into college, Mun Wah suggested, "Maybe they should work a little harder." Christiansen's face lit up because he realized he had been saying that to the men of color in the group.

The choice of accepting the demographic reality of welcoming and collaborating with people from different cultural traditions into the fabric of our society lies before us. Or we can choose the path of resistance and embrace the white supremacist perception, viewing this phenomenon as an "alien" invasion that will forever alter the culture of our society. I am fond of using the multicultural train analogy: It has left the station. We can get on at the next stop and celebrate our diversity, or we can try to pull it back.

But there are contradictions in the data. We attempted to refute the principal assumption and complaint of white supremacists—that the West, including Europe and the United States, will be overrun by people of color who will replace them. If one looks at data from Central and South America, where many immigrants to North America come from, projections indicate that the average age of the population in this region will soon be the oldest in the world, with a current population growth rate for Central America of 0.88 percent, down from 2.74 percent in 1951, and a South American population growth rate in 2023 of 0.66 percent, down from 2.72 percent in 1951.

Aside from demonstrating that the numbers of people in these previously quickly growing societies will continue to decline, thereby diminishing the number of possible immigrants seeking to enter predominantly white societies, the data also indicate that the wisest and most effective method for curbing the number of immigrants to Western countries would be the development of programs within donor countries to make their homelands more hospitable to them and their families. Instead of punitive policies and laws that perpetuate racist stereotypical images of immigrants that limit their freedom, Western leaders would do well to promote programs in their homelands that improve the quality of their lives so they choose to remain there. We should also recognize the important roles that immigrants play in providing work and services that are indispensable to our society, although they are frequently exploited while performing these jobs.[40]

The Future of Asian American Relations in the United States

In the final analysis, acceptance and rejection of Asian Americans in this country may depend on developments beyond their control. We would be disingenuous for attempting to diminish the conflict between the People's Republic of China led by its President, Xi Jinping, and the West, especially the United States. The last few years have revealed numerous areas of rivalry and conflict between mainland China, that is, the People's Republic of China (PRC), and Western nations. Flash points have occurred over the attempt of the PRC to build islands in the South China Sea. For example, the Spratly archipelago contains three Chinese human-made islands built on coral atolls that have been militarized by the Chinese with warehouses, hangars, runways, seaports, radar, anti-ship and anti-aircraft missile systems, jet fighters, and jamming equipment. Although the Chinese claim sovereignty over the islands and surrounding area, the United States opposes their attempt to gain hegemony over the region, and periodically sails ships into the waters and flies planes over the contested air space to demonstrate that it considers the area international. This situation has resulted in several near misses between Chinese and U.S. ships, and close encounters between Chinese and U.S. planes.[41]

Another area of friction between China and the West concerns the lack of credibility behind Chinese claims about perpetuating liberal political policies, including the freedom of speech, press, and assembly, in Hong Kong. The city of 7.25 million had been under British control since 1841, the time of the first Opium War. It was formally handed over to the PRC on July 1, 1997, with assurances by the PRC that it would remain fairly autonomous, at least for fifty years, as was stipulated in the Sino-British Joint Declaration of 1984 between China and Great Britain that designated Hong Kong as a special administrative region with the understanding of "one country, two systems." However, the intervening years have seen widespread unrest and discontent among Hong Kong residents, mostly around the PRC's attempt to curtail their freedoms. Violent protests erupted in 2003 when the PRC tried to change provisions of Article 23 placing limits on freedoms and to move the city closer into the orbit of the mainland. More than half a million people demonstrated against the changes and they were withdrawn.

In 2012 a controversy arose when the PRC attempted to mandate changes in the public school curriculum that depicted the mainland in a positive light and multiparty countries such as the United States and Britain negatively. Again, massive demonstrations occurred for ten days until the proposal was withdrawn. But just two years later, the PRC attempted to preselect Hong Kong candidates for top offices and three pro-democracy groups tried to paralyze the city's financial district to force free elections. When police tried to clear the area, protesters used umbrellas to shield themselves from their cudgels; hence the name "the umbrella revolution." After seventy-nine days the protesters were cleared, but this time the PRC was successful in securing its objectives, installing the candidate it selected.

But the PRC was not through meddling in the city's affairs. In 2016 protesters again took to the streets to lobby for pro-democracy candidates, and although some were elected, six representatives were disqualified and barred from taking office. Then, in 2019 two million protesters fought the PRC's attempt to impose the extradition of offenders to the mainland, where the system of jurisprudence was dubious. More than 10,000 people were arrested and nearly 3,000 were charged before the bill was withdrawn. However, just a year later, Beijing imposed a national security law in the city under the pretense of restoring order. It made secession, subversion, terrorism, and collusion with foreign powers punishable by life in prison and reintroduced the concept of extraditing accused prisoners to stand trial on the mainland. This draconian law was implemented, and hundreds of political opponents and journalists have been jailed, including Jimmy Lai, the seventy-five-year-old founder of Giordano (a Chinese clothing retailer) and of the *Apple Daily* newspaper, who has been in jail for more than three years with a sentence that will likely see him die there if it is not commuted.[42]

As economic competition between the United States and the PRC intensifies, a significant increase has been occurring in the level of espionage and associated activities between the two countries. Tensions were heightened in February 2023 when a Chinese spy balloon sailed across the continental United States before it was shot down by an American fighter plane. A recent report in *The New York Times* stated that the level of espionage between the two countries now exceeds that between the United States and the former Soviet Union. The Chinese government has been recruiting people to gather information on U.S. military bases, and a great deal of energy is being expended in using electronic communications to gather intelligence information from various sources, such as social media. In return, the CIA and the Pentagon have established new centers to spy on China in a cascading wave of frenetic energy oriented toward the collection of information that may prove useful to intelligence agencies. According to the *New York Times* article, China is surveilling "every facet of national security, diplomacy and advanced commercial technology in the United States and partner nations."[43]

In the process of increasing surveillance, Christopher Wray, the director of the Federal Bureau of Investigation (FBI), cautioned "They're going after everything," and he noted that the FBI "has thousands of open Chinese intelligence investigations, and every one of its 56 field offices has active cases."[44] The danger in this dance of mutual mistrust between the United States and China is that Asian Americans, especially Chinese residents in the United States, may come under scrutiny and suspicion, much as the Japanese did during World War II. Although no Japanese was ever convicted of engaging in espionage against the United States during World War II, pejorative stereotypes about their loyalty to this country prevailed in some segments of our society. Attitudes toward Asian Americans, especially Chinese residents in this country, might well be tainted by the growing economic and political competition between the two nations.

One of the first casualties of this heightened tension between the two nations has been the reduction of PRC-sponsored Confucius Institutes that were designed to teach the Chinese language and culture. At their height in 2017, there were 118 such institutes in the United States, mostly on the campuses of universities, and institutes in 160 countries around the world. These institutes were designed to partner with universities in this country, offering courses taught by Chinese scholars. The Chinese government spent more than $158 million on the institutes between 2006 (their inception) and 2019. Typically, the Chinese government gave a partnering institution $150,000 for the startup and annual operating expenses of $100,000 to $200,000 to provide teachers' salaries, books, scholarships, and computer hard- and software.

U.S. partners usually matched these contributions in kind by providing classrooms, office space, and program staff.

In August 2020, the Trump Administration designated the Confucius Institutes as a "foreign mission" of the PRC, requiring its parent organization, the Confucius Institutes of the United States, to file information about its operations with the U.S. Department of State. The level of mistrust between China and the United States obviously influenced the situation of these institutes. However, there were reports in the media about professors at some universities receiving retainers and fees for being associated with the institutes.

Pressure by the federal government ultimately led to the closure of most of the institutes. Several bills were introduced in Congress in the 117th and 118th sessions because some senators and congressmen perceived the institutes to be "influence agents" of China, designed to sway public opinion toward the PRC and even engage in espionage on U.S. campuses.[45] As of December 2022, there were only seven institutes operating in the United States. Like TikTok, they follow the laws of the host country they are located in, but they are not allowed to contravene PRC laws. Still, the National Academy of Sciences Engineering and Medicine concluded that it was "not aware of any evidence at the unclassified level that [the Confucius Institutes] were associated with espionage or intellectual property theft."[46] As Jonathan Sullivan, a professor at the University of Nottingham in the United Kingdom, ruefully noted, "the scare around the Confucius Institutes is exaggerated, and the fears about what they are doing and are able to achieve are overblown. The harsh reality is that Confucius Institutes/Confucius Classrooms stepped up to fulfill a need that governments were not—and they were happy to accept a 'freebie.' Now that Confucius Institutes have been tainted by wider distaste and suspicion of the Chinese government, the 'freebie' now has a cost."[47]

Even more disconcerting are the ties some U.S. researchers have with the Chinese Talent Program, a project begun by the PRC in 2010 to develop educated and skilled workers and transform China from a manufacturing economy to an engine predicated on generating scientific and technological innovations. With an allocation over $2 trillion a year, the program termed the National Medium- and Long-Term Development Plan (2010–2020) aggressively courted and recruited gifted researchers in the United States. Although some of the scientists were well-paid, they received additional stipends from the PRC and didn't disclose it to their own institutions. For example, the chair of Harvard's chemistry department, Charles Lieber, an international authority on nanotechnology, was receiving $15 million from the U.S. government for his research, but was simultaneously receiving $1.5 million for a research lab at Wuhan University in China and $50,000 a month plus $150,000 in annual living expenses between 2012 and 2017.[48]

Other similar situations were found at the Moffitt Cancer Center in Tampa, Florida, where the president was sacked, and the director was removed when it was discovered that a researcher received $300,000 in salary, research funding, and lab space and $80,000 for living expenses from the PRC under the Talents Program for working six months a year in China and recruiting other researchers. At the MD Anderson Cancer Center in Texas, Zhimin Lu, a researcher, received $14 million to work on federal grants but simultaneously served as chief scientist at China's Qingdao Cancer Institute. Upon closer investigation, it was found that 100 faculty members were involved with the Chinese Talent Program at Texas A&M University but only five of them had disclosed it. A plant pathologist in the Texas university system was offered $250,000 and more than a million dollars in seed money to start a lab with Chinese assistance, but he declined the offer.

While it is not illegal to accept foreign money for services, it must be disclosed when a researcher is receiving taxpayer funds through federal grants. Additionally, such behavior raises the specter of creating dual loyalties that may result in the transferal of information and know-how to adversarial nations. Aside from possibly undermining academic freedom, such behavior calls into question the loyalty and commitment of trusted personnel, be they Asian or not. That is precisely what some federal prosecutors have seized upon. "Chemistry, nanotechnology, polymer studies, robotics, computer science, biomedical research—this is not an accident or coincidence. This is a small sample of China's ongoing campaign to siphon off American technology and know-how for Chinese gain," said Andrew Lelling, a federal prosecutor who commented about the situation.[49]

Spying or Racial Profiling?

Our relationship with mainland China has taken many twists and turns over the decades and with it attitudes toward Asians and Asian Americans. Harsh laws have been implemented to prevent the immigration of Asians to this country and investigations enacted of Asian professors accused of engaging in espionage by collecting and disseminating information about scientific, cultural, and industrial developments in the United States. One of the most egregious cases of purported espionage by a Chinese professor involved Anming Hu, a

Chinese Canadian professor at the University of Tennessee. The FBI investigated Hu as possibly being in the Chinese Talent Program, and he was accused of defrauding NASA by ostensibly hiding his affiliations with a Chinese university.

Since the Trump administration began a "Chinese Initiative" in 2018 for the purpose of combatting "the greatest long-term threat" to the United States, investigations of Chinese scientists and professors like Anming Hu have increased dramatically, despite skepticism about the project by security experts, legal scholars, and activists who consider the initiative misplaced and even a case of racial profiling.[50] Some of them even consider the initiative damaging to United States–China relations. The Hu case was the first "China Initiative" case to go to trial. The jury deadlocked and a mistrial was declared after only one day of deliberations. The principal government witness admitted he gave false information about Professor Hu to the University of Tennessee and spread false information about him that damaged his career, for example that Hu was a military operative of the PRC, which led to him being fired by the University of Tennessee.

This ad hominem attack on an Asian American scientist was not the first nor will it, unfortunately, be the last of its kind. For example, Wen Ho Lee, who was born in Taiwan, became a naturalized U.S. citizen in 1974. He was a professor at the University of California and working as a scientist at the Los Alamos National Laboratory when he was arrested by the FBI and charged in 1999 with stealing secrets for the PRC about the U.S. nuclear arsenal. However, federal investigators were unable to prove their case, and fifty-eight of the fifty-nine charges against him were dropped. Instead, he was charged with improper handling of restricted data—a charge he pleaded guilty to. James A. Parker, the federal judge in charge of the case, apologized to Dr. Lee for denying him bail and keeping him in solitary confinement for 278 days. Lee filed a civil suit against the U.S. government and five media organizations for releasing his name to the press prior to him being formally charged, and he collected $1.6 million from the suit in June 2006. Judge Parker apologized to Lee for denying him bail and putting him in solitary confinement, and criticized the federal government for misconduct and misrepresentation to the court: "top decision makers in the executive branch ... have embarrassed our entire nation and each of us who is a citizen."[51] President Bill Clinton also apologized to Dr. Lee soon thereafter.

Fed by increasing xenophobia and Sinophobia, the pressure to prosecute Asian Americans, especially Chinese, has become relentless. A study by the Committee of 100, "Racial Profiling Among Scientists of

Chinese Descent," noted that the "China Initiative" of the U.S. Department of Justice is having a "chilling effect" on scientific productivity in this country. Young Chinese scholars from the United States and abroad are being discouraged from pursuing scientific careers in this country because of fear of harassment and persecution based on hysteria and racial profiling.[52] Michael German, a former FBI agent and currently a scholar at the Brennan Center for Justice's Liberty and National Security Program, ruefully noted that pressure across the country to develop cases on Chinese espionage is rampant within the FBI "because they have to prove statistical accomplishments."[53]

As former Secretary of Defense Robert Gates noted, many countries, including allies like France, steal U.S. technology, and the conservative Cato Institute found that from 1990 to 2019, excluding violations related to the Arms and Export Control Act, China accounted for only 27.5 percent of convictions, and domestic espionage benefiting U.S. entities, such as corporations, accounted for 30.8 percent.[54] Frank Wu, president of Queens College of the City University of New York, has publicly criticized the stereotype of "ethnic affinity," that is, the belief that Chinese people owe allegiance to Beijing and the PRC. One would think that our experience with Japanese Americans in World War II would have dampened such xenophobia, but the tendency to ostracize and accuse non–Anglos is resistant to change in the United States.

The recent flurry of laws around this country designed to restrict mainland China and Chinese residents here from purchasing land is reminiscent of restrictive land laws at the turn of the 20th century.[55] In May 2023 a Florida law was passed that prohibits most citizens of "foreign countries of concern" from purchasing land on or within 10 miles of any "military installation or critical infrastructure facility," including seaports, airports, and power plants. Upon signing the law, Florida's governor, Ron DeSantis, noted, "Today, Florida makes it very clear: We don't want the (Chinese Communist Party) in the Sunshine State. We want to maintain this as the 'Free State of Florida.'"[56] Asian Americans immediately sued Florida officials over the law's alleged violation of the constitutional rights to due process and equal protection. While there is legitimate concern about spying on sensitive military installations or stockpiling large amounts of fertile land by the Chinese government, the reality is that about 40 million acres of agricultural land in the United States are owned by foreign investors and of that, China owns less than 1 percent. Nevertheless, eight states (and more are considering it) have passed legislation barring or limiting China, Russia, North Korea, Cuba, and Iran from purchasing land here. CNN spoke with other experts on the issue of foreign acquisition of U.S. land and they cautioned that such actions need to be based on evidence, not hysteria. As professor Nancy Qian of the Kellogg School of Management at Northwestern University noted, these actions are often "rooted in racism and xenophobia."[57]

Surveillance, Harassment, and Confusion

Writing about the long history of mistrust and racism toward Asian Americans by the Anglo society in the United States gives one the feeling that a good measure of the suspicion and attacks leveled against them is the result of scapegoating and xenophobia.[58] As the cold war between mainland China and the United States escalates over things like disputed territory, such as the human-made islands in the South China Sea, the treatment of residents of Hong Kong, the political integrity of Taiwan, and economic ascendancy in emerging markets around the world, it is obvious that a good deal of the increasing animosity directed toward mainland China by a growing segment of the population and the government of the United States is a by-product of the struggle between these superpowers. Asian Americans may be stigmatized and discriminated against from the fallout of the perturbations between them.

An observer may have a nagging feeling that the intentions of some PRC leaders toward this country are at times malevolent. There have been near misses with ships and planes near Taiwan, warnings issued by the PRC to the United States about not violating their territorial integrity or our reputed malevolent policies, spy balloons that mysteriously drift over military bases around the United States and elsewhere (at last count forty nations have been surveilled by these balloons), the reneging on promises to continue democratic principles in Hong Kong, the purchase of land near military establishments in the United States, and the possible surreptitious use of the popular social media app TikTok (as of September 2023, nineteen states had issued some sort of ban on the app and federal employees in thirty-four states were prohibited from using it on government devices).

On April 20, 2024, the U.S. House of Representatives passed legislation (360–58) mandating that the app TikTok in use in the United States be sold to non–Chinese ownership within a year, and the U.S. Senate followed suit on April 23, passing the bill 78–18. President Biden signed the legislation on April 24, 2024, but First Amendment challenges under the premise that such action interferes with free speech would have to be resolved before action could be taken. A federal judge blocked the banning of the app in Montana in November 2023, but a suit brought by the Knight First Amendment Institute and Columbia University to prevent Texas from banning the app was rejected in December 2023 by another federal judge. Alex Haurek, a spokesman for TikTok, noted: "It is unfortunate that the House of Representatives is using the cover of important foreign and humanitarian assistance to once again jam through a bill that would trample the free speech right of 170 million Americans, devastate 7 million businesses and shutter a platform that contributes $24 billion to the U.S. economy annually."[59] At the time of this writing (April 2024), the issue was still in doubt.

Although one might be inclined to give the PRC the benefit of a doubt regarding its intentions, the recent revelation that the PRC was surveilling and harassing Chinese dissidents in the United States and in as many as fifty-three other countries in an attempt to muzzle their dissent, including "repatriating" some dissidents to the mainland, is a chilling reminder that some of the activities and actions of the PRC are suspect.[60]

Asian American Assimilation and Integration

This book's discussion of stereotypes about Asian Americans has revealed some of the myths that have been and still are used against them to limit their freedoms and participation in this country. Still, the draconian Chinese Exclusion Acts of the late 19th century and restrictive immigration policies and injunctions preventing Asians from owning land are resurfacing. As competition for world hegemony, especially domination of markets and technological development, becomes ascendant, pressure to conform and assimilate, to look and act American, will increase on Asian Americans. In the process of becoming more like their traditional oppressors, their wide variety of cultures and languages must not be sacrificed on the altar of materialism.

While more work must be done to improve the economic plight of many Asians in the United States, we have seen how successful some Asian Americans have become, and we benefit from their contributions to the scientific, technological, economic, and political spheres of our society. Their works are far-ranging in scope and influence every sector of American life. From agriculture to aerospace, law to medicine, science to technology, Asian Americans' contributions to America and the world have made a transcendent mark on the quality of life for everyone on the planet. We can expect their contributions to continue as their numbers increase over the coming years.

One notable area of Asian American participation that has been increasing in recent years is politics. We now have the first female vice president of the United States, Kamala Harris (born in 1964), whose father, Donald, was Jamaican and an economics professor at Stanford University, and whose mother, a cancer researcher from India, became a tenured professor at McGill University in Canada. Andrew Yang (born in 1975), a Chinese American businessman and attorney, ran for U.S. President in the 2020 Democratic primary. One of his pivotal policy promises was to provide a universal basic income of $1,000 a month to every adult in this country. He is also the founder of Ventures for America (VFA), which connects young professionals to innovative companies in economically distressed cities.

While Harris and Yang are affiliated with the mainline Democratic Party, Pramila Jayapal, born in 1965 in Madras, India (now Tamil Nadu), and is the leader of the Congressional Progressive Caucus in the U.S. House of Representatives, where she has been elected to represent the region that includes Seattle, Washington, since 2016. She became a naturalized citizen in 2000, is an activist for immigrants and women's rights, and wields considerable influence on Capitol Hill.

As we have seen, there is wide diversity in interests among Asian Americans, and they are also represented by diverse political approaches and styles. Nikki (Nimarata) Haley (born in 1972) was governor of South Carolina from 2011 to 2017 and served in the Trump Administration as ambassador to the United Nations for two years. A daughter in a Sikh family, she was the second person of Indian ethnicity (after Bobby Jindal, born in 1971, who served as governor of Louisiana from 2008 to 2016) to be elected governor of a state in this country, and she ran

Vice President Kamala Harris. She also ran as the presidential candidate of the Democratic Party in 2024 (Library of Congress).

8. The Future of Asians in American Society

for the presidency as a member of the Republican Party during the 2024 election campaign. She was joined by Vivek Ramaswamy (born in 1985), who made a fortune as a biotech executive. His parents came legally to the United States from southern India, and he graduated as a biology major from Harvard and then earned a law degree from Yale. Although his parents are not citizens, he was born in the United States and has citizenship by birthright. The conservative Ramaswamy unsuccessfully sought the Republican nomination for presidency in the 2024 election. We can expect the political contributions from these and other Asian Americans to continue, and we should also welcome the diversity of their ideas and their desire to become an integral part of the American social system, always keeping in mind the words of the Rev. Dr. Martin Luther King, Jr., that we should not judge a person by the color of their skin, but by the content of their character.

Representative Pramila Jayapal (Library of Congress, photo by George Skidmore).

Chapter Notes

Preface

1. Mia Tuan, *Forever Foreign or Honorary White? The Asian Ethnic Experience Today*. New Brunswick, NJ: Rutgers University Press, 1998, p. 28.

Introduction

1. For a comprehensive review that attempts to pinpoint the origin of the Covid-19 pandemic (without reaching a definitive conclusion) see David Quammen, "Points of Origin," *The New York Times Magazine*, July 30, 2023, pp. 20–27, 42–43, 45.
2. Edwin Rios, "Hate Incidents Against Asian Americans Continue to Surge, Study Finds," *The Guardian*, July 21, 2022.
3. Cathy Park Hong, *Minor Feelings* (New York: One World, 2020), p. 202.
4. *Ibid.*, p. 13.
5. *Ibid.*, pp. 9–10.
6. Rosalind S. Chou and Joe R. Feagin, *The Myth of the Model Minority: Asian Americans Facing Racism* (Boulder, CO: Paradigm Publishers, 2010).
7. Wesley Yang, *The Souls of Yellow Folk: Essays* (New York: W.W. Norton and Company, 2018); Charles Yu, *Interior Chinatown: A Novel* (New York: Vintage, 2020); Cathy Park Hong, note 3; Julia Lee, *Biting the Hand: Growing Up Asian in Black and White America* (New York: Henry Holt and Company, 2023); Jay Caspian Kang, *The Loneliest Americans* (New York: Crown Publishing Group, 2021).
8. Hong, note 3, p. 90.
9. *Ibid.*, p. 35.

Chapter 1

1. For insight into human evolution see Matt Ridley, *Genome: The Evolution of a Species in 23 Chapters* (New York: HarperCollins, 2000); John H. Relethford, *Reflections of Our Past: How History Is Revealed in Our Genes* (Cambridge, MA: Westview Press, 2003); Yuval Noah Harari, *Sapiens: A Brief History of Humankind* (New York: Harper Perennial, 2018).
2. Replacement theory holds that black and brown people will be replacing whites in society because of lax immigration policies in the United States and Europe coupled with the low birth rate of whites. Derived from the writing of Jean Raspail in 1973 in his novel *The Camp of the Saints* (Paris: Editions Robert Laffont), and expanded by Renaud Camus's 2012 treatise, *The Great Replacement* (France: Chez L'auteur, 2019), the theory has been embraced by white supremacists in the United States and Western Europe as a foundation for their racist, exclusionary immigration policies and behavior.
3. This information was gathered from the U.S. Census Bureau: census.gov/library/stories/2021/08/improved-race-ethnicity-measures-reveal-united-states-population-much-more-multiracial.html.~:text=Asian%20Population.people%20(4.8%25)%20. Retrieved 5/5/22.
4. Abby Budiman and Neil G. Ruiz,

"Key Facts about Asian Americans, a Diverse and Growing Population," Pew Research Center, April 29, 2021, https://www.pewresearch.org/fact-tank/2021/04/29/key-facts-about-asian-americans.

5. There are approximately fifty Chinatowns dotting the U.S. landscape, but the Covid pandemic led to a 50–80 percent reduction in foot traffic in them, causing a severe shortfall in small business revenue. See Allison Lau, "Is the U.S. Losing Its Chinatowns?," CNBC, May 28, 2021, cnbc.com/video/2021/05/28/why-the-us-has-so-many-chinatowns.html.

6. One of the most authoritative discussions of the Chinese laborers' role in building the transcontinental railroad is the award-winning book by Gordon Chang, *Ghosts of Gold Mountain* (New York: Mariner Books, 2019). See also Mae Ngai, *The Chinese Question* (New York: W.W. Norton, 2021). She described the discrimination Chinese immigrants faced in the gold fields and mines in California, South Africa, and Australia.

7. For a glimpse of Marco Polo's adventures in the Far East, see *Book of the Travels of Marco Polo*, available online at Gutenberg.org/files/10636/10636-h/10636-h.htm. While Polo's description of his journey is at times illuminating, the names of places have changed over the centuries, often obscuring the places he visited. Indeed, the editor's notes trying to explain his statements and clarify his travel are often confusing, contradictory, and much longer than Polo's narrative.

8. Pearl Buck's book *The Good Earth* can be accessed online at archives.org/details/goodearth00buck_1/page/n5/mode/2up.

9. Stuart C. Miller, *The Unwelcome Immigrant: The American Image of the Chinese, 1785–1882* (Berkeley: University of California Press, 1969).

10. *Ibid.*, p. 73.

11. "China," from *Encyclopedia Britannica*, 7th edition, vol. VI, 1842. Quoted in Miller, note 9, p. 83.

12. Miller, note 9, pp. 87–88. Compare the contemporary QAnon's assertions about Democrats' obsession with obtaining adrenochrome from children.

13. See the comprehensive analysis of British, American, Australian, and South African motivation toward China in Ngai, note 6. She provides an interesting history of British subjugation of the East Indian economy for the purpose of producing opium that was traded by the company to the Chinese for silk and silver, in the process destroying Indian and Chinese lives through unhealthy work environments and addiction.

14. Ngai noted that a quarter million Chinese indentured laborers worked in European plantation colonies in the Caribbean after the abolition of slavery. This phenomenon was referred to as the "coolie trade." See Ngai, *ibid.*, p. 3.

15. Madison Grant, *The Passing of the Great Race* (New York: Charles Scribner's Sons, 1916).

16. Lothrop Stoddard, *The Rising Tide of Color Against White World-Supremacy* (New York: Charles Scribner's Sons, 1920).

17. Quoted in Miller, note 9, p. 190.

18. Herbert Spencer, *The Synthetic Philosophy* (New York: D. Appleton and Co., 1921; first published in 1896).

19. See Ngai, note 6, pp. 138–143, 163–164, for a historical analysis of the concept of coolieism and racist attitudes toward the Chinese in the United States, Australia, and South Africa.

20. Quoted in Miller, note 9, p. 168.

21. Cf. the comments of Donald Trump in his presidential announcement speech on June 16, 2015: "When Mexico sends its people, they're not sending their best. They're not sending you. They're sending people that have lots of problems, and they're bringing those problems with us. They're bringing drugs. They're bringing crime. They're rapists. And some, I assume, are good people." His entire speech can be seen at YouTube.com/watch?v=apjNfKysjbM.

22. Miller, note 9, pp. 180–181.

23. Linda Perrin, *Coming to America: Immigrants from the Far East* (New York: Delacorte Press, 1980), p. 5.

24. From the *Irish Citizen*, July 9, 1870, quoted in *ibid.*, p. 198.

25. From *McGee's Illustrated Weekly*, vol. 1, 1877, quoted in *ibid.*, p. 199.

26. "The cheap labor cry was always a falsehood. [Our] labor was never cheap, and is not cheap now. It has always commanded the highest market price. But

the trouble is that the Chinese are such excellent and faithful workers that bosses will have no others when they can get them. It was the jealousy of laboring men of other nationalities—especially the Irish—that raised all the outcry against the Chinese. No one would hire an Irishman, German, Englishman or Italian when he could get a Chinese, because our countrymen are so much more honest, industrious, steady, sober and painstaking. Chinese were persecuted, not for their vices, but for their virtues." Quoted in Perrin, note 23, p. 27.

27. Chang, note 6.
28. *Ibid.*, p. 144–145.
29. *Ibid.* p. 166.
30. Ngai, note 6, p. 51.
31. A popular ditty of the time, "Twelve Hundred More," is worth recounting here:

"O workingmen dear, and did you hear
The news that's goin' round?
Another China steamer
Has been landed here in town.
Today I read the papers,
And it grieved my heart full sore
To see upon the title page,
O, just 'Twelve Hundred More!'
O, California's coming down,
As you can plainly see.
They are hiring all the Chinamen
and discharging you and me;
But strife will be in every town
Throughout the Pacific shore,
And the cry of old and young shall be,
'O, damn, 'Twelve Hundred More.'"
[Quoted in Perrin, note 23, pp. 32–34.]

32. Bill Lee, *Chinese Playground: A Memoir* (Scotts Valley, CA: CreateSpace, 2014).
33. For more information on Donaldina Cameron see Kristin Wong and Kathryn Wong, *Fierce Compassion: The Life of Abolitionist Donaldina Cameron* (Encinitas, CA: New Earth Enterprises, 2012).
34. For a discussion of the Chinese boycott of U.S. goods see Ngai, note 6, pp. 294–298.
35. For a review of the Chinese Exclusion Act and its implications for the United States see Yuning Wu and Adam Augustyn, "Chinese Exclusion Act," at Britannica.com/biography/Chester-A-Arthur.

36. The Economist Intelligence Unit, *From Foundation to Frontiers: Chinese American Contributions to the Fabric of America* (New York: The Committee of 100, July 2, 2021), aasforum.org/2021/07/02/from-foundations-to-frontiers-chinese-american-contributions-to-the-fabric-of-america.
37. This study was authored by Qin Gao, Jennifer So, and Stacey Tao of Columbia University and Sam Collitt of the Committee of 100. It was based upon a nonrepresentative sample from around the United States and reflects the diversity of the Chinese American population: "The Fight for Representation: The State of Chinese Americans 2022" (New York: Columbia University, 2023).
38. Global Chinese Philanthropy Initiative, 2022, globalchinesephilanthropy.org/gcpi/report/178333.
39. *Ibid.*
40. The subject of government surveillance of Chinese American researchers is discussed later in this book. See Chapter 8.
41. The Economist Intelligence Unit, note 36.
42. Report of the Immigration Commission 349, U.S. Senate, 1911. Italics added.
43. "The Formation of Human Populations in South and Central Asia," *Science*, volume 365, September 6, 2019, p. 7487ff.
44. Today this group is known as the Dalits.
45. The Puritan Doctrine of the Elect, which had a significant influence on the behavior and industriousness of adherents, was also a potent method of social control. See Max Weber, *The Protestant Ethic and the Spirit of Capitalism*: and Other Writings, ed. Peter Baehar and Gordon S. Wells (New York: Penguin Twentieth-Century Classics Edition, 2002). The sermon delivered by the Rev. Jonathan Edwards, "Sinners in the Hands of an Angry God" (July 8, 1741, in Enfield, CT), is a classic example of the Puritan influence on our society through spiritual social control. Available at blueletterbible.org/Comm/Edwards_Jonathan/Sermons/sinners.cfm. Recently, historian Isabel Wilkerson applied the caste structure to the United States. See Isabel

Wilkerson, *Caste: The Origins of Our Discontents* (New York: Random House, 2020).

46. Ravi Shankar, "It's All in the Genes: Does DNA Call the Bluff on Aryan Invasion Theory?," *The New India Express*, September 15, 2019.

47. Sumitra Badrinathan, Devesh Kapur, Jonathan Kay, and Milan Vaishnav, "Social Realities of Indian Americans: Results of the 2020 Indian American Attitude Survey," Carnegie Endowment for International Peace, June 19, 2021, https://carnegieendowment.org/research/2021/06/social-realities-of-indian-americans-results-from-the-2020-indian-american-attitudes-survey?lang=en.

48. Officer Murphy was shot fifteen times but recovered. He was given $10,000 by Sikhs for Justice, a New York-based organization and $100,000 by two Sikhs from Yuba City, California. For more information on crimes against Sikhs see Moni Basu, "15 Years After 9/11, Sikhs Still Victims of Anti-Muslim Hate Crimes," CNN.com/2016/09/15/us/sikh-hate-crime-victims/index.html. Information about Sikhs can be obtained from the Sikh American Legal Defense and Education Fund (SALDEF), saldef.org/archive/learn-about-sikhs/#.WaR7qyiGOM9.

49. For more information about hate crimes perpetrated against Sikhs see "Hate Crime Tracking and Prevention," The Sikh Coalition, sikhcoalition.org/our-work/preventing/hate-and-discrimination/hate-crime-tracking-and-prevention.

50. For a readable summary of the origins and uniqueness of East Indian society see Akhilesh Pillalamarri, "Where Did Indians Come From?," *The Diplomat*, parts 1–4, 2019, thediplomat.com/2019/01/unraveled-where—indians-come-from-part-1/.

51. Research found that skin tone among African Americans predicted many forms of discrimination and even affected health outcomes for research subjects. See Ellis P. Monk, Jr., "The Cost of Color: Skin Color, Discrimination, and Health Among African Americans," *American Journal of Sociology* vol. 121, #2 (September 2015), pp. 396–444. See also Jairo N. Fuertes et al., "A Meta-Analysis of the Effects of Speakers' Accents on Interpersonal Evaluations," *European Journal of Social Psychology* vol. 42, October 26, 2011.

52. Jessica Wolf, "2021 Hollywood Diversity Report: Audiences Showed Up for Diverse Films in Theaters, Online," *UCLA Newsroom*, April 22, 2021, newsroom.ucla.edu/releases/2021-hollywood-diversity-report.

53. The Sikhs were highly decorated and respected for their assistance to the British in World War I. About 130,000 Sikhs served in the British Indian Army, composing almost 20 percent of it, and nearly 300,000 Sikhs served in the British Army during the Second World War. They experienced 83,000 killed and 109,000 wounded in the two wars.

54. For example, the gift of $200 million by Drs. Kiran and Pallavi Patel to Nova Southeastern University was the largest in the school's history. For details see nova.edu/patelgift/index.html.

55. Badrinathan et al., note 47.

56. Neha Mishra, "India and Colorism: The Finer Nuances," *Washington University Global Studies Law Review* vol. 14, no. 4, 2015, pp. 725–50.

57. https://www.statista.com/statistics/1071134/philippines-value-cash-remittances-overseas-filipino-workers-usa/.

58. Demographic information about Filipinos is derived from Abby Budiman, "Filipinos in the U.S. Fact Sheet," Pew Research Center, April 29, 2021, pewresearch.org/social-trends/fact-sheet/Asian-americans-filipinos-in-the-u-s. Information on the history of the Philippines is derived from Office of the Historian, "The Philippine-American War, 1899–1902," history.state.gov/milestones/1899–1913/war. Migration information was derived from Lisa H. Gallardo and Jeanne Batalova, "Filipino Immigrants in the U.S.," Migration Policy Institute, July 15, 2020, migrationpolicy.org/article/filipino-immigrants-united-states-2020.

59. For the extended list of Filipino notables who contributed to U.S. society see "List of Filipino Americans," *Wikipedia*, en.wikipedia.org/wiki/List_of_Filipino_Americans.

60. For a list of Vietnamese

Americans and their accomplishments see en.wikipedia.org/wiki/List_of_Vietnamese_Americans.

61. For more information on the history of Korean immigration in the United States see "In Observance of Centennial of Korean Immigration to the U.S.," ed. John H. Kim et al., www.naka.org/resources/briefhistory.htm.

62. For a lengthy list of Korean American notables and their contributions see en.wikipedia.org/wiki/List_of_Korean_Americans.

63. "The U.S. Mainland: Growth and Resistance," Library of Congress, loc.gov/classroom-materials/immigrantion/Japanese/the-us-mainland-growth-and-resistamce (no date).

Chapter 2

1. Chris Hedges, "What Every Person Should Know About War," *The New York Times*, July 6, 2003.

2. Stephen Devereux, "Famine in the Twentieth Century," Social Sciences in Humanitarian Action Platform, https://www.socialscienceinaction.org/resources/famine-in-the-twentieth-century.

3. Jonathan Sperber, "Infectious Diseases in the Twentieth Century," University of Missouri, College of Arts and Sciences, May 16, 2020, history.missouri.edu/node/141; and "Control of Infectious Diseases, 1900–1999," Centers for Disease Control and Prevention, September 15, 1999, jamanetwork.com/journal/jama/fullarrticle/191692.

4. For a dated but at the time revelatory view of this conundrum, see Paul and Anne Ehrlich, *The Population Bomb* (New York: Ballantine Books, 1968).

5. Feng Wang, "China's Population Destiny: The Looming Crisis," Brookings Inst., September 30, 2010, brookings.edu/articles/chinas-population-destiny-the-loomiong-crisis. See also Roland Rajah and Alyssa Leng, "Revising Down the Rise of China," Lowy Institute, March 15, 2022, lowyinstitute.org/publications/revising-down-rise-China.

6. See H. Roy Kaplan, *Understanding Conflict and Change in a Multicultural World* (Lanham, MD: Rowman & Littlefield, 2014), pp. 80–85. For a recent look at attempts to revitalize Chinatowns see Lydia Lee, "The Future of Chinatowns," *Preservation* (Spring 2024), pp. 18–27.

7. William F. Ogburn, *Social Change*, rev. ed. (New York: Viking, 1950).

8. The acronym MAD is used by many anti-nuke advocates. It stands for mutual assured destruction—the belief that a nuclear war would result in the destruction of all parties in the exchange—and hence the concept has been used as a deterrent.

9. While it seems heretical for contemporary economists to adopt a slow or no-growth perspective, economist E.F. Schumacher published his essays on the virtue of controlled growth, *Small Is Beautiful*, in 1973 (New York: HarperCollins).

10. It is rather ironic that Marxists and the Catholic Church both contend that poverty is not preordained but the result of maldistribution of resources, although their prescriptions for resolving the problem are different.

11. The influx of Irish immigrants into New York City was described by Randi Minetor, *New York Immigrant Experience* (Guilford, CT: Globe Pequot Press, 2010.)

12. The *1619 Project: A New Origin Story* provides insight into the origin of class antagonisms in the United States. Of special import to our discussion was the process that led to the investiture of "whiteness" and privilege (as opposed to "blackness" and deprivation) utilized by affluent whites in the early years of our nation. See Nikole Hannah-Jones et al. (eds.), *The 1619 Project* (New York: One World, 2021).

13. For a discussion of the despoliation of Native American lands by encroaching white settlers in the formative years of this nation see H. Roy Kaplan, *American Indians at the Margins: Racist Stereotypes and Their Impacts on Native Peoples*. (Jefferson, NC: McFarland and Company, 2022).

14. Abigail Johnson Hess, "13 U.S. Workers Die on the Job Per Day on Average and These Are the Most Dangerous Jobs," *Make it*, December 29, 2021, cnbc.com/2021/12/29/bis-estimates-that-13-

us-workers-die-on-the-job-per-day-on-average.html#.

15. Giovanni Peri, "Do Immigrant Workers Depress Wages of Native Workers?," IZA World of Labor, May 2014, Wol.iza.org/uploads/articles/42/pdfs/do-immigrant-workers-depress-the-wages-of-native-workers.pdf. (Italics added). See also Alan de Brauw, "Does Immigration Reduce Wages?," *Cato Journal* vol. 37, no. 3, Fall 2017, pp. 473–480. For a different perspective see the work of economist George Borjas, e.g., *Unraveling the Immigration Narrative* (New York: W.W. Norton, 2016).

16. Madison Grant, *The Passing of the Great Race: Or the Racial Basis of European History*, 4th ed. (New York: Charles Scribner's Sons, 1921; originally published in 1914). Carl C. Brigham, *A Study of American Intelligence* (London, England: Forgotten Books, 2017; originally published In 1923). Lothrop Stoddard, *The Rising Tide of Color Against White World-Supremacy* (New York: Charles Scribner's Sons, 1920).

17. The classic treatise on white antipathy toward black labor was authored by W.E.B. Du Bois, *Black Reconstruction in America, 1860–1880* (New York: The Free Press, 1998; originally published in 1935).

18. Tyler Stovall, *White Freedom: The Racial History of an Idea* (Princeton, NJ: Princeton University Press, 2021).

19. "Over 200,000 Green Cards Wasted in 2021 as Backlog Explodes," *Boundless*, January 1, 2022, boundless.com/blog/uscis-wastes-200k-green-cards-backlog-triples/#.

20. Patrick Lyons, "Trump Wants to Abolish Birthright Citizenship. Can He Do That?," *The New York Times*, August 22, 2019.

21. UNHCR, "Global Displacement Hits Another Record, Capping Decade-Long Rising Trend," June 16, 2022, UNHCR.org/en-us/news/press/2022/6/62a9d2b04/unhcr-global-displacement-hits-record-capping-decade-long-rising-trend.html.

22. For example, see "Migration and Gender," *Pew Research Center*, July 5, 2006, pewresearch.org/Hispanic/2006/07/0a5/ii-migration-and-gender; "Gender and Migration," Global Migration Data Portal, International Organization for Migration, 2021, migrationdataportal.org/themes/gender-and-migration.

23. "Poverty Myth: Immigrants Come to the U.S. to Use Welfare," *ATD Fourth World USA*, September 6, 2018, 4thworldmovement.org/immigrants-come-use—welfare.

24. https://www.cato.org/blog/cis-exaggerates-cost-immigrant-welfare-use.

25. "Adding Up the Billions in Tax Dollars Paid by Undocumented Immigrants," *American Immigration Council*, April 4, 2016, https://www.americanimmigrationcouncil.org/sites/default/files/research/adding_up_the_billions_in_tax_dollars_paid_by_undocumented_immigrants.pdf.

26. Ibid.

27. Francine J. Lipman, "The Illegal Tax," *Connecticut Public Interest Law Journal* vol. 11, no. 1, 2012, pp. 93–131, Cpilj.law.uconn.edu/wp-content/uploads/sites/2515/2018/10/11.1-The-"Illegal"-Tax-by-Francine-J.-Lipman.pdf.

28. "Boundless Releases 2022 Immigrant Income and Taxation Report," *Boundless*, April 14, 2022, http://www.boundless.com/blog/boundless-releases-2022-immigrant-income-taxation-report.

29. *Ibid.*

30. *Ibid.*

31. Alex Nowrasteh, "Immigration and Crime—What the Research Says," *Cato Institute*, July 14, 2015, cato.org/blog/immigration-crime-what-research-says.

32. Michael T. Light, Jingying He, and Jason P. Robey, "Comparing Crime Rates Between Undocumented Immigrants and Native-Born U.S. Citizens in Texas," December, 22, 2020, *Proceedings of the National Academy of Sciences* vol. 117, no. 51, https://doi.org/10.1073/pnas.2014704117.

33. *Ibid.*

34. See note 16.

35. See the treatise on the decline of the Anglo human species in Joseph-Arthur Comte de Gobineau, *The Inequality of Human Races*, trans. Adrian Collins (London: William

Heinemann, 1915). Also see the work of Houston Stewart Chamberlain, a leading scientific racist, *Foundations of the Nineteenth Century*, trans. John Lees (London: John Lane, 1911).

36. Howard Markel and Alexandra M. Stern, "The Foreignness of Germs: The Persistent Association of Immigrants and Disease in American Society," *Milbank Quarterly* vol. 80, no. 4 (December 2022), pp. 757–788, ncbi.nim.nih.gov/pmc/articles/PMC2690128.

37. The United Nations' World Health Organization (WHO) sought unsuccessfully to eliminate the disease by 2020. Although it has declined, there is no vaccine to prevent it.

38. The cosponsor of the Nationality Act of 1952, Senator Pat McCarran of Nevada (Democrat) observed on the floor of the United States Senate: "I believe that this nation is the last hope of western civilization and if this oasis of the world shall be overrun, perverted, contaminated or destroyed, then the last flickering light of humanity will be extinguished.…we have in the United States today hardcore, indigestible blocs which have not become integrated into the American way of life, but which, on the contrary are its deadly enemies. Today, as never before, untold millions are storming our gates for admission and those gates are cracking under the strain." *Congressional Record*, Senate, March 2, 1953, p. 1518.

39. Eli Watkins and Abby Phillip, "Trump Decries Immigrants From 'Shithole Countries' Coming to the U.S.," *CNN*, January 12, 2018, cnn.com/2018/01/11/politics/immigrants-shithole-countries-trump/index.html.

40. For a review of Dobbs's contretemps see David Leonhardt, "Truth, Fiction and Lou Dobbs," *The New York Times*, May 30, 2007, nytimes.com/2007/05/30/business/30leonhardt.html.

Chapter 3

1. "Crime in the United States, 2019," Uniform Crime Report, FBI, Table 43, ucr.fbi.gov/crime-in-the-u.s./2019/topic-pages/tables/table-43.

2. B.C.E. (before the common era) and C.E. (common era) are the contemporary terms, instead of B.C. (before Christ) and A.D. (anno domini, in the year of our lord, or since Jesus' birth).

3. John A. Price, "Gambling in Traditional Asia," *Anthropologia vol.*14 (1972), pp. 157–180.

4. For a review of the deterioration of gambling revenues in Macau and shifting Chinese government policies about gambling there see Chad De Guzman, "'An Empty Shell of What It Used to Be': Asia's Gambling Mecca Gets a China-Backed Makeover," *Time*, November 3, 2022, time.com/6227922/macau-gambling-capital-casino-china.

5. Widespread prevalence of gambling among Chinese in California was reported in *Gamblers of the Old West* (Alexandria, VA: Time-Life Books, 1977), pp. 85–97. San Francisco was the focal point of gambling among Chinese immigrants, with an estimated 200 illegal gambling casinos operating in Chinatown in that city in the latter part of the 19th century.

6. Analucia A. Alegria et al., "Disordered Gambling Among Racial and Ethnic Groups in the United States: Results from the National Epidemiologic Survey on Alcohol and Related Conditions," *CNS Spectrums* vol. 14, no. 3 (March 2009), pp. 132–143.

7. See Donald E. Nowak and Ariel M. Aloe, "The Prevalence of Pathological Gambling Among College Students: A Meta-Analytic Synthesis, 2005–2013," *Journal of Gambling Behavior* vol. 30 (2014), pp. 819–843. This study found the prevalence of pathological gambling among students to be 10.23 percent—several times higher than the general population.

8. Susan E. Luczak and Tamara L. Wall, "Gambling Problems and Comorbidity with Alcohol Use Disorders in Chinese-Korean, and White-American College Students," *American Journal of Addictions*, vol. 3 (April 25, 2016), pp. 195–202, pubmed.ncbi.nim.nih.gov/26935871.

9. Alan K.K. Chan et al., "Personal Gambling Expectancies Among Asian American and White College Students,"

Journal of Gambling Studies vol. 31 (May, 2015), pp. 33–57.

10. Dipali V. Rinker et al., "Racial and Ethnic Differences in Problem Gambling Among College Students," *Journal of Gambling Studies* vol. 32 (June, 2016), pp. 581–590.

11. Daniel Nam and George Hicks. "2018 Asian Gambling Prevention Project," Asian American Community Services, Maryhaven, OH.

12. Wooksoo Kim, "Acculturation and Gambling Among Asian Americans: When Culture Meets Availability," *International Gambling Studies* vol. 12 (2012), pp. 69–88.

13. *Ibid.*

14. C.N. Le, "Lunar New Year, Las Vegas Style," Asian Nation: The Landscape of Asian America, http://www.asian-nation.org/headlines/2009/03/lunar-new-year-las-vegas-style/ (August 24, 2024).

15. Mathew Mathews and Rachel Volberg, "Impact of Problem Gambling on Financial, Emotional and Social Well-Being of Singaporean Families," *International Gambling Studies*, October 31, 2012, pp. 127–140.

16. Jasmine M.Y. Loo, Namrata Raylu, and Tian Po S. Oei, "Gambling Among the Chinese: A Comprehensive Review," *Clinical Psychology Review* vol. 28, no.7 (October 2008), pp. 1152–1166.

17. Kim, note 12.

18. In 1989, Clifford Chi Fai Wang, identified as the head of the Tung On Gang by the U.S. Department of Justice, was put on an exclusion list by the New Jersey Casino Control Commission. He had previously provided bus trips to casinos for Asians. Peter Chan, another shadowy underworld figure, was engaged in booking and managing Asian entertainers in Atlantic City casinos at that time.

19. David Ballingrud, Nicole Christian, and Bill Duryea, "Holdups Raise Fears of Asian Gangs," *St. Petersburg Times*, December 18, 1992.

20. Betty Lee Sung, *The Story of Chinese in America* (New York: Collier Books, 1967), p. 168.

21. *Ibid.*

22. *Ibid.*, p. 173.

23. *Wikipedia*, "Gangs in the United States," en.wikipedia.org/wiki/Gangs_in_the_United_States.

24. T. Wing Lo and Sharon Ingrid Kwok, "Triads and Tongs," in *Encyclopedia of Criminology and Criminal Justice*, ed. G. Bruinsma and D. Weisburd, November 27, 2018, pp. 5330–5343.

25. Ko-lin Chin, *Chinatown Gangs: Extortion, Enterprise and Ethnicity* (New York: Oxford University Press, 1994).

26. Frederick Thrasher, *The Gang: A Study of 1,313 Gangs in Chicago* (Chicago: University of Chicago Press, 1938).

27. Phone interview with Professor Ko Lin Chin of Rutgers University, Newark, NJ, on March 10, 2023.

28. Contacts were made with police departments in San Jose, San Francisco, Fremont, Los Angeles, New York City, Boston, Seattle, Chicago, and Newark. Although gang activities, especially violence and homicides linked to them, are still a primary focus of police in these areas, Asian gang activity has waned and been surpassed by the activities of black and Latino groups. See, for example, the report by Professor Anthony Braga of Northeastern University, done for the San Francisco Police Department, "Understanding Serious Violence in San Francisco 2017–2020," *California Partnership for Safe Communities* and the *San Francisco Police Department*, March 4, 2021.

29. For personal accounts of former Chinese gang members in New York City whose exploits spanned the 1970s through the 1990s, see *Chinatown Gang Stories* on YouTube, produced by Michael Moy.

30. Information about the yakuza is partially derived from "Yakuza" in *Wikipedia*, en.wikipedia.org/wiki/Yakuza; A. Johnson, "Yakuza: Past and Present," U.S. Department of Justice, Office of Justice Programs, NCJ number 166177.

31. See "U.S. Attorney Announces Arrests of Yakuza Leader and Affiliates for International Trafficking of Narcotics and Weapons, Including Surface-to-Air Missiles" (April 7, 2022), justice.gov/usao-sdny/pr/Manhattan-us-attorney-announces-arrests-yakuza-leader-and-affiliates-international.

Chapter 4

1. "Remembering Pearl Harbor, A Pearl Harbor Fact Sheet," The National WWII Museum, www.nationalww2museum.org. Ironically, two Japanese diplomats, Ambassador Kichisaburo Nomura (1877–1964), an admiral in the Japanese Imperial Navy, and Saburō Kurusu (1886–1954) a Japanese career diplomat who had lived in the United States and was married to an American woman, were negotiating with Cordell Hull, the U.S. Secretary of State, and President Roosevelt at the time of the attack, ostensibly to avoid war between the nations. The terms for peace presented by the Americans, that Japan withdraw its forces from China and renounce ties to Germany and Italy, were rejected by the Japanese. The Japanese diplomats denied knowledge of the attack on Pearl Harbor and were interned in Hot Springs, Virginia, until an exchange of diplomats was accomplished in 1942. For an interesting perspective about the detention of foreign adversarial diplomats during World War II see Harvey Solomon, *Such Splendid Prisons: Diplomatic Detainment in America During World War II* (Lincoln: University of Nebraska Press, 2020). John Koster alleges that a Soviet spy within the Roosevelt administration helped orchestrate the failed reconciliation between the two nations as an intended communist conspiracy to further Russian objectives. It's an interesting but questionable hypothesis. See John Koster. *Operation Snow: How a Soviet Mole in FDR's Whitehouse Triggered Pearl Harbor* (Washington, D.C.: Regnery, 2012).

2. In recent years there has been a reemergence of laws against land ownership by Asians. This is addressed in Chapter 8.

3. This discussion of restrictive "alien" land laws draws from material presented in "The U.S. Mainland: Growth and Resistance," Library of Congress, loc.gov/classroom-materials/immigration//japanese/the-us-mainland-growth-and-resistance, and the *Densho Encyclopedia,* which is the publication of a Japanese nonprofit organization committed to informing the American public about the bias against Japanese in World War II that led to their incarceration and, hopefully, avoid something like that happening here again. In Japanese, *densho* means "to pass on to future generations." For information on "alien" land laws see "Alien Land Laws," encyclopedia.densho.org/Alien%20land%20/laws/?_ga2.94433055.2045226408.1669850486.753267949.1669663536. For information about the award-winning Densho organization see "Densho: The Japanese American Legacy Project," *Wikipedia,* en.wikipedia.org/wiki/Densho:_The_Japanese_American_Legacy_Project.

4. Attorney General Francis Biddle, under President Franklin D. Roosevelt, wrote a note to him in 1943 :"You signed the original Executive Order permitting the exclusions so the Army could handle the Japs. It was never intended to apply to Italians and Germans." Quoted in en.wikipedia.org/wiki/Executive_order_9066.

5. Gwendolyn M. Jensen, "The Experience of Injustice: Health Consequences of the Japanese American Internment," *Dissertation Abstracts International, Section A: Humanities and Social Sciences* 58 (7-A) (1998), 2718.

6. There was a case involving three Japanese sisters who helped two German POWs escape from a Colorado prisoner of war camp. They were convicted of being disloyal to the United States in October 1943, but a review of the case by Eric L. Muller, "Betrayal on Trial: Japanese American Treason in World War II," *North Carolina Law Review* vol. 82, no. 5 (2004), revealed the government's case was devoid of evidence linking the women to assisting the Axis powers, despite the jury's conviction of them for treason. Their primary motivation was a romantic involvement.

7. Joan I. Miller, "Spies in America: German Espionage in the United States 1935–1945," *Dissertations and Theses,* paper 3579 (1984), https://doi.org/10.15760/etd.5463. During World War II approximately 11,000 Germans (mostly ethnic Germans) were detained by the U.S. government, and in contrast to the Japanese Americans, relatively few of these individuals were sent to internment camps under the aegis of

the U.S. Department of Justice. However, J. Edgar Hoover, who directed the FBI for forty-eight years, was suspicious of Germans and Italians who resided in the United States in the 1930s and was placed in charge of keeping abreast of their behavior by President Roosevelt in 1939. The Alien Registration Act of 1940 required registration and fingerprinting of all resident aliens, which wasn't enough for the jingoistic Hoover, who contended that "the naturalized citizen ... is dangerous to the nation's security." Though the focus of his organization's attention, along with the Immigration and Naturalization Service, was on ethnic Germans, a number of German Jewish immigrants also came under scrutiny and suspicion, hinting at the age-old antisemitism that was rife within our society. Ethnic Germans and Italians were removed from coastal regions on the U.S. mainland and imprisoned in camps similar to the Japanese under the auspices of the War Relocation Agency, but the sheer number of Germans and Italians in our society mitigated against their wholesale internment. For more on this subject see "German and Italian Detainees" by Alan Rosenfeld, encyclopedia.densho.org/German%20Italian%20detainees?_ga=2.5702515.1588215905.1670451422–1324868818.1670451422. Also see Arnold Krammer, *Undue Process: The Untold Story of America's German Alien Internees* (Lanham, MD: Rowman & Littlefield, 1997), and Stephen Fox, *Uncivil Liberties: Italian Americans Under Siege During World War II* (Parkland, FL: Universal Publishers, 2000).

8. Renee Romano, "The Trauma of Internment," *The Washington Post*, June 25, 2018.

9. Gwendolyn M. Jensen, "The Experience of Injustice: Health Consequences of the Japanese American Internment," *Dissertation Abstracts International, Section A: Humanities and Social Sciences* 58 (7-A) (1997), 2718.

10. Nobu Miyoshi, "Identity Crisis of the Sansei and the Concentration Camp," Sansei Legacy Project, 1994.

11. Donna K. Nagata, *Legacy of Injustice: Exploring the Cross-Generational Impact of Japanese American Internment* (New York: Plenum Press, 1993).

12. Jean Wakatsuki Houston and James D. Houston, *Farewell to Manzanar* (New York: Dell Laurel-Leaf, 1973), p. 158.

13. George Takei, Justin Eisinger, Steven Scott, and Harmony Becker, *They Called Us Enemy* (San Diego, CA: Top Shelf Productions, 2019).

14. Listen to or read the transcript of the podcasts about the camps by Noah and Hana Maruyama, "Campu," densho.org/campu. For more information about sexual assaults at the camps see Nina Wallace, "Sexual Violence, Silence, and Japanese American Incarceration," densho.org/catalyst/sexual-violence-silence-japanese-american-incarceration. Wallace contends that "Sexual assault and rapes were under-reported and covered up by the WRA." "The frightened anxiety many women felt as they marched through the camps was survival instinct honed by a lifetime spent navigating a world where such violence is norm not aberration. They experienced incarceration not just as a violation of their civil rights but of their physical safety and bodily autonomy, their freedom of movement constricted not just by barbed wire and high desert but by the constant threat of sexual violence."

15. Noah and Hana Maruyama, *Campu* podcast, at Densho.org/campu: "Latrines."

16. The historical novel by Edward Miyakawa, *Tule Lake*, provides a graphic picture of life in the Tule Lake "relocation center" and discusses the motivation of Japanese internees to refuse to cooperate with the WRA and resist induction into the armed services. After reading this you will understand why many Japanese refer to the camps as "concentration camps." See Edward Miyakawa, *Tule Lake* (Waldport, OR: House by the Sea Publishing Company, 1979).

17. Half the detainees at Manzanar responded "No" to questions 27 and 28, but only 2 percent replied that way at Minidoka. Overall, 6,700 detainees replied "No" to question 28 but 65,000 replied "Yes." There was some consternation among U.S. authorities concerning how to deal with respondents who

refused to declare their loyalty to this country. On December 10, 1942, some of them along with inmates deemed trouble makers by the U.S. government were transferred to a former Civilian Conservation Corps Camp in Moab, Utah, and then to a former boarding school on the Navajo reservation in Leupp, Arizona. The men did not receive hearings and were unable to challenge the War Relocation Authority's decisions about them. Many of the men who were transferred were No Nos who refused to answer the loyalty questions or respond affirmatively. Eventually, most of these internees were transferred to the Tule Lake facility in northern California, which housed more than 18,000 inmates and was plagued by unsanitary conditions and overcrowding. The U.S. Army entered the Tule Lake facility on November 4,1943, with tanks and declared martial law. The facility did not revert to civilian control until January 15, 1944. For more information on Japanese American dissent in the camps and the No Nos see https://www.aasc.ucla.edu/storybooks/suyana/lc_nonos.aspx. The novel by John Okada, *No-No Boy* (Seattle: University of Washington Press, 1979), is a poignant statement about the effects of Japanese American political dissent during and after World War II.

Social scientists debated about the interpretation of detainees' responses to the loyalty oath, observing that many reasons may have influenced their responses, including the violation of their rights as well as their enforced removal to the camps. No doubt existent racism against the Japanese was heightened by the Pearl Harbor attack, which led to the passage of the first law in the United States that allowed citizens to renounce their citizenship during wartime—on July 1, 1944, Public Law 78–405, the Denaturalization Act, was signed by President Roosevelt.

18. The National Park Service with the help of the Western Archaeological and Conservation Center compiled a list of detention facilities. There were ten Relocation Centers, two Isolation Centers, three War Relocation Authority Facilities, fifteen Assembly Centers, sixteen Department of Justice and U.S. Army facilities, and three Federal Bureau of Prisons facilities involved in the detention of Japanese and Japanese Americans in World War II. For further information see Jeffery F. Burton, Mary M. Farrell, Florence B. Lord, and Richard W. Lord, *Confinement and Ethnicity: An Overview of WWII Japanese American Relocation Sites* (Seattle, University of Washington Press, 2002). See the film *Honor Bound: A Personal Journey*, directed by Joan Saffa and written by Wendy Hanamura about her father's experiences in the 442nd during World War II.

19. At the time of this writing (December 2022), news headlines proclaim a recent dinner between Donald Trump and rapper Ye (aka Kanye West), and Nick Fuentes, a known white supremacist and Holocaust denier. The hallmark slogan of Holocaust survivors, "Never Again," was a motivating factor in the creation of the Densho archives about the fate of interned Japanese Americans in the United States during World War II. Yet Ron DeSantis, governor of Florida, and Greg Abbott, governor of Texas, were, late in 2022, engaged in shuttling undocumented immigrants to northern cities without providing them with information about their destinations or social supports such as living quarters, jobs, and other humane amenities.

20. Justia U.S. Supreme Court, *Ex parte Endo*,323 U.S. 283 (1944), supreme.justia.com/cases/federal/us/323/283.

21. Legal Information Institute, "Ex parte Mitsuye Endo," law.cornell.edu/supremecourt/text/323/283.

22. *Ibid.*

23. See his statement at https://www.fordlibrarymuseum.gov/sites/default/files/pdf_documents/library/document/0159/1670001.pdf.

24. Summary of the Commission on Wartime Relocation and Internment of Civilians, archives.gov/files/research/japanese-americans/justice-denied/summary.pdf.

25. Findings from the report by Lt. Commander Kenneth D. Ringel are at famous-trials.com/Korematsu/2567-ringel-report-on-japanese-internment-12–30–1941.

26. See Curtis B. Munson in "Report

on Japanese on the West Coast of the United States," Hearings, 79th Congress, 1st sess., Joint Committee of the Investigation of the Pearl Harbor Attack, Washington, D.C.: Govt. Printing Office, 1946, lib.washington.edu/specialcollections/collections/exhibits/harmony/exhibit/intro#:~text=%20not%20Japanese%20in%20culture.

27. Craig Collisson, "Japanese American Wartime Incarceration in Oregon," *Oregon Encyclopedia*, oregonencyclopedia.org/articles/Japanese_internment/#.Y6dFR3bMKOO.

28. For more information on this finding and Katyal's statement see U.S. Department of Justice Archives, justice.gov/archives/opa/blog/confession-error-solicitor-generals-mistakes-during-japanese-american-internment-cases.

29. "Remarks on Signing the Bill Providing Restitution for the Wartime Internment of Japanese-American Civilians," National Archives, https://www.reaganlibrary-gov/archives/speech/remarks-signing-bill-providing-restitution-wartime-internment-japanese-american

30. Robert Jay Lifton and Greg Mitchell, *Hiroshima in America: Fifty Years of Denial* (New York: G.P. Putnam and Sons, 1995).

31. *Ibid.*, p. 176.

32. *Ibid.* p. 182.

33. These phrases were used by conservative columnist George Will to describe the Smithsonian's original exhibit.

34. Lifton and Mitchell, note 30, p. xv.

35. *Ibid.*

36. *Ibid.*, p. 83.

37. *Ibid.*

38. Unfortunately, such attitudes persist to this day, as later chapters verify.

39. Cited in Lifton and Mitchell, note 30, p. 31.

40. *Ibid.*

41. *Ibid.*, p. 72.

42. Lifton and Mitchell, note 30, p. 60.

43. The blockbuster film *Oppenheimer*, starring Cillian Murphy, directed by Christopher Nolan, and released by Universal Pictures in July 2023, was a fairly good representation of Oppenheimer's role in making the atomic bombs that were used against the Japanese, but it omitted the horror of the destruction wreaked by their use.

44. For more information on Dr. Seuss's patriotic antifascist activities see Richard H. Minear, *Dr. Seuss Goes to War: The World War II Editorial Cartoons of Theodor Seuss Geisel* (New York: The New Press, 2001). The University of California San Diego has holdings of Dr. Seuss in their special collections. See library.uscd.edu/speccoll/dswenttowar/index.html#intro.

45. Lifton and Mitchell, note 30, p. 36.

46. *Ibid.*, p. 46.

47. Hersey's work was published as a book, *Hiroshima* (Alfred A. Knopf), in 1946. In 1999, a 36-member panel of journalists at New York University judged the work to be the finest piece of American journalism of the 20th century.

48. See, for example, the recollection of Monica Sone in her *Nisei Daughter* (Seattle: University of Washington Press, 1953) about the refusal of landlords to rent to her family: "we scoured the neighborhood with no success. Every time it was the same story," until someone told them candidly, "I'm sorry, but we don't want Japs around here" (pp. 113–114).

49. Herbert Nicholson, an ardent supporter of Japanese Americans during World War II, recalled the defacing of homes owned by professors who housed Japanese students (one owned by the eminent Linus Pauling) with the words scribbled in yellow paint "Jap Lover." See Herbert Nicholson, *Valiant Odyssey: Herbert Nicholson in and out of America's Concentration Camps*, ed. Michi Weglyn and Betty E. Mitson (Upland, CA: Brunk's Printing, 1978). As Jean Wakatsuki Houston recalled, at the time of her mandatory relocation, "They wouldn't see me, they would see the slant-eyed face, the Oriental. This is what accounts, in part, for the entire evacuation." She noted wistfully, "I smiled and sat down, suddenly aware of what being of Japanese ancestry was going to be like. I wouldn't be faced with physical attack, or with overt shows of hatred. Rather, I would be seen as someone foreign, or as someone other than American, or perhaps not be seen at all." Jean Wakatsuki Houston and

James D. Houston, *Farewell to Manzanar* (New York: Dell Laurel-Leaf, 1973), p. 158.

Chapter 5

1. See "Killing of Vincent Chin" in *Wikipedia*, en.wikipedia.org/wiki/killing_of_Vincent_Chin.
2. Ken Waite, "The Bloody History of Anti-Asian Violence in the West," *National Geographic*, May 10, 2021, nationalgeographic.com/history/article/the-bloody-history-of-anti-asian-violence-in-the-west.
3. For an overview of Asian contributions to the United States society see Jeff Yang, Phil Yu, and Philip Wang, *Rise: A Pop History of Asian America from the Nineties to Now* (New York: Mariner Books, 2022).
4. Even though the World Health Organization (WHO) took the lead in labeling Covid-19 as a pandemic and threat to humans, Trump was displeased with the organization and initiated the withdrawal of the United States membership in the organization in 2020. The Biden Administration restored the ties between the United States and WHO in 2021.
5. Yulin Hswen et al., "Association of 'Covid-19 Virus' 'Chinesevirus' with Anti-Asian Sentiments on Twitter: March 9–23, 2020," *American Journal of Public Health*, May 2021, ajph.aphapublications.org/doi/10.2105/AJPH.2021.306154.
6. "Two Years and Thousands of Voices: What Community-Generated Data Tells Us About AAPI Hate," StopAAPI Hate, National Report, October 2022. The groups that formed the coalition to create this organization are the AAPI Equity Alliance, the San Francisco State University Asian American Studies Department, and Chinese for Affirmative Action.
7. See a summary of the ADL's achievements at adl.org/who-we-are/history.
8. We discuss this phenomenon in Chapter 8 under the topic of replacement theory.
9. "History of Lynching in America,"

NAACP, naacp.org/find-resources/history-explained/history-lynching-america.
10. For more information about hate crime statistics see the FBI Press Release, "FBI Releases 2021 Hate Crime Statistics," March 13, 2023, fbi.gov/news/press-releases/fbi-releases-supplemental-2021-hate-crime-statistics. It should noted that the FBI switched to a new reporting system, the National Incident-Based Reporting System, and some large police departments did not initially submit their data to the organization.
11. "Audit of Antisemitic Incidents, 2022," ADL, adl.org/resources/report/audit-antisemitic-incidents-2022. There has been another dramatic increase in antisemitic activities since the onset of the Israel–Hamas War in October 2023.
12. "Hate Crime Victimization 2005–2019," Bureau of Justice Statistics, U.S. Department of Justice, September 13, 2021, bjs.ojp.gov/press-release/hate-crime-victimization-2005–2019. See also Nathan Sandholtz, Lynn Langton, and Michael Planty, "Hate Crime Victimization, 2003–2011," U.S. Department of Justice, Bureau of Justice Statistics, March, 2013.
13. Paul Sniderman and Thomas Piazza, *The Scar of Race* (Boston: Belknap Press, 1995).
14. Deanna Pan, "Asians Are an Afterthought: Asian American Students at BPS Report Feeling Less Safe, More Undervalued," *Boston Globe*, March 20, 2023, bostonglobe.com/2023/03/20/metro/Asian-students-bps-report/.
15. Michele Lee, "China Has Opened Police Stations in U.S. and Canada to Monitor Chinese Citizens: Report," September 29, 2022, Foxnews.com/world/china-opened-overseas-police-stations-us-canada-monitor-chinese-citizens.
16. Article 7 of the National Intelligence Law states "any organization or citizen shall support, assist and cooperate with the state intelligence work in accordance with the law." And the 2014 Counter-Espionage Law states that individuals and organizations "shall provide it [data] truthfully and may not refuse."
17. Martin Thorley, professor at the

University of Nottingham, and an international expert on engagement with China, stated that refusals of requests for data from the Chinese Communist Party would be unrealistic, noting that "one must submit to the Party if called upon." Further, "For anyone at Huawei to oppose a serious request from the Party would require bravery bordering on recklessness—what do you do when your adversary is the police, the media, the judiciary and the government?" Quoted in Arjun Kharpal, "Huawei Says it Would Never Send Data to China's Government. Experts Say it Wouldn't Have a Choice," CNBC, March 5, 2019, cnbc.com/2019/03/0a5/Huawei-would-have-to-give-data-to-china-government-if-asked-experts.html.

18. Cecilia Kang, "ByteDance Inquiry Finds Employees Obtained User Data of Two Journalists," *The New York Times*, December 22, 2022.

19. Joseph Pisani and Theo Francis, "TikTok Stars Who Made More Money than Many of America's Top CEOs," *The Wall Street Journal*, January 13, 2023, foxbusiness.com/technology/tiktok-stars-who-made-more-money-than-many-of-americas-top-ceos. See also Abram Brown and Abigail Freeman, "Top-Earning TikTok-ers 2022. Charlie and Dixie D'Amelio and Addison Rae Expand Fame—and Paydays," *Forbes*, January 7, 2022.

20. See Adam Xu, "China-Owned Parent Company of TikTok Among Top Spenders on Internet Lobbying," *Voice of America*, February 13, 2023, https://www.voanews.com/a/china-owned-parent-company-of-tiktok-among-top-spenders-on-internet-lobbying-/6961891.html.

21. *Ibid*. It bears noting that the Committee on Foreign Investment in the United States (CFIUS), an interagency organ of the U.S. Treasury Department, ordered ByteDance to divest TikTok in 2020, to no avail. They are reportedly still in negotiations. For a summary of TikTok's origin and current dilemma see Alex W. Palmer, "How TikTok Became a Diplomatic Crisis," *The New York Times Magazine*, December 25, 2022, pp. 22–27, 46–49.

22. "A Tik-Tok-ing Timebomb: How Tik Tok's Global Platform Anomalies Align with the Chinese Communist Party's Geostrategic Objectives," *Intelligence Report*, December 2023, Rutgers Miller Center on Policing and Community Resilience.

23. Two other people were also killed by Long, but they were not Asians.

24. Fujii, who arrived in the United States when he was twenty-one, spent his life trying to combat discriminatory laws against Asians. After years of trying, he became a U.S. citizen at the age of 73. Because of racial prejudice, he was not allowed to enter the California Bar, but was admitted posthumously to the Bar in 2017. For a summary of the case, *Fujii v. California* (38 Cal 2nd 718), see *Densho Encyclopedia*, encyclopediadensho.org/Fujii_v._California.

25. These nations are euphemistically referred to as "adversarial nations," presumably because they are suspected of engendering hostile feelings about the United States.

26. In fact, North America has been the recipient of China's smallest land expenditures of any continent. See Noah Wicks, "Despite Holding Little U.S. Land, China Remains Focus of Foreign Ownership Discussion," *Agri Pulse*, December 1, 2021, agri-pulse.com/articles/16846-despite-holding-little-us-land-china-remains-focus-of-foreign-farmland-ownership-discussion.

27. *Ibid*.

28. *Ibid*.

29. Noah Wicks, "Bill Banning Foreign Governments from Buying Farmland Nears Passage in N.D.," *Agri Pulse*, April 6, 2023, agri-pulse.com/articles/19205-bill-prohibiting-foreign-government-from-purchasing-farmland-nears-passage-in-north-dakota.

30. Although Till's accuser, Carolyn Bryant Donham, recanted her testimony in a 2017 book, Till's murderers, her husband and his step-brother, were not convicted of the crime. She died in April 2023.

31. As the Civil Rights Movement gained momentum for African Americans, it generated interest and enthusiasm for Native Americans (the Red Power movement) and Asian Americans (the Yellow Power movement).

32. See Lee's famous description of the tragedy: John H. Lee, "Understanding the Riots Part 4: Seeing Ourselves: Koreatown: Together We Suffer," *Los Angeles Times*, May 14, 1992, latimes.com/archives/la-xpm-1992-05-14-ss-3085-story.html. For a visual account of the rioting see the film "Clash of Colors: LA Riots of 1992" directed by David D. Kim. Books and articles have been written about the uniqueness of this event. See the compilation of papers on this topic edited by Arnold Pan, "Reflections on the L.A. Civil Unrest: Thirty Years After 4/29/92," *Amerasia Journal*, May 10, 2022, tandfonline.com/journals/ramj20/collections/reflections_on_the_LA_civil_unrest. In a 2002 article that was somewhat of an apologia for his and other journalistic approaches to the rioting, Lee noted that he still felt the pain caused by the rioting and regretted the lack of empathy evinced by white Americans about it. He acknowledged that he should have done a better job of reporting the situation: "I had the chance to write a definitive chapter in Korean-American immigration history. And I blew it. I came to the riots with all the intentions of contributing something constructive through my reporting. And still, somehow, I feel responsible for there being next to nothing on record." Lee was also critical of Koreans for their "collective amnesia" that led them to forget about the event in their attempt to blend into American society. See John H. Lee, "The Untold Story," *LA Weekly*, April 26–May 2, 2002.

33. For a personal account of the destruction of Koreatown in Los Angeles see Julia Lee, *Biting the Hand: Growing Up Asian in Black and White America*. (New York: Henry Holt and Company, 2023), chapter five.

34. O'Shea Jackson (aka Ice Cube) later tempered his remarks and engaged in community dialogues with members of the Los Angeles Korean community.

35. Se-Hyoung Yi and William T. Hoston, "Demystifying Americanness: The Model Minority Myth and the Black-Korean Relationship," *Journal of Ethnic and Cultural Studies* vol. 7, no. 2 (2020), p. 84.

36. Jay Caspian Kang, *The Loneliest Americans* (New York: Crown, 2021), pp. 46–49.

37. *Ibid.*, pp. 98–99.
38. *Ibid.*, pp. 92–93.
39. *Ibid.*, p. 161.

Chapter 6

1. Jay Caspian Kang, *The Loneliest Americans* (New York: Crown, 2021), p. 3.

2. Frank Chin, *Bulletproof Buddhists and Other Essays* (Honolulu: University of Hawaii Press, 1993), p. 98.

3. *Ibid.*, p. 99.

4. Earl Derr Biggers, *The Chinese Parrot*, in *Charlie Chan: Five Complete Novels* (New York: Avenel Books, 1981), p. 162.

5. Earl Derr Biggers, *Keeper of the Keys*, in *Charlie Chan: Five Complete Novels* (New York: Avenel Books, 1981), p. 609.

6. *Ibid.*, p. 614.

7. Earl Derr Biggers, *Charlie Chan Carries On* (Chicago: Academy Chicago Publishers), p. 236.

8. Earl Derr Biggers, *The Black Camel*, in *Charlie Chan: Five Complete Novels* (New York: Avenel Books, 1981), p. 483.

9. *Charlie Chan Carries On*, note 7, p. 207.

10. Earl Derr Biggers, *Keeper of the Keys*, in *Charlie Chan: Five Complete Novels* (New York: Avenel Books, 1981), p. 581.

11. *Ibid.*, p. 699.

12. Yunte Huang, *Charlie Chan* (New York: W.W. Norton, 2010), p. 285. I am indebted to Huang for providing an historical overview of the Charlie Chan story that has been summarized here.

13. Frank Chin, note 2, pp. 95–98.

14. Yunte, note 12, p. 284. The *Hollywood Diversity Report, 2023*, Part 1: Film, published by the UCLA Entertainment and Media Research Institute, revealed a current persistent shortfall of actors of color in leading motion pictures: "With the exception of total streaming film actors (42.5 percent), people of color remained underrepresented on every industry employment front" (p. 3). Although the motion picture industry was attempting to improve the situation,

the COVID pandemic and the predominance of white males in decision-making roles in the industry were singled out as being responsible for the lack of progress.

15. Lan Cao and Himilce Novas, *Everything You Need to Know About Asian-American History* (New York: Penguin, 1996), p. 60.

16. Earl Derr Biggers, *The House Without a Key* (New York: Grosset & Dunlap, 1925), p. 76.

17. *Ibid.*, p. 83.
18. *Ibid.*, p. 119.
19. *Ibid.*, p. 311.
20. *Ibid.*, p. 311.
21. Huang, note 12, p. 286.
22. *Ibid.*, p. 287. Italics in original.
23. Cited in Ken Hanke, *Charlie Chan at the Movies: History, Filmography, and Criticism* (Jefferson, NC: McFarland and Company, 1989), p. xiii. Luke left the series after the death of Warner Oland in 1937 and returned in 1948.
24. *Ibid.*, p. xv.
25. *Ibid.*, p. xvi.
26. *Ibid.*, p. 261.
27. Cao and Novas, note 15, p. 25.
28. Sax Rohmer, *The Mystery of Dr. Fu-Manchu* (London: Methuen, 1913), p. 20.
29. *Ibid.*
30. *Ibid.*, p. 43.
31. Sax Rohmer, *The Return of Dr. Fu-Manchu* (New York: A.L. Burt and Company, 1916), p. 204.
32. Rohmer, *The Mystery of Dr. Fu-Manchu*, note 28, p. 7.
33. *Ibid.*, p. 84.
34. *Ibid.*, p. 21.
35. *Ibid.*
36. *Ibid.*
37. *Ibid.*, p. 209.
38. Cay Van Ash, a friend and assistant to Rohmer, authored two additional Fu Manchu novels after Rohmer's death and was working on a third book when he died in Paris in 1994.
39. For an overview of the books and films pertaining to Dr. Fu Manchu see "Books and Films of Fu Manchu," fumanchu.seriesbooks.info. Also see Charles Largent, "The Fu Manchu Cycle—1965–1969," October 31, 2020, trailersfromhell.com/the-fu-manchu-cycle-1965-1969.
40. Jack Adrian cited in David Pringle's review in *St. James Guide to Horror,*

Ghost and Gothic Writers (London: St. James Press, 1998), pp. 482–484.

41. For a fuller explanation of this phenomenon see "Bushido" in *Wikipedia*, en.wikipedia.org/wiki/bushido.

42. "39 Martial Arts Industry Statistics to Know," *Gymdesk*, gymdesk.com/blog/martial-arts-industry-statistics.

43. For a review of the series see en.wikipedia.org/wiki/Kung_Fu_(19p72_TV_series. For a discussion of the Shaolin Monastery see "Shaolin Monastery," *Wikipedia*, org/wiki/shaolin_monastery.

44. For a summary of Bruce Lee's life see Adam Augustyn, "Bruce Lee: American-Born Actor," *Britannica*, July 16, 2023, Britannica.com/biography/Bruce-Lee; Clay Eals, "Remembering Bruce Lee, and His Time In Seattle, on the 80th Anniversary of his Birth," *The Seattle Times*, November 12, 2020.

45. The author drew from the following sources for this summary of TMNT: "Teenage Mutant Ninja Turtles," *Wikipedia*, en.wikipedia.org/wiki/Teenage_mutant_Ninja_Turtles; Andrew Farago, *Teenage Mutant Ninja Turtles: The Ultimate Visual History* (Portland, OR: Image Editions, 2014).

46. Jackie Manno and Jessica White, "Everything to Know About American Ninja Warrior Season 15," *NBC Insider,* nbc.com/nbc-insider/everything-to-know-about-american-ninja-warrior-season-15.

47. For a fuller discussion of the history and contemporary status of the Power Rangers, see "Power Rangers," *Wikipedia*, en.wikipedia.org/wiki/Power_Rangers.

48. For a fuller discussion of Yang's work, see Jamie Fisher, "The Discomfort Artist," *The New York Times Magazine*, May 28, 2023, pp. 42–45.

49. For a review of these media, see Madeline Dunnett, "Manga's Growth in Popularity is Here to Stay, Industry Leaders Predict," *Anime News Network*, May 11, 2022; and "Anime Popularity in America Statistics and Trends in 2023," Gitnux Marketdata, blog.gitnux.com/popularity-in-america-statistics. We should not ignore the impact of the other blockbuster franchise, *Transformers*, also of Japanese origin, which has

produced the thirteenth highest grossing film series, garnering over $5 billion and giving Hasbro Inc. over $14 billion for toys and associated merchandise. See Matthew Townsend, "How the Battling Robots of Transformers Built a $14 Billion Empire," *Bloomberg News*, https://www.bloomberg.com/news/articles/2018-12-20/hasbro-reboots-transformers-for-gen-x-dads-and-their-daughters#xj4y7vzkg. And, of course, there is the ever-present influence of the Japanese-originated monster—Godzilla! For a review of the history of anime and suggestions about what to view, see Yang, Yu, and Wang, *Rise*, note 3, pp. 166–169.

50. For a comparison of the major game devices see T.J. Donegan, "Nintendo vs. XBOX vs. PlayStation: Here's How They All Compare," *Reviewed*, reviewed.usatoday.com/televisions/features/Nintendo-vs-xbox-vs-playstation-heres-how-they-all-compare. Estimates of the number of video game players and revenue can be found in Adam Bankhurst, "Three Billion People Worldwide Now Play Video Games, New Report Shows," August 14, 2020, ign.com/articles/three-billion-people-worldwide-now-play-vide-games-new-report-shows; and *Statista*, statista.com/forecasts/1196090/revenue-video-game-consoles-worldwide. Meta is promoting its virtual reality *Oculus*, which may cut into the video game market, and Microsoft manufactures Xbox. Of the three billion people who are playing video games, it is estimated that 240 million are dedicated video console players. The number of people who have played popular video games is astounding: *Tetris* has had 520 million players, followed by *Minecraft* with 238 million players, *Grand Theft Auto V* with 170 million, *Wii Sports* with 83 million, *Pub G* with 75 million, *Mario Kart 8 + Delux* with 64 million, *The Elder Scrolls V: Skyrim* with 60 million, *Red Dead Redemption 2* with 50 million, and *Overwatch* also with 50 million. One of the most popular games ever developed, with a committed legion of followers, is *The Legend of Zelda*, developed by Shigeru Miyamoto, with music by Koji Kondo, both Japanese. Nearly 19 million copies of the game have been sold.

51. See, for example, this passage in Eddie Huang's *Fresh Off the Boat* (New York: Spiegel and Grau, 2013), pp. 30–31.

52. See H. Roy Kaplan, *Failing Grades: How Schools Breed Frustration, Anger, and Violence and How to Prevent It* (Lanham, MD: Scarecrow Education, 2004), pp. 63–87.

53. "Saving Animals from China's Dog and Cat Meat Trade," *Humane Society International*, 2023, his.org/news-resources/saving-dogs-from-chinas-dog-meat-trade.

54. *Ibid.*

55. *Ibid.*; "Dog Meat Consumption in South Korea," *Wikipedia*, https://en.wikipedia.org/wiki/Dog_meat_consumption_in_South_Korea.

56. "A Summary Report on Dog and Cat Meat Consumption in Vietnam," *Four Paws*, January 2021, dogcatmeat.four.paws.org/the-truth/a-summary-report-on-dog-and-cat-meat-consumption-in-vietnam.

57. "Cancer and Asian Americans," Office of Minority Health, U.S. Department of Health and Human Services, hhs.gov./omh/browse.aspx?lvl=4&lvllD=46.

58. For a summary of Asian predilections for meals, see Cathy Margolin, "10 Things You Need to Know About the Asian Diet," *Huffington Post*, October 8, 2013.

59. Brahmjot Kaur, "Why South Asian Americans Stan Taco Bell," *NBC News*, May 26, 2023, nbcnews.com/news/Asian-america/south-asian-americans-stan-taco-bell-rcha86318.

60. For a discussion of the popularity of Asian food in the United States, see Matt Hilburn, "Asian Cuisine Fastest-Growing in U.S.," *VOA*, July 15, 2018, learningenglish.voanews.com/a/Asian-cuisine-fastest-growing-in-u-s/4480072. Also see Cheuk Kwan, *Have You Eaten Yet? Stories from Chinese Restaurants Around the World* (Vancouver: Douglas and McIntyre, 2022).

61. "President Trump Signs the Farm Bill Making Dog and Cat Meat Illegal in the United States," Associated Press, December 21, 2018, wrdw.com/content/news/President-Trump-signs-the-farm-bill-making-dog-and-cat-meat-illegal-in-the-united-states-503308841.html.

62. Amy Chua, *Battle Hymn of the Tiger Mother* (New York: Penguin, 2011),

pp. 3–4. There are many similarities in this book with the Indian American Prachi Gupta's book, *They Called Us Exceptional: and Other Lies that Raised Us* (New York: Crown, 2023). However, her traditional East Indian upbringing was also influenced by her father, who had mental health issues.

63. Laura Dang, "Here's What Happened to the Daughters of the Original 'Tiger Mom,'" *Next Shark*, January 28, 2016, nextshark.com/anychua-tiger-mom-daughters.

64. Chua, note 62, p. 29.

65. *Ibid.*, p. 52.

66. A.S. (Alexander Sutherland) Neill, *Summerhill: A Radical Approach to Child Rearing* (Oxford, UK: Hart Publishing Company, 1960), and later revised to *Summerhill School: A New View of Childhood* (New York: St. Martin's Griffin, 1995).

67. Chua, note 62, p. 101.

68. Even Chua notes that "the kids [her two daughters] were definitely mad at me. But as a Chinese mother, I put that out of my head." *Ibid.*, pp. 106–7. And she butted heads on many occasions with her recalcitrant daughters: "Lulu never wants to do anything I propose, so naturally I ignored her." *Ibid.*, p. 131.

69. Yang, Yu, and Wang, note 3.

70. Chua, note 62, p. 148.

71. *Ibid.*, p. 167.

72. *Ibid.*, p. 205. See also their comments on pp. 168 and 170, and Chua's admission to a friend that revealed her own second thoughts about the process: "I'm just not so sure anymore" (p. 201).

73. For an review of the folly inherent in positing differences in intellectual and athletic accomplishments based on ethnicity, see H. Roy Kaplan, *Understanding Conflict and Change in a Multicultural World* (Lanham, MD: Rowman & Littlefield, pp. 13–44).

74. *Ibid.* Important societal contributions have been disproportionally made by Jews, and this can be explained by cultural and environmental differences, especially in childrearing, not unlike the Chinese parenting model espoused by Chua. See, for example, Andrew Cherlin and Carin Celebuski, "Are Jewish Families Different? Some Evidence from the General Social Survey," *Journal of Marriage and the Family* vol. 45, no. 4 (1983), and Richard Nisbett, *Intelligence and How to Get It: Why Schools and Culture Count* (New York: W.W. Norton and Company, 2009).

75. New York: Doubleday, 2013. The novel sold 1.5 million copies and the film, released in 2018, grossed more than $238 million on a budget of $30 million. For an analogous fictionalized discussion of a similar phenomenon among East Indian Americans, see Jhumpa Lahiri's Pulitzer Prize-winning *Interpreter of Maladies* (Boston: Houghton Mifflin, 1999).

76. R. Varisa Pataporn, Paul Ong, and Chhandara Pech, "Wealth Inequality Among Asian Americans: The Continuing Significance of Ethnicity and Immigration," *Asian American Policy Review*, April 16, 2021, aapr.hkspublications.org/2021/04/16/wealth-inequality-among-asian-americans-the-continuing-significance-of-ethnicity-and-immigration.

77. A more current analysis of this situation yielded similar results. See Priya Anand and Ellen Huet, "Why Silicon Valley's Many Asians Still Feel Like a Minority," *Bloomberg Businessweek*, August 6, 2021, Bloomberg.com/news/features/2021-08-06/why-silicon-valley-s-asian-americans-still-feel-like-a-minority.

78. Matthew A. Painter, Malcolm D. Holmes, and Jenna Bateman, "Skin Tone, Race/Ethnicity, and Wealth Inequality Among New Immigrants," *Social Forces* vol. 94, no. 3, March 1, 2016, pp. 1153–1185.

79. *Ibid.*, p. 1174.

80. Huang, note 51.

81. He is bitter about white racism, as can be seen from this passage: "To this day, I wake up at times, look in the mirror, and just stare, obsessed with the idea that the person I am in my head is something entirely different than what everyone else sees. That the way I look will prevent me from doing the things I want [he was offered a position and then rejected as a reporter for the *Orlando Sentinel* when his prospective manager realized he was Chinese]; that there really are sneetches with stars and I'm not one of them. I touch my face, I feel my skin, I check my color every day, and I

swear it feels all right. But then someone says something and that sense of security and identity is gone before I know it." *Ibid.*, p. 45. Further, "We live in a world that treated us like deviants and we were outcasts" (p. 60). And, "Every time an Edgar or Billie called me a 'chink' or 'Chinaman' or 'Ching Chong' it took a piece out of me" (p. 81). His initial rejection of white culture might be summed up thusly: "I wanted my dignity, my identity, and my pride back; I wanted them to know that there were repercussions to the things they said. There were no free passes on my soul and everything they stole from me I decided to take back double" (*Ibid.*). "I wanted to hurt people like they hurt me" (p. 90).

82. See for example the work of Claude Steele and Joshua Aronson, "Stereotype Threat and the Intellectual Test Performance of African Americans," *Journal of Personality and Social Psychology* vol. 69, no. 5 (1995), 797–811.

83. For firsthand reports of these contretemps see Cerrissa Kim, "Koreans and Camptowns: Reflections of a Mixed-Race Korean," *Korean American Story*, November 4, 2015, koreanamericanstory.org/written/the-conference-that-introduced-me-to-the-legacy-of-being-a-mixed-race-korean; and Erin Raftery, "Korean War Babies Still Searching for G.I. Fathers," *USA Today*, usatoday.com/story/news/nation/2015/07/26/Korean-war-orphans/306301611.

84. For a discussion of this phenomenon see Joel L.A. Peterson, "The Surprising Facts Behind Korean Child Abandonment," *Huffpost*, October 10, 2017, huffpost.com/entry/the-surprising-facts-behind-Korean-child-abandonment_b_59doc0516e4b0b48cd8e0a5be. According to a *New York Times* article by Choe Sang-Hun ("A Painful Past Behind South Korean Adoptions," September 17, 2023, pp. 1, 16), the South Korean government began an investigation of the sordid history of past South Korean adoptions in 2022. These adoptions, facilitated by agencies, were often characterized by fraud and deceit, with babies being sent abroad to adoptive parents around the world, often without parental knowledge or consent.

85. For a discussion of this phenomenon, see Samantha Raphelson, "One Man's Mission to Bring Home 'Amerasians' Born During Vietnam War," *National Public Radio*, July 12, 2018, npr.org/2018/07/12/628398153/one-mans-mission-to-bring-home-amerasians-born-during-vietnam-war.

Chapter 7

1. William Pettersen, "Success Story: Japanese-American Style," *The New York Times Magazine*, January 9, 1966.

2. See Frances Kai-Hwa Wang, "#Remodel Minority," January 11, 2016, nbcnews.com/news/Asian-america/50-years-later-challenging-model-minority-myth-through-remodelminority-n493911.

3. Cathy Park Hong, *Minor Feelings: An Asian American Reckoning* (New York: One World, 2020), pp. 40–41.

4. Jay Caspian Kang, *The Loneliest Americans* (New York: Crown, 2021), p. 15.

5. Cited in Kang, *ibid.*, p. 93.

6. Hong, note 3, p. 35. She contends that the treatment Asian Americans get from whites is like being ghosted, "where deprived of all social cues, I have no relational gauge for my own behavior. I ransack my mind for what I could have done, could have said. I stop trusting what I see, what I hear. My ego is in freefall while my superego is boundless, railing that my existence is not enough, never enough, so I become compulsive in my efforts to do better, *be* better, blindly following this country's gospel of self-interest, proving my individual worth by expanding my net worth, until I vanish."

7. Wesley Yang, *The Souls of Yellow Folk/Essays* (New York: W.W. Norton, 2018), pp. 207–208.

8. Some of the most important contributions to the field of physics were made by Chien-Shiung Wu, also known as "The First Lady of Physics." Although she was revered, and her writing is still studied today, she did not receive the Nobel Prize for her work. President Gerald Ford awarded her the Presidential Medal of Science in 1976.

9. Jane Hyun, *Breaking the Bamboo Ceiling: Career Strategies for Asians* (New York: Harper Business, 2006).

10. Priya Arnand and Ellen Huet, "Why Silicon Valley's Many Asians Still Feel Like a Minority," *Bloomberg Businessweek,* August 6, 2021, Bloomberg.com/news/features/2021-08-06/why-silicon-valley-s-asian-americans-still-feel-like-a-minority.

11. U.S. Bureau of Labor Statistics, BLS Report, January, 2023, bls.gov/opub/report/race-and-ethnicity/2021/home.htm.

12. See also "College Professor Demographics and Statistics in the U.S.," zippia.com/college-professor-jobs/demographics.

13. Just 3 percent of new college and university presidents in the United States between June 2020 and November 2021 were Asian, compared to 25.3 percent black, 6.8 percent Latino, and 65.8 percent white. Doug Lederman, "Diversity on the Rise Among College Presidents," *Inside Higher Education,* February 13, 2022, insidehighered.com/news/2022/02/14/colleges-have-hired-more-minority-presidents-amid-racial-reckoning. Interestingly, the proportion of women hired as college and university presidents actually *declined* during this time, but they were more racially diverse.

14. Asian Americans have the highest median income in the United States of any group and the lowest unemployment rates. Numerous federal government reports demonstrate these facts. See, for example, "The State of U.S. Science and Engineering 2022," National Science Foundation, Science and Engineering Indicators, ncses.nsf.gov/pubs/nsb20221/executive-summary. Data on the number of Asian physicians in 2021 (173,283 out of 841,322 or 20.6 percent for all specialties) can be found at aamc.org/data-reports/workforce/data/active-physicians-asian-2021.

15. Jackson G. Lu, Richard E. Nisbett, and Michael W. Morris, "Why East Asians but Not South Asians Are Underrepresented in Leadership Positions in the U.S.," *Psychological and Cognitive Sciences* vol. 17, no. 9 (February 18, 2020), pp. 4590–4600, https://doi.org/10.1073/phas.1918896117.

16. A similar sentiment was expressed by distinguished Asian American leaders in higher education during a recent forum on the "glass" or "bamboo ceiling." Sponsored by the Committee of 100, a predominantly Chinese American organization, and broadcast over Zoom on July 20, 2023, Frank Wu, President of Queens College of the City University of New York, proudly observed, "I wouldn't be here if it weren't for consideration of diversity." And he noted wryly, "No amount of hard work overcomes other peoples' prejudices." Gordon Chang, professor of history at Princeton University, along with the others, confirmed that some Asian Americans are less assertive and that may hamper their progress. "Enough of this humble Asian shit. Just take the job!" But the participants also noted increasing suspicion about Asian Americans by xenophobic whites as the competition increases between mainland China and the United States. (We explore this phenomenon in the next chapter.)

17. See, for example, Committee of 100 Asian American Career Ceilings Initiative Webinars.

18. Margaret M. Chin, *Stuck: Why Asian Americans Don't Reach the Top of the Corporate Ladder* (New York: New York University Press, 2020).

19. *Ibid.,* p. 8.

20. *Ibid.,* p. 39.

21. See, for example, Lu, Nisbett, and Morris, note 15.

22. Chin, note 18, p. 66.

23. For evidence of the positive relationship between academic achievement and lifetime earnings, see "Education and Lifetime Earnings," Research Statistics and Policy Analysis, Social Security Administration, November 2015, ssa.gov/policy/docs/research-summaries/education-earnings-html. Data indicate that men with bachelor's degrees earn $900,000 more in median lifetime earnings than high school graduates and women with bachelor's degrees earn $630,000 more. Men with graduate degrees earn $1.5 million more in median lifetime earnings than high school graduates and women with graduate degrees earn $1.1 million more in median lifetime earnings.

24. Robert VerBruggen, "Racial Preferences on Campus: Trends in Asian Enrollment at U.S. Colleges," The Manhattan Institute, April 2022,

media4.manhattan-institute.org/sites/default/files/verbruggen-trends-in-asian-enrollment-at-us-colleges.pdf.

25. Kimmy Yam, "70% of Asian Americans Support Affirmative Action. Here's Why Misconceptions Persist," NBC News, November 14, 2020, nbcnews.com/news/Asian-America/70-asian-americans-support-affirmative-action-here-s-why-misconceptions-n1247806.

26. Supremecourt.gov/opinions/22pdf/20-1199_hgdj.pdf, pp. 1–8 (Syllabus statement).

27. *Ibid.*, p. 7.

28. *Ibid.*, p. 29.

29. See Cornel West, *Race Matters* (Boston: Beacon Press, 1993).

30. Supremecourt.gov, note 26, p. 2.

31. *Ibid.*

32. *Ibid.*, p. 14.

33. *Ibid.*, p. 16.

34. *Ibid.*, p. 21.

35. Cf. Thomas R. Jimenez and Adam Horowitz, "When White is Just Alright: How Immigrants Redefine Achievement and Reconfigure the Ethnoracial Hierarchy," *American Sociological Review* vol. 78, no. 5 (2013), pp. 849–871. See also Chin, note 18, p. 45.

36. See Elie Mystal, "Conservatives Don't Actually Have an Argument for Killing Affirmative Action," *The Nation*, November 11, 2022; Kali Holloway, "Affirmative Action Is in the Supreme Court's Crosshairs," *The Nation*, June 22, 2023; Kali Holloway, "In the Right's Web," *The Nation*, July10/ 17, 2023, pp. 8–9; and Kali Holloway, "I Needed Asian Plaintiffs," *The Nation*, August 21/28, 2023, pp. 25–28.

37. Peter Arcidiacono, Josh Kinsler, and Tyler Ransom, "Legacy and Athletic Preferences at Harvard," Working Paper 26316, *National Bureau of Economic Research*, Cambridge, MA, September 2019.

38. *Ibid.*

39. Alexa Lee, "South Korea's Plastic Surgery Boom: A Quest to be 'Above Normal,'" *HuffPost*, September 18, 2019, huffpost.com/entry/Korea-plastic-surgery_1_5d72afboe4b07521022cOOe1. Also see Beatrice Hazelhurst, "How Our Fascination with Ethnic Ambiguity Affects Plastic Surgery Trends," *Allure*, June 20, 2021, allure.com/story/Asian-american-plastic-surgery-trends; and a U.S. national survey of 2020 people by RealSelf, which found that 24 percent of people in the United States had at least one cosmetic procedure and 12 percent had two or more, with blacks and Hispanics having twice the amount of plastic surgery as whites. See Alex Tunell, "The Real Self Culture Report: How Americans Feel About Plastic Surgery," realself.com/news/culture-report.

40. Jack Graham, "For Korean Americans a Popular Surgery Shrouded in Shame," *The Seattle Globalist*, June 24, 2014 (archived).

41. Jeff Yang, Phil Yu, and Philip Wang, *Rise: A Pop History of Asian America from the Nineties to Now* (New York: Mariner Books, 2022).

42. "Plastic Surgery Statistics Report," American Society of Plastic Surgeons, 2023, plasticsurgery.org/documents/News/Statistics/2020/plastic-surgery-statistics/2020/plastic-surgery-statistics-full-report-2020.pdf. Ironically, a new fad among some white women is to have their eyes shaped like almonds, Asian-style.

43. See, for example, our earlier discussion of the importance of building trust and the right amount of assertiveness to progress up the corporate ladder.

44. RealSelf poll, note 39.

45. Some writers estimate the industry is in the billions of dollars. See Priya Arora and Sapna Maheshwari, "Tracing the Multi-Billion Dollar Fairness Cream Market in India," *India Forbes*, June 26, 2020, forbesindia.com/article/special/tracing-the-multibillion-dollar-fairness-cream-market-in-india/60371/1.

46. Pavitha Rao, "Paying a High Price for Skin Bleaching," *Africa Renewal*, April 9, 2019, un.org/africarenewal/magazine/April-2019-july-2019/paying-high-price-skin-bleaching.

47. Sunny Jain, Unilever's President of Beauty and Personal Care, conceded that "We recognize that the use of the words 'fair,' 'white,' and 'light' suggest a singular ideal of beauty that we don't think is right, and we want to address this." Arora and Maheshwari, note 45.

48. *Ibid.* Unilever's new names for skin whitening products are "Glow and Lively" for women and "Glow and

Handsome" for men. See also Lauren Frayer, "Black Lives Matter Gets Indians Talking About Skin Lightening and Colorism," *National Public Radio*, July 9, 2020, npr.org/sectional/goats and soda/2020/07/09/860912124/black-lives-matter-gets-indians-talking-about-skin-lightening-and-colorism. See also Sameer Yasir and Jeffrey Gettleman, "India Debates Skin-Tone Bias as Beauty Companies Alter Ads," *The New York Times*, June 28, 2020, nytimes.com/2020/06/28/world/asia/india-skin-color-unilever.html.

49. Philosophical differences are emerging that seem to contradict the infatuation with Western looks, although light skin is still more highly prized than dark skin, perhaps indicating a continuing racist phenomenon that may be universal. For South Korea see J. Elfving-Hwang, "Media, Cosmetic Surgery and Aspirational Beauty Aesthetics of the Ageing Body in South Korea," *Asian Studies Review* vol. 45, no. 2 (2021), pp. 238–252; for East Asia see D. Henley and N. Porath, "Body Modification in East Asia: History and Debates," *Asian Studies Review* vol. 45, no. 2 (2021), pp. 198–216; for Thailand see D.B. Kang, "The Duty to Transform: Properly Refining the Body and (Re)defining Oneself in Thailand, *Asian Studies Review* vol. 45, no. 2 (2021), pp. 272–289; for Japan see L. Miller, "Deracialization or Body Fashion? Cosmetic Surgery and Body Modification in Japan," *Asian Studies Review* vol. 45, no. 2 (2021), pp. 217–237; for China see H. Wen, "Gentle Yet Manly: xiao xian rou, Male Cosmetic Surgery and Neoliberal Consumer Culture in China," *Asian Studies Review* vol. 45, no. 2 (2021), pp. 253–271. For an overview of this issue see J. Yip, S. Ainsworth, and M.T.H. Hugh, "Beyond Whiteness: Perspectives on the Rise of the Pan-Asian Beauty Ideal," in G.D. Johnson, K.D. Thomas, A.K. Harrison, and S.A. Grier, eds., *Race in the Marketplace: Crossing Critical Boundaries* (New York: Palgrave Macmillan, 2019).

50. Anthony Kuhn, "South Korean Women 'Escape the Corset' and Reject Their Country's Beauty Ideals," National Public Radio, May 6, 2019, npr.org/2019/05/06/703749983/south-korean-women-escape-the-corset-and-reject-their-country's-beauty-ideals. See also Abbie Sharp, "Escape the Corset," *Leeds Human Rights Journal*, November 29, 2019, hrj.leeds.ac.uk/2019/11/29/escape-the-corset.

Chapter 8

1. For a brief synopsis outlining black/white disparities in these areas, see the statement of U.S. Supreme Court Justice, Ketanji Brown Jackson. Trial Reports of the Supreme Court, June 29, 2023, vol. 600 U.S. Part 1, October term, 2022, *Students for Fair Admission Inc. v. President and Fellows of Harvard University*, pp. 383–412 at supremecourt.gov/opinions/22pdf/600us/r53_4g15.pdf.

2. At the time of this writing, Florida continues to refuse to accept $50 billion from the federal government to expand its Medicaid program. Former Florida governor Rick Scott also refused to accept the federal Medicaid funds. The other nine states refusing federal matching funds for Medicaid are Wyoming, Kansas, Texas, Wisconsin, Tennessee, Mississippi, Alabama, Georgia, and South Carolina. It is estimated that 2.1 million people in these states would benefit from Medicaid expansion under provisions of the Affordable Care Act, and the federal government would match states' contributions up to 95 percent.

3. This phrase was lifted from the 1947 film by that name starring Gregory Peck. The film's title was taken from Laura Hobson's novel of the same name. For a summary of the way African Americans and other ethnic minorities were systematically discriminated against in the United States by the federal government, see Ira Katznelson, *When Affirmative Action Was White* (New York: W.W. Norton, 2005); Carol Anderson, *Eyes Off the Prize* (New York: Cambridge University Press, 2003).

4. During World War II the U.S. State Department, under the leadership of Breckinridge Long, refused to recognize the plight of European Jewry and resisted disseminating information to President Roosevelt and other key administration members who might have relaxed U.S. immigration policy toward them.

Notes—Chapter 8

5. Camus has written other books and essays since then affirming his belief in the moral and cultural superiority of the white race. See *You Will Not Replace Us!* (Paris: published by the author, November, 2018).

6. See, for example, the works of John Relethford, *Reflections of Our Past* (Cambridge, MA: Westview Press, 2003); Spencer Wells, *The Journey of Man* (Princeton, NJ: Princeton University Press, 2003); Steve Olson, *Mapping Human History* (Boston: Mariner Books, 2002); Yuval Noah Harari, *Sapiens: A Brief History of Humankind* (New York: Signal Books, 2014).

7. New York: John Lane, 1911.

8. London: G. Bell and Sons, Ltd., 1920.

9. New York: Charles Scribner's Sons, 1920.

10. New York: Charles Scribner's Sons, 1922.

11. To see film of the event, see the Oscar-winning documentary "A Night at the Garden," Youtube.com/Watch?v=r4zR7XLYSA&t=37s.

12. For an award-winning treatise on the topic of medical atrocities committed by the Nazis, see Robert Jay Lifton, *The Nazi Doctors: Medical Killing and the Psychology of Genocide* (New York: Basic Books, 2nd ed., 2017).

13. The practice of forcibly sterilizing people was rejected in the U.S. Supreme Court decision (*Skinner v. Oklahoma*, 1942), but it took other forms, as can be seen by recent allegations in the following: Victoria Belkiempis, "More Immigrant Women Say They Were Abused by ICE Gynecologist," *The Guardian*, December 22, 2020, https://www.theguardian.com/us-news/2020/dec/22/ice-gynecologist-hysterectomies-georgia. Also see Sanjana Manjeshwar, "America's Forgotten History of Forced Sterilization," *Berkeley Political Review*, September 8, 2023, bpr.berkeley.edu/2022/11/04/Americas-forgotten-history-of-forced-sterilization. California's "asexualization acts" accounted for around 20,000 sterilizations of mostly black and Mexican women. Even Hitler was impressed, noting that the process helped to create a better citizenry. Under the Nixon Administration, thousands of black women on Medicaid were sterilized, and nearly a quarter of Indigenous (Native American) women were sterilized in the 1960s and 1970s.

14. The first quote is from the racist and eugenicist Madison Grant, written in the early part of the 20th century—Madison Grant, *The Passing of the Great Race* (London: G. Bell and Sons, Ltd. 1920), p. 16—and the second quote is from the Frenchman Renaud Camus, "The Great Replacement," Lecture delivered on November 26, 2010, in Lunel, France, p. 27, docdroid.net/8tGi9Vx/camus-r-2021-the-great-replacement-pdf#page=7.

15. Carl Brigham, *A Study of American Intelligence* (Princeton, NJ: Princeton University Press, 1923).

16. Arthur Jensen, "How Much Can We Boost IQ and Scholastic Achievement?," *Harvard Education Review* vol. 39, no. 1 (1969), pp. 1–123.

17. See, for example, the complete collection of papers and Jensen's rejoinders at "The Harvard Educational Review 1969 Debate," arthurjensen.net/?p=838.

18. Richard J. Herrnstein and Charles Murray, *The Bell Curve: Intelligence and Class Structure in American Life* (New York: Free Press, 1994).

19. Steven Pinker, *The Blank Slate: The Modern Denial of Human Nature* (New York: Penguin Press Science, 2003).

20. Ali Vitali, Kasie Hunt, and Frank Thorp V, NBC News, January 11, 2018, nbcnews.com/politics/white-house/trump-referred-haiti-african-countries-shithole-nations-n836946.

21. Camus, note 14.

22. For example, the Manhattan Institute, the Heritage Foundation, and the Hudson Institute. Even some higher education institutions advocate promoting the individual over the commonweal, e.g., Claremont McKenna College, George Mason University. Youthful proponents of rightist ideology, such as Christopher Rufo, who advises governor of Florida and 2024 Republican Presidential candidate Ron DeSantis, as well as revered television hosts and former hosts on the FOX Television channel, e.g., Laura Ingram and Tucker Carlson, are fond of spinning Horatio Alger myths in ways that often blend into replacement theory. Governor DeSantis

has carried the banner of conservative anti–intellectualism and replacement theory to extreme in his state, banning corporations from considering diversity, equity, and inclusion (DEI) in decision making regarding hiring and promotions, and banning diversity training. When he signed HB 7 into law on April 22, 2022 (at times referred to as the Anti-Woke Law), he commented, "No one should be instructed to feel as if they are not equal or ashamed because of their race. In Florida, we will not let the far-left woke agenda take over our schools and workplaces. There is no place for indoctrination or discrimination in Florida." See his full comments at flgov.com/2022/04/22/governor-ron-desantis-signs-legislation-to-protect-floridians-from-discrimination-and-woke-indoctrination. He then replaced six members of the Board of Trustees at the highly respected, left-leaning, New College in Sarasota, appointed a political crony as interim president of the school at double the salary of his predecessor, and set about infusing the pedagogical principles of the conservative and religiously oriented Michigan-based Hillsdale College there and in Florida's public schools. This act was followed by the banning of the College Board's Advanced Placement course on African American history in public schools, the introduction of the ideologically conservative anti-climate-change Prager school curriculum in Florida's schools, and the option of substituting the religiously oriented Classic Learning Test for the SAT and ACT entrance exams to higher educational institutions in Florida. See Dana Goldstein, "Florida Approves New Test For College Admissions Use," *The New York Times*, September 10, 2023, sec. N, p. 18. Other states such as Arkansas, under the leadership of Governor Sarah Huckabee Sanders, are following DeSantis's lead.

23. Lorin Utsch, "Migrant Smuggling Across the Mediterranean Sea," Ballard Briefs, Spring 2021, ballardbrief.byu.edu/issue-briefs/migrant-smuggling-across-the-mediterranean-sea#~text=since%20 2014%2C%20over%2019%2C000%20 migrants%20have%20died%20crossing %20the%20Mediterranean.

24. See Lorenzo Tondo and Emmanuel Akinwotu, "People of Colour Fleeing Ukraine Attacked by Polish Nationalists," *The Guardian*, March 2, 2022, theguardian.com/global-development/2022/mar/02/people-of-colour-fleeing-Ukraine-attacked-by-Polish-nationalists.

25. For polling data on the acceptance of Christian nationalism in the United States, see Gregory A. Smith, Michael Rotolo, and Patricia Tevington, "3. Views of the U.S. as a 'Christian Nation' and Opinions About 'Christian nationalism,'" Pew Research Center, October 27, 2022, pewresearch.org/religion/2022/10/27/views-of-the-u-s-as-a-christian-nation-and-opinions-about-christian-nationalism. See also Robert P. Jones, "The Roots of Christian Nationalism Go Back Further Than You Think," *Time*, August 31, 2023, and his book, *White Too Long: The Legacy of White Supremacy in American Christianity* (New York: Simon & Schuster, 2020). Also, see the statement by Americans United for the Separation of Church and State about the new education curriculum in Florida at au.org/the-latest-/press/Christian-nationalism-florida-curriculum/#.

26. https://www.adl.org/resources/report/audit-antisemitic-incidents-2023.

27. Camus, note 14, pp. 10, 11, 23.

28. Groups such QAnon, Oath Keepers, Three Percenters, Boogaloo.

29. A phrase used by former Algerian President Houari Boumediene in a United Nations speech on April 10, 1974: "One day millions of men will leave the southern hemisphere to go to the northern hemisphere. And they won't go there as friends. Because they will go there to conquer. And they will conquer it by populating it with their sons. It is the belly of our women that will grant us victory." Cited in Camus, note 14, 2011.

30. Thomas R. Malthus, *An Essay on the Principle of Population as it Affects the Future Improvement of Society* (London: J. Johnson, 1798).

31. Nor did the dire predictions of demographer Paul R. Erlich in his *The Population Bomb* (New York: Ballantine Books, 1971).

32. The top eight countries in population growth are respectively Syria

(4.98 percent annual population growth rate); Moldova (4.98 percent); Niger (3.8 percent); Democratic Republic of the Congo (3.28 percent); Chad (3.13 percent); Somalia (3.1 percent); Angola (3.08 percent); and Mayotte (3.03 percent). All but the top two of these are in Africa.

33. For example, a Club of Rome report predicts a dramatic reduction in the world's population as technological and medical innovations become widely accepted. See Ben Turner, "World's Population Could Plummet to 6 Billion by the End of the Century, Study Suggests," *Live Sciences*, March 27, 2023, livescience.com/worlds-population-could-plummet-to-six-billion-by-the-end-of-the-century-new-study-suggests. See "Limits and Beyond," The Club of Rome, Exapt Press, https://exapt.press/limits-and-beyond.

34. The use of the word "alien" by white supremacists and some politicians is off-putting and inaccurate when describing illegal immigrants. The word is often used to denote someone from outside, a stranger, but it also connotes a nonhuman. To infer that illegal immigrants lack humanity is a ploy that allows them to be viewed and treated inhospitably, overlooking their humanity, and rationalizing their circumstances so they may be treated disparagingly.

35. John Gramlich and Alissa Scheller, "What's Happening at the U.S.–Mexico Border in 7 Charts," Pew Research Center, November 9, 2021, pewresearch.org/short-reads/2021/11/09/whats-happening-at-the-u-s-mexico-border-in-7-charts.

36. Mary Hanna and Jeanne Batalova, "Immigrants from Asia in the United States," *Migration Policy Institute*, March 10, 2021, migrationpolicy.org/article/immigrants-Asia-United-States-2020.

37. William H. Frey, "The Nation Is Diversifying Even Faster than Predicted, According to New Census Data," *Brookings*, July 1, 2020, brookings.edu/articles/new-census-data-shows-the-nation-is-diversifying-even-faster-than-predicted.

38. Ibid.

39. Peggy McIntosh, "White Privilege: Unpacking the Invisible Knapsack," *Peace and Freedom*, July/August, 1989, Psychology.umbc.edu/wp-content/uploads/sites/57/2016/10/white=-Privilege_mcintosh-1989.pdf. Her article triggered a furious debate about whether the phenomenon was real. In 2023, the state of Florida, under pressure from the DeSantis administration, banned the teaching of the concept, and other states are following suit. See her article for illustrations about how white privilege works in everyday life.

40. For a riveting account about the exploitation of East Indian workers in the United States by a large construction company, see Saket Soni, *The Great Escape: The True Story of Forced Labor and Immigrant Dreams in America* (Chapel Hill, NC: Algonquin Books, 2023).

41. See the interview with Admiral John C. Aquilino, head of the U.S. Indo-Pacific Command, in *The Guardian*, March 20, 2022, theguardian.com/world/2022/mar/21/China-has-fully-militarized-three-islands-in-south-china-sea-us-admiral-says.

42. This summary of PRC interference in Hong Kong was derived from Dylan Butts, Molpasorn Shoowong, and Meredith Chen, "Hong Kong's 25 Years Under China: Protests, Politics, and Tightening Laws," NBC News, July 1, 2022, nbcnews.com/news/world/hong-kong-25-years-china-protests-politics-tightening-laws-rcna36284.

43. Julian E. Barnes and Edward Wong, "Global Espionage Grows Between U.S. and China," *The New York Times*, September 17, 2023, pp. 1, 12.

44. Ibid., p. 12.

45. For a review of this phenomenon see "Confucius Institutes in the United States: Selected Issues," Congressional Research Services, May 2, 2023, crsreports.congress.gov/product/pdf/IF11180.

46. Ibid.

47. Lin Yang, "Controversial Confucius Institutes Returning to U.S. Schools Under New Name," *VOA*, June 27, 2022, voanews.com/a/controversial-confucius-institutes-returning-to-u-s-schools-under-new-name/6635906.htm.

48. Aruna Viswantha and Kate O'Keeffe, "Harvard Chemistry Chairman

Charged on Alleged Undisclosed Ties to China," *Wall Street Journal*, January 28, 2020, wsj.com/articles/harvards-chemistry-chair-charged-on-alleged-undisclosed-ties-to-china-11580228768?mod=article_online. For information about the National Medium- and Long-Term Development Plan see: Huiyao Wong, "China's National Talent Plan: Key Measures and Objectives," Brookings, November 23, 2010, brookings.edu/articles/chinas-national-talent-plan-key-measures-and-objectives.

49. Viswantha and O'Keeffe, note 48.

50. It should be noted that the Obama administration had already begun prosecutions of alleged theft of trade secrets prior to the implementation of the "China Initiative," but under President Trump, the level of vitriol was increased. For example, then Attorney General William Barr asserted that China was engaged in "an aggressive, orchestrated, whole-of-government (indeed, whole-of-society) campaign ... to surpass the United States as the world's preeminent technological superpower." The "China Initiative" emanated from this type of xenophobia. For more on this phenomenon see Karen Hao and Eileen Cho, "The FBI Accused Him of Spying for China. It Ruined His Life," *MIT Technology Review*, June 27, 2021, technologyreview.com/2021/k06/27/1027350/anming-hu-china-initiative-research-espionage-spying/.

51. "Wen Ho Lee," *Wikipedia*, en.wikipedia.org/wiki/Wen_Ho_Lee.

52. See the paper by Jenny K. Lee and Xiaojie Li for more information on the adversarial climate being created by this initiative. Their survey of 2,000 scientists across the nation revealed that nearly half (42 percent) of the Chinese scientists felt racially profiled by the U.S. government, and 30 percent reported difficulty in obtaining research funds. Even so, 41 percent of the scientists reported having limited communication with China, and 42 percent reported that FBI investigations affected their plans to stay in the United States. See Dong Liu, "Committee of 100 Survey," Committee 100.org/wp-content/uploads/2021/10/translation-the-paper-coverage-of-10_28-Arizona.pdf.

53. Hao and Cho, note 50.

54. *Ibid.*

55. CNN reported more than 24 states have passed legislation limiting or prohibiting the Chinese government from purchasing land in the United States. See Sydney Kashiwagi, "States Accelerate Efforts to Block Chinese Purchases of Agricultural Land," CNN, June 19, 2023, cnn.com/2023/06/19/politics/Chinese-land-purchases/indes.html. The Committee of 100 published data indicating that 32 states and 36 bills limiting purchase of land by Asians and other foreign adversaries had passed by April 2024. For a list of these see the statement of the Committee of 100, May 9, 2024, and for a detailed analysis of the exclusionary behavior go to their webpage at Committee100.org/our-work/federal-and-state-bills-prohibiting-property-ownership-by-foreign-individuals-and-entities/?mc_cid=46c9eb254a&mc_eid-=8c647a5f7d.

56. *Ibid.*

57. *Ibid.* In December, 2023, the Committee of 100 launched a database that identifies restrictive land legislation around the United States, including an interactive map that denotes the location and types of restrictions related to land ownership. To see this material see committee100.org/our-work/federal-and-state-bills-prohibiting-property-ownership-by-foreign-individuals-and-entities.

58. A recent initiative by Stop AAPI Hate is known as "Stop the Blame." It is focused on reducing anti-Asian scapegoating in American politics. For more information see stopaapihate.org/2023/09/21/stop-the-blame-press-releas.

59. Mary Clare Jalonick and Haleluya Hadero, "House Votes Possible TikTok Ban in U.S., but Don't Expect the App to Go Away Anytime Soon," ABC Eyewitness News, Chicago, April 20, 2024, abc7chicago.com/house-of-representatives-passed-foreign-aid-bills-that-includes-tiktok-ban-provision-aid-to-taiwan/14702642. United States Senator Maria Cantwell (D-Washington), Chair of the Senate Commerce Committee, said at the time, "Congress is acting to prevent foreign adversaries from conducting

espionage, surveillance, maligned operations, harming vulnerable Americans, our servicemen and women, and our U.S. government." Bobby Allyn, "President Biden Signs Law to Ban TikTok Nationwide Unless It is Sold," NPR, April 24, 2024, npr.org/2024/04/24/1246663779/biden-ban-tiktok-us.

60. For information about the PRC's pursuit of so-called "fugitives" through the use of INTERPOL "Red Notices" by using extralegal and even illegal methods to apprehend them, see the report by Safeguard Defenders, "No Room to Run: China's Expanded Mis(Use) of INTERPOL Since the Rise of Xi Jinping," safeguarddefenders.com/sites/default/files/pdf/No%20Room%20to%20Run.pdf. See also Hannah Rabinowitz, Evan Perez, and Lauren del Valle, "FBI Arrests Two Alleged Chinese Agents and Dozens With Working Inside U.S. to Silence Dissidents," CNN, April 18, 2023, cnn.com/2023/04/17/politics/fbi-chinese-agents/index.html. Research by Lauren Harth revealed that the Chinese use a variety of techniques to "persuade" dissidents to return to the mainland for trial, such as prolonged detention, arbitrary arrests of ethnic and religious minorities, improper use of INTERPOL "Red Notices" to identify and induce dissidents to return, and harassment of the families of dissidents on the mainland. The FBI has identified more than 100 Chinese-backed police stations in foreign countries and arrested two New York City residents for conspiring to act as agents of China and obstructing justice. It is estimated that in one recent year more than 230,000 Chinese nationals were "persuaded" to return to the mainland to stand trial. The Chinese government contends that individuals conducting such activities in other countries are volunteers, the centers were created to assist people after the pandemic, and people they are seeking are fugitives who had engaged in illegal activities on the mainland. See Masood Fariver, "China Steps Up Intimidation, Harassment of Chinese Dissidents in U.S.," VOA, July 13, 2022, voanews.com/a/us-officials-warn-of-chinese-s-transnational-repression-operations/6658166.html; and Holly Henderich, "FBI Makes Arrests Over Alleged Secret Chinese 'Police Stations' in New York," BBC News, bbc.com/news/world-us-canada-65305415. The horror of Tiananmen Square in 1989 provides an example of the way dissidents have been treated by the PRC.

Bibliography

*Online citations were correct at the time of retrieval and have been updated, but they may change over time.

Alegria, Analucia, et al. "Disordered Gambling Among Racial and Ethnic Groups in the United States: Results from the National Epidemiologic Survey on Alcohol a Related Conditions." *CNS Spectrum* vol. 14, no. 3 (March 2009), pp. 132–143.
American Immigration Council. "Adding Up Billions in Tax Dollars Paid By Undocumented Immigrants." April 4, 2016. https://www.americanimmigrationcouncil.org/sites/default#files/research/adding_up_the_billions_in_tax_dollars_paid_by_undocumented_immigrants.pdf.
Americans United for Separation of Church and State. "Americans United Launches Investigation of White Christian Nationalism in Florida Education Curriculum." July 1, 2022. Au.org/the-latest-press/Christian-nationalism-florida-curriculum/#.
Anand, Priya, and Ellen Huet. "Why Silicon Valley's Many Asians Still Feel Like a Minority." *Bloomberg Business Week*, August 6, 2021. Bloomberg.com/News/features/2021-08-06/why-silicon-valley-s-asian-americans-still-feel-Like-a-minority.
Anderson, Carol. *Eyes Off the Prize*. New York: Cambridge University Press, 2003.
"Anime Popularity in America Statistics and Trends in 2023." *Gitnux Market Data*. blog.gitnux.com/popularity-in-america-statistics.
Anti-Defamation League. Adl.org/resources/press-release/us-antisemitic-Incidents-hit-highest-level-ever-recorded-adl-audit-finds.
———. "Audit of Antisemitic Incidents 2022." adl.org/resources/report/audit-Antisemitic-incidents-2022.
———. "Summary of Achievements." adl.org/who-we-are/history.
Aquillino, John C. "China Has Fully Militarized Three Islands in South China Sea, US Admiral Says." *The Guardian*, March 20, 2022. Theguardian.com/world/2022/mar/21/china-has-fully-militarized-three-islands-in-south-china-sea-us-admiral-says.
Arcidiacono, Peter, John Kinsler, and Tyler Ransom. "Legacy and Athletic Preferences at Harvard." Working Paper 26316, September, 2019. National Bureau of Economic Research, Cambridge, MA.
Arora, Priya, and Sapna Maheshwari. "Tracing the Multi-Billion Dollar Fairness Cream Market in India." *India Forbes*, June 26, 2020. Forbesindia.Com/article/special/tracing-the-multibillion-dollar-fairness-cream-marketIn-india-60371/1.
Asian-nation.org/headlines/las-vegas-style/#sthash.PsNxcuhd.dpbs. (This blog was written by C.N. on March 3, 2007, in *Asian Nation*.)
Association of American Medical Colleges. "Active Physicians who Identified as Asian, 2021." aamc.org/data-reports/workforce/data/active-physicians-asian-2021.

Bibliography

Augustyn, Adam. "Bruce Lee: American-Born Actor." *Britannica*, July 16, 2023. Britannica.com/biography/Bruce-Lee.

Badrinathan, Sumitra, Devesh Kapur, Jonathan Kay, and Milan Vaishhav. "Social Realities of Indian Americans: Results of the 2020 Indian American Attitude Survey." Carnegie Endowment for International Peace, June 19, 2021. Carnegieendowment.org/2021/06/09/social-realities-of-indian-americans-results-from-2020-indian-attitudes-survey-pub-84667.

Ballingrud, David, Nicole Christian, and Bill Duryea. "Holdups Raise Fears of Asian Gangs." *St. Petersburg Times*, December 18, 1992.

Bankhorst, Adam. "Three Billion People Worldwide Now Play Video Games, New Report Shows." August 14, 2020. Ign.com/articles/three/billion-people-worldwide-now-play-video-games-new-study-shows.

Barnes, Julian E., and Edward Wong. "Global Espionage Grows Between U.S. and China." *The New York Times*, September 17, 2023, pp. 1, 12.

Basu, Moni. "15 Years After 9/11, Sikhs Still Victims of Anti-Muslim Hate Crimes." CNN, September 15, 2016. cnn.com/2016/09/15/us/sikh-hate-crime-victims/index.html.

Belkiempis, Victoria. "More Immigrant Women Say They Were Abused by ICE Gynecologist." *The Guardian*, December 22, 2020. https://theguardian.com/us-news/2020/dec/22/ice-gynecologist-hysterectomies-georgia.

Biggers, Earl Derr. *The Black Camel*. In *Charlie Chan: Five Complete Novels*. New York: Avenel Books, 1981.

———. *Charlie Chan Carries On*. Chicago: Academy Chicago Publishers, 1930.

———. *The Chinese Parrot*. In *Charlie Chan: Five Complete Novels*. New York: Avenel Books, 1981.

———. *The House Without a Key*. New York: Grosset & Dunlap, 1925.

———. *Keeper of the Keys*. In *Charlie Chan: Five Complete Novels*. New York: Avenel Books, 1981.

Bingham, Carl. *A Study of American Intelligence*. Princeton: Princeton University Press, 1923.

"Books and Films of Fu Manchu." n.d. Fumanchu.seriesbooks.info.

Borjas, George. *Understanding the Immigration Narrative*. New York: W.W. Norton, 2016.

Boumediene, Houari. *United Nations Speech*, April 10, 1974.

Boundless. "Over 200,000 Green Cards Wasted in 2021 as Backlog Explodes." January 1, 2022. boundless.com/blog/uscis-wastes-200k-green-cards-backlog-triples.

"Boundless Releases 2020 Immigrant Income and Taxation Report." Boundless. April 14, 2022. http://www.boundless.com/blog/boundles-releases-2022-Immigrant-income-taxation-report.

Braga, Anthony. "Understanding Serious Violence in San Francisco 2017–2020." California Partnership for Safe Communities and the San Francisco Police Department, March 4, 2021.

Brown, Abram, and Abigail Freeman. "Top-Earning TikTok-ers 2022. Charlie and Dixie D'Amelio and Addison Rae Expand Fame—and Paydays." *Forbes*, January 7, 2020.

Buck, Pearl S. *The Good Earth*. Archive.org/details/goodearthoobuck_1/page/n5/mode/2up.

Budiman, Abby. "Filipinas in the U.S. Fact Sheet." Pew Research Center, April 29, 2021. pewresearch/org/social-trends/fact-sheet/asian-americans-filipinos-in-the-u-s.

Budiman, Abby, and Neil G. Ruiz. "Key Facts About Asian Americans, A Diverse and Growing Population." Pew Research Center, April 29, 2021. https://www.pewresearch.org/fact-tank/2021/04/29/key-facts-about-asian-americans.

Burton, Jeffrey F., Mary M. Farrell, Florence B. Lord, and Richard W. Lord. *Confinement and Ethnicity: An Overview of World War II Japanese American Relocation Sites*. Seattle: University of Washington Press, 2002.

Butts, Dylan, Molpasorn Shoowong, and Meredith Chen. "Hong Kong's 25 Years Under

Bibliography 215

Protests, Politics, and Tightening Laws." NBC News, July 1, 2021. nbcnews.com/news/world/hong-kong-25-years-china-protests-politics-Tightening-laws-rcna.36284.
Camus, Renaud. *The Great Replacement.* France: Chez L' auteur, 2019.
_____. *You Will Not Replace Us!* Self-published, 2018.
"Cancer and Asian Americans." Office of Minority Health, U.S. Department of Health and Human Services. hhs.gov/cancer-and-asian-americans.
Cao, Lan, Himilce Novas, and Rosemary Silva. *Everything You Need to Know About Asian-American History.* New York: Penguin, 1996.
Centers for Disease Control and Prevention. "Control of Infectious Diseases, 1990–1999." iamanetwork.com/journal/jama/fullarticle/191692.
Cerrissa, Kim. "Koreans and Camptowns: Reflections of a Mixed-Race Korean." *Korean American Story,* November 4, 2015. koreanamericanstory.org/written/the-conference-that-introduced-me-to-the-legacy-of-being-a-mixed-race-korean.
Chamberlain, Houston S. *Foundations of the Nineteenth Century,* trans. John Lees. London: John Lane, 1911.
Chan, Alan K.K., et al. "Personal Gambling Expectancies Among Asian American and White College Students." *Journal of Gambling Studies* vol. 31 (May 2015), pp. 33–57.
Chang, Gordon. *Ghosts of Gold Mountain.* New York: Mariner Books, 2019.
Cherlin, Andrew, and Carin Celebusk. "Are Jewish Families Different? Some Evidence from the General Social Survey." *Journal of Nursing and the Family* vol. 45, no. 4 (1983).
Chin, Ava. *Mott Street: A Chinese American Family's Story of Exclusion and Homecoming.* New York: Penguin Press, 2023.
Chin, Frank K. *Bulletproof Buddhists and Other Essays.* Honolulu: University of Hawaii Press, 1998.
Chin, Ko-lin. *Chinatown Gangs: Extortion, Enterprise and Ethnicity.* New York: Oxford University Press, 1994.
Chin, Margaret. *Stuck. Why Asian Americans Don't Reach the Top of the Corporate Ladder.* New York: New York University Press, 2020.
Chou, Rosalind S., and Joe R. Feagin. *The Myth of the Model Minority: Asian Americans Facing Racism.* Boulder, CO: Paradigm Publishers, 2010.
Chua, Amy. *Battle Hymn of the Tiger Mother.* New York: Penguin, 2011.
Club of Rome. "Limits and Beyond." Exapt Press, May 2023. https://exapt.press/limits-and-beyond.
"College Professor Demographics and Statistics in the US." zippia.com/college-professor-jobs/demographics.
Collisson, Craig. "Japanese American Wartime Incarceration in Oregon." *Oregon Encyclopedia.* oregonencyclopedia.org/articles/Japanese_internment/#.Y6dFR3bMKOO.
Committee of 100. "Forum on Bamboo Ceiling," July 20, 2023.
Congressional Research Service. "Confucius Institutes in the United States: Selected Issues." May 2, 2023. crsreports.congress.gov/product/pdf/IF/IF11180.
"Crime in the United States, 2019." *Uniform Crime Report,* FBI, Table 43. ucr.fbi.gov/crime-in-the-u.s./2019/topic-pages/tables/table-43.
Dang, Laura. "Here's What Happened to the Daughters of the Original 'Tiger Mom.'" *Next Shark,* January 28, 2016. nextshark.com/amy-chua-tiger-mom-daughters.
de Brau, W. "Does Immigration Reduce Wages?" *Cato Journal* vol. 37, no. 3 (Fall 2017), pp. 473–480.
de Gobineau, Joseph Comte. *The Inequality of Human Races,* trans. Adrian Collins. London: William Heinemann, 1915.
De Guzman, Chad. "'An Empty Shell of What It Used to Be': Asian's Gambling Mecca Gets a China-Backed Makeover." *Time,* November 3, 2022. time.com/6227922/macau-gambling-capital-casino-china.
Demographics of Asian Americans. *Wikipedia.* en.wikipedia.org/wiki/demographics_of_asian_americans.
Densho Encyclopedia. "Alien Land Laws." encyclopedia.densho.org/Alien_land_laws.

DeSantis, Ron. "Anti-Woke Legislation Comments." flgov.com/2022/04/22/governor-ron-desantis-signs-legislation-to-protect-floridians-from-discrimination-and-woke-indoctrination.

Devereux, Stephen. "Famine in the Twentieth Century." *Social Sciences in Humanitarian Action Platform.* socialsciencesinaction.org/resources/famine-in-the-twentieth-century.

"Dog Meat Consumption in South Korea." *Wikipedia.* en.wikipedia.org/wiki/Dog_meat_consumption_in_South_Korea.

Donegan, T.J. "Nintendo vs. Xbox vs. Playstation: Here's How They All Compare."usatoday.com/televisions/features/Nintendo-vs-xbox-vs-playstationheres-how-they-all-compare.

Du Bois, W.E.B. *Black Reconstruction in America: 1860–1880.* New York: The Free Press, 1998.

Dunnett, Madeleine. "Manga's Growth in Popularity Is Here to Stay, Industry Leaders Predict." *Anime News Network,* May 11, 2022.

Eals, Clay. "Remembering Bruce Lee and His Time in Seattle, on the 80th Anniversary of his Birth." *The Seattle Times,* November 20, 2020.

"Education and Lifetime Earnings." Research Statistics and Policy Analysis. Social Security Administration, November, 2015. ssa.gov/policy/docs/research-Summaries/education-earnings.html.

Edwards, Jonathan. "Sinners in the Hands of an Angry God." July 8, 1741. blueletterbible.org/comm/edwards.jonathan/sermons/sinners.cfn.

Ehrlich, Paul, and Anne Ehrlich. *The Population Bomb.* New York: Ballantine Books, 1968.

Elfving, Hwang. "Media, Cosmetic Surgery and Aspirational Beauty Aesthetics of the Aging Body in South Korea." *Asian Studies Review* vol. 45, no. 2 (2021), pp. 238–252.

Executive Order 9066. *Wikipedia.* en.wikipedia.org/wiki/Executive_order_9066.

Farago, Andrew. *Teenage Mutant Ninja Turtles: The Ultimate Visual History.* Portland, OR: Image Editions, 2014.

Fariver, Masood. "China Steps Up Intimidation, Harassment of Chinese Nationalists in US." VOA, July 13, 2022. voanews.com/a/us-officials-warn-of-chinese-s-transnational-repression-operations/6658166.html.

FBI. "FBI Releases 2021 Hate Crime Statistics," March 13, 2023. fbi.gov/news/press-releases/fbi-releases-supplemental-2021-hate-crime-statistics.

Feurtes, Jairon, et al. "A Meta-Analysis of the Effects of Speakers' Accents on Interpersonal Evaluations." *European Journal of Social Psychology* vol. 42 (October 26, 2011).

"The Formation of Human Populations in South and Central America." *Science* vol. 365 (September 6, 2019), p. 7487ff.

Four Paws. "Dogmeat." January 2021. four-paws.org/the-truth/a-summary-report-on-dog-and-cat-meat-consumption-in-vietnam.

Fox, Stephen. *Uncivil Liberties: Italian Americans Under Siege During World War II.* Parkland, FL: Universal Publications, 2000.

Frayer, Lauren. "Black Lives Matter Gets Indians Talking About Skin Lightening and Colorism." National Public Radio, July 9, 2020. npr.org/sectional/goatsandsoda/2020/07/09/860912124/black-lives-matter-gets-indians-talking-about-skin-lightening-and-colorism.

Frey, William F. "The Nation Is Diversifying Even Faster Than Predicted, According to New Census Data." Brookings Institution, July 1, 2020. brookings.edu/articles/new/census/data/shows-the-nation-is-diversifying-even-faster-than-predicted.

Fujii v. California. Densho Encyclopedia. encyclopedia.densho.org/Fujii_v._california.

Gallardo, Lisa, and Jeanne Batlova. "Filipino Immigrants in the U.S." Migration Policy Institute, July 15, 2020. Migrationpolicy.org/article/Filipino-Immigrants-united-states-2000.

Gamblers of the Old West. Alexandria, VA: Time-Life Books, 1977.

"Gangs in the United States." *Wikipedia.* en.wikipedia.org/wiki/gangs_in_the_United_States.

Gao, Qin, Jennifer So, Stacey Tao, and Sam Collitt. "The Fight for Representation: The State of Chinese Americans 2022." The Committee of 100. New York: Columbia University, 2023.
"Gender and Migration." Global Migration Data Portal, International Organization for Migration, 2021. migrationportal.org/themes/gender-and-migration.
Glionna, John. "Gambling Addiction and Asian Culture." *Los Angeles Times,* January 16, 2006.
"Global Chinese Philanthropy Initiative, 2022." Globalchinesephilanthropy.org/gcp/report/178333.
Goldstein, Dana. "Florida Approves New Test for College Admissions Use." *The New York Times,* September 10, 2023, sec. N, p. 18.
Graham, Jack. "For Korean Americans, a Popular Surgery Shrouded in Shame." *The Seattle Globalist,* June 24, 2014.
Gramlich, John, and Alissa Scheller. "What's Happening at the U.S.-Mexico Border in 7 Charts." Pew Research Center, November 9, 2021. pewresearch.org/short-reads/2021/11/09/whats-happening-at-the-u-s-mexico-border-in-7-charts.
Grant, Madison. *The Passing of the Great Race.* New York: Charles Scribner's Sons, 1916.
Gymdesk. "39 Martial Arts Industry Statistics to Know." Gymdesk.com/blog/martial-arts-industry-statistics.
Hanke, Ken. *Charlie Chan at the Movies: History, Photography, and Criticism.* Jefferson, NC: McFarland, 1989.
Hanna, Mary, and Jeanne Batalova. "Immigrants from Asia in the United States." Migration Policy Institute, March 10, 2021. migrationpolicy.org/article/immigrants-asia-united states-2020.
Hao, Karen, and Eileen Cho. "The FBI Accused Him of Spying for China. It Ruined His Life." *MIT Technology Review,* June 27, 2021. technologyreview.com/2021/k06/27/1027350/anming-hu-china-initiative-research-espionage-spying.
Harari, Yural N. *Sapiens: A Brief History of Humankind.* New York: Harper Perennial, 2018.
"The Harvard Educational Review 1969 debate." arthurjensen.net/?p=838.
"Hate Crime Victimization, 2005–2019." Bureau of Justice Statistics, U.S. Department of Justice, September 13, 2021. bjs.ojp.gov/press-release/hate-crime-victimization-2005-2019.
Hazelhurst, Bruce. "How Our Fascination with Ethnic Ambiguity Affects Plastic Surgery Trends." *Allure,* June 20, 2021. allure.com/story/Asian-american-Plastic-surgery-trends.
Hedges, Chris. "What Every Person Should Know About War." *The New York Times,* July 6, 2003.
Henderich, Holly. "FBI Makes Arrests Over Alleged Secret Chinese 'Police Stations' in New York." BBC News. bbc.com/news/world-us-canada-65305415.
Henley, D., and N. Porath. "Body Modification in East Asia: History and Debates." *Asian Studies Review* vol. 45, no. 2 (2021), pp. 198–216.
Herrnstein, Richard J., and Charles Murray. *The Bell Curve: Intelligence and Class Structure in American Life.* New York: The Free Press, 1994.
Hersey, John. *Hiroshima.* New York: Alfred A. Knopf, 1946.
Hess, Abigail J. "13 U.S. Workers Die on the Job Per Day, on Average, and These Are the Most Dangerous Jobs." Make It, December 29, 2021. cnbc.com/2021/12/29/bis-estimates-that-13-us-workers-die-on-the-job-per-day-on-average.html.
Hilborn, Matt. "Asian Cuisine Fastest Growing in US." VOA, July15, 2018. EarningEnglish.voanews.com/a/Asian-cuisine-fastest-growing-in-u-s/4480072.
"History of Lynching in America." NAACP. NAACP.org/find-resources/history-explained/history-lynching-america.
Holloway, Kali. "Affirmative Action is in the Supreme Court's Crosshairs." *The Nation,* June 22, 2023.
_____. "I Needed Asian Plaintiffs." *The Nation,* August 21–28, 2023, pp. 25–28.

———. "In the Right's Web." *The Nation,* July 10–17, 2023, pp. 8–9.
"The Hollywood Diversity Report." UCLA Entertainment and Media Research Institute, 2023.
Hong, Cathy Park. *Minor Feelings.* New York: One World, 2020.
Houston, Jean Wakatsuki, and James D. Houston. *Farewell to Manzanar.* New York: Dell Laurel-Leaf, 1973.
Hswen, Yulin, et al. "Association of COVID-19 Virus 'Chinesevirus' with Anti-Asian Sentiments on Twitter: March 9–23, 2020." *American Journal of Public Health,* May 2021. ajph.alphapublications.org/doi/10.2105/AJPH.2021.306154.
Huang, Yunte. *Charlie Chan.* New York: W.W. Norton, 2010.
Humane Society International. "Saving Animals from China's Dog and Cat Meat Trade." 2023. his.org/news-resources/saving-dogs-from-Chinas-dog-meat-trade.
Hyun, Jane. *Breaking the Bamboo Ceiling: Career Strategies for Asians.* New York: Harper Business, 2006.
Jensen, Arthur. "How Much Can We Boost IQ and Scholastic Achievement?" *Harvard Educational Review* vol. 39, no. 1 (1969), pp. 1–123.
Jensen, Gwendolyn. "The Experience of Injustice: Health Consequences of the Japanese American Internment." *Dissertation Abstracts International, Section A: Humanities and Social Sciences* 58 (7-A) (1998), p. 2718.
Jimenez, Thomas R., and Adam Horowitz. "When White Is Just Alright: How Immigrants Redefine Achievement and Reconfigure the Ethnoracial Hierarchy." *American Sociological Review* vol. 78, no. 5 (2013), pp. 849–871.
Johnson, A. "Yakuza: Past and Present." U.S. Department of Justice, Office of Justice Programs, NCJ, no. 166177.
Jones, Nikole-Hannah, et al. *The 1619 Project: A New Origin Story.* New York: One World, 2021.
Jones, Robert P. "The Roots of Christian Nationalism Go Back Further Than You Think." *Time,* August 31, 2023.
———. *White Too Long: The Legacy of White Supremacy in American Christianity.* New York: Simon & Schuster, 2020.
Justia US Supreme Court. Ex Parte Endo, 323 U.S. 283, 1944. Justia.com/cases/federal/us/323/283.
Kang, Cecilia. "ByteDance Inquiry Finds Employees Obtained User Data of Two Journalists." *The New York Times,* December 22, 2022.
Kang, D.B. "The Duty to Transform: Properly Refining the Body and (Re)Defining Oneself in Thailand." *Asian Studies Review* vol. 45, no. 2 (2021), pp. 273–289.
Kang, Jay Caspian. *The Loneliest Americans.* New York: Crown Publishing Group, 2021.
Kaplan, H. Roy. *American Indians at the Margins: Racist Stereotypes and Their Impacts on Native Peoples.* Jefferson, NC: McFarland, 2022.
———. *Failing Grades: How Schools Breed Frustration, Anger and Violence and How to Prevent It.* Lanham, MD: Scarecrow Education, 2004.
———. *Understanding Conflict and Change in a Multicultural World.* Lanham, MD: Rowman & Littlefield, 2014.
Kashiwagi, Sydney. "States Accelerate Efforts to Block Chinese Purchases of Agricultural Land." CNN, June 19, 2023. edition.cnn.com/2023/06/19/politics/Chinese-land-purchases/index.html.
Katyal, Neal. Statement regarding incarceration of Japanese in WWII. Justice.gov/Archives/opa/blog/confession-error-solicitor-generals-mistakes-during-Japanese-american-internment-cases.
Katznelson, Ira. *When Affirmative Action Was White.* New York: W.W. Norton, 2005.
Kaur, Brahmjot. "Why South Asian Americans stan Taco Bell." NBC News, March 26, 2023. nbcnews.com/news/Asian-america/south-asian-americans-stan-taco-bell-rcha86318.
Kharpal, Arjun. "Huawei Says It Would Never Send Data to China's Government. Experts Say It Wouldn't Have a Choice." CNBC, March 5, 2019. cnbc.com/2019/03/05/Huawei-would-have-to-give-data-to-china-government-If-asked-experts.html.

"Killing of Vincent Chin." *Wikipedia*. en.wikipedia.org/wiki/killing_of_Vincent_Chin.
Kim, John H., et al., eds. "In Observance of Centennial of Korean Immigration to the U.S." www.naka.org/resources/briefhistory.htm.
Kim, Wooksoo. "Acculturation and Gambling Among Asian Americans: When Culture Meets Availability." *International Gambling Studies* vol. 12 (2012), pp. 69–88.
Koster, John. *Operation Snow: How a Soviet Mole in FDR's White House Triggered Pearl Harbor*. Washington, D.C.: Regnery, 2012.
Krammer, Arnold. *Undue Process: The Untold Story of America's German Alien Interns*. Lanham, MD: Rowman & Littlefield, 1997.
Kuhn, Anthony. "South Korean Women 'Escape the Corset' and Reject Their Country's Beauty Ideals." *National Public Radio*, May 6, 2019. npr.org/2019/05/06/703749983/south-korean-women-escape-the-corset-and-reject-their-country's-beauty-ideals.
Kung Fu Series. *Wikipedia*. en.wikipedia.org/wiki/kung_fu_(1972_TV_series).
Kwan, Kevin. *Crazy Rich Asians*. New York: Doubleday, 2015.
Largent, Charles. "The Fu Manchu Cycle—1965–1969." October 31, 2020. trailersfromhell.com/the-fu-manchu-cycle-1965–1969.
Lau, Allison. "Is the U.S. Losing Its Chinatowns?" CNBC, May 28, 2021. cnbc.comvideo/2021/05/28/why-the-us-has-so-many-chinatowns.html.
Lederman, Doug. "Diversity on the Rise Among College Presidents." *Inside Higher Education*, February 13, 2022. insidehighered.com/news/2022/02/14/colleges-have-hired-more-minority-presidents-amid-racial/rekoning.
Lee, Alex. "South Korea's Plastic Surgery Boom: A Quest to be Above Normal." *Huffpost*, September 18, 2019. huffpost.com/entry/korea-plastic-surgery_1_5d72afb0e4b07521022c00e1.
Lee, Bill. *Chinese Playground: A Memoir*. Scotts Valley, CA: CreateSpace, 2014.
Lee, Jenny K., Xiaojie Li, and Dong Liu. "Committee of 100 Survey." committee100.org/wp-content/uploads/2021/10/translation-the-paper-coverage-of-10–28-Arizona.pdf.
Lee, John H. "Understanding the Riots Part 4: Seeing Ourselves: Koreatown: Together We Suffer." *Los Angeles Times*, May 14, 1992. latimes.com/Archives/la-xpm-1992-05-14-ss-3085-story.html.
———. "The Untold Story." *LAWeekly*, April 26–May 2, 2002.
Lee, Julia. *Biting the Hand: Growing Up Asian in Black and White America*. New York: Henry Holt and Company, 2023.
Lee, Michele. "China Has Opened Police Stations in US and Canada to Monitor Chinese Citizens: Report." Fox News, September 29, 2022. foxnews.com/world/chinaopened-overseas-police-stations-us-canada-monitor-chinese-citizens.
Legal Information Institute. "Ex parte Mitsuye Endo." law.cornell.edu/supremecourt/text/323/283.
Leonhardt, David. "Truth, Fiction, and Lou Dobbs." *The New York Times*, May 30, 2007. nytimes.com/2007/05/business/30Leonhardt.html.
Lifton, Robert J. *The Nazi Doctors: Medical Killing and the Psychology of Genocide*, 2nd ed. New York: Basic Books, 2017.
Lifton, Robert J., and Gregg Mitchell. *Hiroshima in America: Fifty Years of Denial*. New York: G.P. Putnam and Sons, 1995.
Light, Michael T., Jingying He, and Jason P. Robey. "Comparing Crime Rates Between Undocumented Immigrants and Native-Born US Citizens in Texas." *Proceedings of the National Academy of Sciences* vol. 117, no. 5 (December 22, 2020). pnas.org/doi/pdf/10.1073/pnas.2014704117.
Lipman, Francine J. "The 'Illegal' Tax." *Connecticut Public Interest Law Journal* vol. 11, no. 1 (2012), pp. 93–131. papers.ssrn.com/so13/papers.cfm?abstract_id=2025449.
List of Filipino Americans. *Wikipedia*. en.wikipedia.org/wiki/list_of_Filipino_Americans.
List of Korean Americans. *Wikipedia*. en.wikipedia.org/wiki/list_of_Korean_Americans.
List of Vietnamese Americans. *Wikipedia*.en.wikipedia.org/wiki/list_of_Vietnamese Americans.

Lo, T. Wing, and Sharon Ingrid Kwok. "Triads and Tongs." In G. Bruinsma and D. Weisbrud, eds., *Encyclopedia of Criminology and Criminal Justice,* November 27, 2018, pp. 5330–5343.
Loo, Jasmine M. Y., Namrata Raylu, and Tian Pos Oei. "Gambling Among the Chinese: A Comprehensive Review." *Clinical Psychology Review* vol. 28, no. 7 (October, 2008), pp. 1152–1166.
Lu, Jackson, Richard Nisbett, and Michael Morris. "Why East Asians but Not South Asians are Underrepresented in Leadership Positions in the U.S." *Psychological and Cognitive Sciences* vol. 17, no. 9, February 18, 2020, pp. 4590–4600. https://doi.org/10.1073/phas.1918896117.
Luczak, Susan E., and Tamara L. Wall. "Gambling Problems and Comorbidity with Alcohol Use Disorders in Chinese-, Korean-, and White-American College Students." *American Journal of Addictions* vol. 3 (April 25, 2016), pp. 195–202. pubmed.ncbi.nim.nih.gov/269358711.
Malthus, Thomas R. *An Essay on the Principle of Population as It Affects the Future Improvement of Society.* London: J. Johnson, 1798.
Manjeshwar, Sanjana. "America's Forgotten History of Forced Sterilization." *Berkeley Political Review,* September 8, 2023. bpr.berkeley.edu/2022/11/04/America's-forgotten-history-of-forced-sterilization.
Mano, Jackie, and Jessica White. "Everything to Know About American Ninja Warrior Season 15." NBC Insider. nbc.com/nbc-insider/everything-to-know-about-American-ninja.
Marco Polo Book of the Travels. Gutenberg.org/files/10636/10636-h.htm.
Margolin, Cathy. "10 Things You Need to Know About the Asian Diet." *Huffington Post,* October 8, 2013.
Markel, Howard, and Alexandra M. Stern. "The Fairness of Germs: The Persistent Association of Immigrants and Disease in American Society." *Milbank Quarterly* vol. 80, no. 4 (December, 2002), pp. 757–788. Onlinelibrary.wiley.com/doi/10.1111/1468–0009.00030.
Maruyama, Noah. "Identity Crisis of the Sansei and the Concentration Camp." Sansei Legacy Project, 1994.
Mathews, Mathew, and Rachel Volberg. "Impact of Problem Gambling on Financial, Emotional and Social Well-Being of Singaporean Families." *International Gambling Studies* vol. 13, no. 1 (October 31, 2012), pp. 127–140.
["McCarran-Walter Act"]. *Congressional Record—Senate,* March 2, 1953, p. 1518.
McIntosh, Peggy. "White Privilege: Unpacking the Invisible Knapsack." *Peace and Freedom,* July/August, 1989. psychology.umbc.edu/wp-content/uploads/sites/57/2016/10/white=privilege_mcintosh-1989.pdf.
"Migration and Gender." Pew Research Center. July 5, 2006. pewresearch.org/Hispanic/2006/07/Oa5/ii-migration-and-gender.
Miller, Joan I. "Spies in America: German Espionage in the United States 1935–1945." MA thesis, Portland State University, 1984. https://doi.org/10.15760/etd.5463.
Miller, L. "Deracialization or Body Fashion? Cosmetic Surgery and Body Modification in Japan." *Asian Studies Review* vol. 45, no. 2 (2021), pp. 217–237.
Miller, Stuart C. *The Unwelcome Immigrant: The American Image of the Chinese, 1785–1882.* Berkeley: University of California Press, 1969.
Minear, Richard H. *Dr. Seuss Goes to War: The World War II Editorial Cartoons of Theodor Seuss Geisel.* New York: The New Press, 2001.
Minetor, Randi. *New York Immigrant Experience.* Guilford, CT: Globe Pequot Press, 2010.
Mishra, Neha. "India and Colorism: The Finer Nuances." *Washington University Global Studies Law Review* vol. 14, no. 4 (2015), pp. 725–750.
Miyakawa, Edward. *Tule Lake.* Waldport, OR: House by the Sea Publishing Company, 1979.
Miyoshi, Nobu. "Identity Crisis of the Sansei and the Concentration Camp." Sansei Legacy Project, 1994.

Monk, Jr., Ellis P. "The Cost of Color: Skin Color, Discrimination, and Health Among African Americans." *American Journal of Sociology* vol. 121, no. 2 (September 2015), pp. 396–444.
Moy, Michael. "Chinatown Gang Stories." YouTube.
Muller, Eric L. "Betrayal on Trial: Japanese Treason in World War II." *North Carolina Law Review* vol. 82, no. 5 (2004).
Munson, Curtis B. "Report on Japanese on the West Coast of the United States." *Hearings, 79th Congress, 1st Session. Joint Committee of the Investigation of the Pearl Harbor Attack.* Washington, D.C.: U.S. Government Printing Office, 1946. lib.washington:edu/special/collections/exhibits/Harmony/exhibit/intro#~text=%20not%20 japanese%20in%20culture.
Murphy, Frank. *San Diego Tribune.* sandiegotribune.com/news/local-history/story/2021-02-19/from-the-archives-1976-wwii-japanese-internment-order-Resented#~text=Ford%20signed%20a%20proclamation%20formally.sh...
Mystal, Elie. "Conservatives Don't Actually Have an Argument for Killing Affirmative Action." *The Nation*, November 11, 2022.
Nagata, Donna K. *Legacy of Injustice: Exploring the Cross-Generational Impact of Japanese American Internment.* New York: Plenum Press, 1993.
Nam, Daniel, and George Hicks. "2018 Asian Gambling Prevention Project." Asian American Community Services, Maryhaven, OH.
National Archives. "Remarks on Signing the Bill Providing Restitution for the Wartime Internment of Japanese American Civilians." https://www. reaganlibrary-gov/archives/speech/remarks-signing-bill-providing-restitution-wartime-internment-japanese-american.
Neill, Alexander Sutherland. *Summerhill: A Radical Approach to Child Rearing.* Oxford: Hart Publishing Company, 1960.
_____. *Summerhill School: A New of Childhood.* New York: St. Martin's Griffin, 1995.
Ngai, Mae. *The Chinese Question.* New York: W.W. Norton, 2021.
Nicholson, Herbert. *Violent Odyssey: Herbert Nicholson in and Out of America's Concentration Camps,* eds. Michi Weglyn and Betty E. Mitson. Upland, CA: Brinks Printing, 1978.
Nisbett, Richard. *Intelligence and How to Get It: Why Schools and Culture Count.* New York: W.W. Norton, 2008.
NoNo Boys. https://www.aasc.ucla.edu/storybooks/suyana/lc_nonos.aspx.
Nowak, Donald E., and Ariel M. Aloe. "The Prevalence of Pathological Gambling Among College Students: A Meta Analytic Synthesis, 2005–2013." *Journal of Gambling Behavior* vol. 30 (2014), pp. 819–843.
Nowrasteh, Alex, and Robert Orr. "Immigration and the Welfare State: Immigrant and Native Use Rates and Benefit Levels for Means Tested Welfare and Entitlement Programs," May 10, 2018, *Immigration and Policy Brief #5.* At: cato.org//immigration-research-policy-brief/immigration-welfare-state-immigrant-native-use-rates-benefit.
Nowrasten, Alex. "Immigration and Crime—What the Research Says." catoinstitute.org/blog/migration-crime-what-research-says.
"Number of Recorded Deaths of Migrants in the Mediterranean Sea." statista.com/statistics/1082077/deaths-of-migrants-in-the-Mediterranean-Sea.
Ogburn, William F. *Social Change,* rev. ed. New York: Viking, 1950.
Okada, John. *No-No Boy.* Seattle: University of Washington Press, 1979.
Olsen, Steve. *Mapping Human History.* Boston: Mariner Books, 2002.
Painter, Matthew A., Malcolm P. Holmes, and Jenna Bateman. "Skin Tone, Race/Ethnicity, and Wealth Inequality Among New Immigrants." *Social Forces* vol. 94, no. 3 (March 1, 2016), pp. 1153–1185.
Palmer, Alex W. "How TikTok Became a Diplomatic Crisis." *The New York Times Magazine*, December 25, 2022, pp. 22–27,46–49.
Pan, Arnold. "Reflections on the L.A. Civil Unrest: Thirty Years After 4/29/92." *Amerasia Journal*, May 10, 2022. tandfonfile.com/journals/ramj20/Collections/reflections_on_the_LA_civil_unrest.

Pan, Deanna. "Asians Are an Afterthought: Asian American Students at BPS Report Feeling Less Safe, More Undervalued." *Boston Globe*, March 20, 2023. bostonglobe.com/2023/03/20/metro/Asian-students-bps-report.

Patraporn, R. Varisa, Paul Ong, and Chhandara Pech. "Wealth Inequality Among Asian Americans: The Continuing Significance of Ethnicity and Immigration." *Asian American Policy Review*, April 16, 2021. aapr.hkspublications.org/2021/04/16/wealth-inequality-among-asian-americans-the-continuing-significance-of-ethnicity-and-immigration.

Peri, Giovanni. "Do Immigrant Workers Depress Wages of Native Workers?" *IZA World of Labor*, May 2014. wol.iza.org/uploads/articles/42/pdfs/do-immigrant-workers-depress-the-wages-of-native-workers.pdf.

Perrin, Linda. *Coming to America: Immigrants from the Far East*. New York: Delacorte Press, 1980.

Petersen, William. "Success Story: Japanese-American Style." *The New York Times Magazine*, January 9, 1966.

Peterson, Joel. "The Surprising Facts Behind Korean Child Abandonment." *Huffpost*, October 10, 2017. huffpost.com/entry/the-surprising-facts-behind-Korean-child-abandonment_b_59dc0516e4bOb48cd8eOa5be.

"Philippine-American War, 1899–1902." Office of the Historian. history.state.gov/milestones/1899–1913/war.

Pillalamarri, Akhilesh. "Where Did Indians Come From?" *The Diplomat*, part 1, 2019. thediplomat.com/2019/01/unraveled-where-indians-come-from-part 1.

Pinker, Steven. *The Blank Slate: The Modern Denial of Human Nature*. New York: Penguin Press Science, 2003.

Pisani, Joseph, and Theo Francis. "These TikTok Stars Made More Than CEOs." *The Wall Street Journal*, January 13, 2023. https://www.wsj.com/story/these-tiktok-stars-made-more-than-ceos-d5bb8fd2.

"Plastic Surgery Statistics Report." American Society of Plastic Surgeons, 2023. plasticsurgery.org/documents/news/statistics/2020/plastic-surgery-statistics/2020/plastic-surgery-statistics-full-report-2020.pdf.

"Poverty Myth: Immigrants Come to the U.S. to Use Welfare." ATD Fourth World U.S.A., September 6, 2018. atdfourthworld-usa.org/latest-news/immigrants-come-use-welfare.

"Power Rangers." *Wikipedia*. en.wikipedia.org/wiki/power_rangers.

"President Trump Signs the Farm Bill Making Dog and Cat Meat Illegal in the United States." Associated Press, December, 21, 2018. wrdw.com/content/News/President-Trump-signs-the-farm-bill-making-dog-and-cat-meat-illegal-in-the-united-states-503308841.html.

Price, John A. "Gambling in Traditional Asia." *Anthropologia* vol. 14 (1972), pp. 157–180.

Pringle, David. *St. James Guide to Horror, Ghost and Gothic Writers*. London: St.James Press, 1998.

Quammen, David. "Points of Origin." *The New York Times Magazine*, July 30, 2023, pp. 20–27, 42–43, 45.

Rabinowitz, Hannah, Evan Perez, and Lauren del Valle. "FBI Arrests Two Alleged Chinese Agents and Dozens With Working Inside US to Silence Dissidents." *CNN*, April 18, 2023. cnn.com/2023/04/17/politics/fbi-chinese-agents/indes.html.

Raftery, Erin. "Korean War Babies Still Searching for G.I. Fathers." *USA Today*. usatoday.com/story/news/nation/2015/07/26/Korean-war-orphans/30630161.

Raija, Richard, and Alyssa Leng. "Revising Down the Rise of China." Lowry Institute, March 15, 2022. lowryinstitute.org/publications/revising-down-rise-china.

Rao, Pavitha. "Paying a High Price for Skin Bleaching." *Africa Renewal*, April 9, 2019. un.org/africarenewal/magazine/April-2019-july-2019/paying-high-price-skin-bleaching.

Raphelson, Samantha. "One Man's Mission to Bring Home 'Americans' Born During Vietnam War." *National Public Radio*, July 12, 2018. npr.org/2018/07/12628398153/one-mans-mission-to-bring-home-americans-born-during-vietnam-war.

Raspail, Jean. *The Camp of the Saints*. France: Robert Laffont, 1973.
Relethford, John. *Reflections of Our Past: How History Is Revealed in Our Genes*. Cambridge, MA: Westview Press, 2003.
"Remembering Pearl Harbor. A Pearl Harbor Fact Sheet." The National WWII Museum. www.nationalww2museum.org.
"Revenue of the Video Game Consoles Market Worldwide from 2019 to 2029." June 2024. https://www.statista.com/forecasts/1196090/revenue-video-game-consoles-worldwide.
Ridley, Matt. *Genome: The Evolution of a Species in 23 Chapters*. New York: HarperCollins, 2000.
Ringle, Kenneth D. "Ringle Report on Japanese Internment (12/30/1941)." famous-trials.com/korematsu/2567-ringle-report-on-japanese-internment-12-30-1941.
Rinker, Dipali, et al. "Racial and Ethnic Differences in Problem Gambling Among College Students." *Journal of Gambling Studies* vol. 332 (June 2016), pp. 581–590.
Rios, Edwin. "Hate Incidents Against Asian Americans Continue to Surge, Study Finds." *The Guardian*, July 21, 2022.
Rohmer, Sax. *The Mystery of Dr. Fu-Manchu*. London: Methuen, 1913.
———. *The Return of Dr. Fu-Manchu*. New York: A.L. Burt and Company, 1916.
Romano, Renee. "The Trauma of Internment." *The Washington Post*, June 25, 2018.
Rosenfeld, Alan. "German and Italian Detainees." *Encyclopedia Densho*. https://encyclopedia.densho.org/German_and_Italian_detainees.
Safeguard Defenders. "No Room to Run: China's Expanded Mis(use) of INTERPOL Since the Rise of Xi Jinping." 2021. https://safeguarddefenders.com/en/no-room-run.
Saffa, Joan. *Honor Bound: A Personal Journey*. Film, 1995.
Sandholtz, Nathan, Lynn Langton, and Michael Planty. "Hate Crime Victimization, 2003–2011." US Department of Justice, Bureau of Justice Statistics, March, 2013.
Sang-Hun, Choe. "A Painful Past Behind South Korean Adoptions." *The New York Times*, September 17, 2023, pp. 1, 16.
Schumacher, E.F. *Small Is Beautiful*. New York: HarperCollins, 1973.
Shankar, Ravi. "It's All in the Genes: Does DNA Call the Bluff on Aryan Invasion Theory?" New Indian Press, September 15, 2019.
"Shaolin Monastery." *Wikipedia*. wikipedia.org/wiki/shaolin_monastery.
Sharp, Abbie. "Escape the Corset." *Leeds Human Rights Journal*, November, 29, 2019. hrj.leeds.ac.uk/2019/11/29/escape-the-corset.
Sikh American Legal Defense and Education Fund. Sa/def.org/our-history.
Sikh Coalition. sikhcoalition.org/our-work/preventing/hate-and-discrimination/hate-crime-tracking-and-prevention.
Smith, Gregory A., Michael Rotolo, and Patricia Tevington. "3 Views of the U.S. as a 'Christian Nation' and Opinions About 'Christian Nationalism.'" Pew Research Center, October, 27, 2022. pewresearch.org/religion/2022/10/27p/views-of-the-us-as-a-christian-nation-and-opinions-about-christian-nationalism.
Sniderman, Paul, and Thomas Piazza. *The Scar of Race*. Boston: Belknap Press, 1995.
Solomon, Harvey. *Such Splendid Prisons: Diplomatic Detainment in America During World War II*. Lincoln: University of Nebraska Press, 2020.
Sone, Monica. *Nisei Daughter*. Seattle: University of Washington Press, 1953.
Soni, Saket. *The Great Escape: The True Story of Forced Labor and Immigrant Dreams in America*. Chapel Hill, NC: Algonquin Books, 2023.
Spencer, Herbert. *The Synthetic Philosophy*. New York: Appleton and Company, 1921.
Sperber, Jonathan. "Infectious Diseases in the Twentieth Century." University of Missouri College of Arts and Sciences, May 16, 2020. history.missouri.edu/node/14.
"The State of Science and Engineering 2022." National Science Foundation, Science and Engineering Indicators. ncses.nsf.gov/pubs/nsb20221.
Stoddard, Lothrop. *The Rising Tide of Color Against White World Supremacy*. New York: Charles Scribner's Sons, 1920.
Stop AAPI Hate. "Stop the Blame." stopaapihate.org/2023/09/21/stop-the-blame-press-release.

———. "Two Years and Thousands of Voices: What Community-Generated Data Tells Us About AAPI Hate." National Report, October 2022.
Stovall, Tyler. *White Freedom: The Racial History of an Idea*. Princeton: Princeton University Press, 2021.
"Summary of the Commission on Wartime Relocation and Internment of Civilians." archives.gov/files/research/Japanese-americans/justice-denied/summary.pdf.
Sung, Betty Lee. *The Story of the Chinese in America*. New York: Collier Books, 1967.
Supreme Court. justice.gov/sites/default/files/briefs/2022/08/23/20–1199_Harvard-final-revised-pdf.
Takei, George, Justin Eisinger, Steven Scott, and Harmony Becker. *They Called Us Enemy*. San Diego: Top Shelf Productions, 2019.
"Teenage Mutant Ninja Turtles." Wikipedia. en.wikipedia.org/wiki/teenage_Mutant_Ninja_turtles.
Thrasher, Frederick. *The Gang: A Study of 1313 Gangs in Chicago*. Chicago: University of Chicago Press, 1938.
Tondo, Lorenzo, and Emmanuel Akinwotu. "People of Color Fleeing Ukraine Attacked by Polish Nationalists." *The Guardian*, March 2, 2022. theguardian.com/global-development/2022/mar/02/people-of-colour-fleeing-ukraine-attacked-by-polish-nationalists.
Townsend, Matthew. "How the Battling Robots of Transformers Built a $14 Billion Empire." *Bloomberg News*. https://www.bloomberg.com/news/articles/2018-12-20/Hasbro-reboots-transformers-for-gen-x-dads-and-their-daughters#xj4y7vzkg.
Trump, Donald. "Presidential Announcement." YouTube.com/watch?v=apjnfkysibm.
Tuan, Mia. *Forever Foreigners or Honorary Whites? The Asian Ethnic Experience Today*. New Brunswick: Rutgers University Press, 1999.
Tunell, Alex. "The Real Self Culture Report: How Americans Feel About Plastic Surgery." realself.com/news/culture-report.
Turner, Ben. "World's Population Could Plummet to 6 Billion by the End of the Century, Study Suggests." *Live Sciences*, March 27, 2023. livescience.com/worlds-population-could-plummet-to-six-billion-by-the-end-of-the-century-new-study-suggests.
UNHCR. "Global Displacement Hits Another Record, Capping Decade-Long Rising Trend." June 16, 2022. unhcr.org/news/unhcr-global-displacement-hits-record-capping-decade-long-rising-trend.
United States Senate. Report of the Immigration Commission 349, 1911.
"U.S. Attorney Announces Arrests of Yakuza Leader and Affiliates for International Trafficking of Narcotics and Weapons Including Surface-to-Air Missiles." April 7, 2022. justice.gov/usa-sdny/pr/Manhattan-us-attorney-announces-arrests-yakuza-leader-and-affiliates-international.
U.S. Bureau of Labor Statistics. BLS Report, January 2023. bls.gov/opub/report/race-and-ethnicity/2021/home.htm.
US Census Bureau. census.gov/library/stories/2021/08/improved-race-ethnicity-measures-reveal-united-states-population-much-more-multiracial.html.
"The U.S. Mainland: Growth and Resistance." Library of Congress. loc.gov/classroom-materials/immigration/Japanese/the-us-mainland-growth-and-resistance.
VerBruggen, Robert. "Racial Preferences on Campus: Trends in Asian Enrollment at US Colleges." The Manhattan Institute, April, 2022. media4.manhattan-institute.org/sites/default/files/vergruggen-trends-in-asian-enrollment-at-us-colleges.pdf.
Viswantha, Aruna, and Kate O'Keeffe. "Harvard Chemistry Chairman Charged on Alleged Undisclosed Ties to China." *Wall Street Journal*, January 28, 2020. wsj.com/articles/harvards-chemistry-chair-charged-on-alleged-undisclosed-ties-to-china-11580228768.
Vitali, Ali, Kasie Hunt, and Frank Thorp V. "Trump Referred to Haiti and African Nations as 'Shithole' Countries." NBC News, January 11, 2018. nbcnews.com/politics/whitehouse/trump-referred-haiti-african-countries-shithole-nations-n836946.
Wagner, Richard. *The Foundations of the Nineteenth Century*. New York: John Lane, 1911.

Waite, Ken. "The Bloody History of Anti-Asian Violence in the West." *National Geographic*, May 10, 2021. nationalgeographic.com/history.article/the-bloody-history-of-antiasian-violence-in-the-west.
Wallace, Nina. "Sexual Abuse, Silence, and Japanese American Incarceration." densho.org/catalyst/sexual-violence-silence-japanese-american-incarceration.
Wang, Feng. "China's Population Destiny: The Looming Crisis." Brookings Institution, September 30, 2010. brookings.edu/articles/chinas-population-destiny-the-looming-crisis.
Wang, Francis Kai-Hwa. "#Remodel Minority." NBC News. nbcnews.com/news/Asian-america/50-years-later-challenging-model-minority-myth-through-Remodelminority-n493911.
Watkins, Eli, and Abby Phillip. "Trump Decries Immigrants from 'Shithole Countries' Coming to the US." *CNN*, January 12, 2018. cnn.com/2018/01/11/politics/immigrants.
Weber, Max. *The Protestant Ethic and the Spirit of Capitalism: and Other Writings*, ed. Peter Baehar and Gordon C. Wells. New York: Penguin Twentieth Century Classics Edition, 2002.
Wells, Spencer. *The Journey of Man*. Princeton: Princeton University Press, 2003.
Wen, H. "Gentle Yet Manly: xiao xian rou-Made Cosmetic Surgery and Neoliberal Consumer Culture in China." *Asian Studies Review* vol. 45, no. 2 (2021), pp. 253–271.
"Wen Ho Lee." *Wikipedia.* en.wikipedia.org/wiki/wen_Ho_Lee.
West, Cornel. *Race Matters*. Boston: Beacon Press, 1993.
Wicks, Noah. "Bill Banning Foreign Governments from Buying Farmland Nears Passage in N.D." *Agri Pulse*, April 6, 2023. agri-pulse.com/articles/19205-bill-prohibiting-foreign-government-from-purchasing-farmland-nears-passage-in-north-dakota.
———. "Despite Holding Little US Land, China Remains Focus of Foreign Ownership Discussion." *Agri Pulse*, December 1, 2021. agri-pulse.com/articles/16846-despite-holding-little-us-land-china-remains-focus-of-foreign-farmland-ownership-discussion.
Wikipedia: "Densho: The Japanese American Legacy Project." en.wikipedia.org/wiki/Densho_/The_Japanese_American_Legacy_Project.
Wolf, Jessica. "2021 Hollywood Diversity Report: Audiences Showed Up for Diverse Films in Theaters, Online." *UCLA Newsroom*, April 22, 2021. newsroom.ucla.edu/releases/2021-hollywood-and-diversity-report.
Wong, Huiyao. "China's National Talent Plan: Key Measures and Objectives." Brookings Institution, November 23, 2010. brookings.edu/articles/chinas-national-talent-plan-key-measures-and-objectives.
Wong, Kristin, and Kathryn Wong. *Fierce Compassion: The Life of Abolitionist Donaldina Cameron*. Encinitas, CA: New Earth Enterprises, 2012.
Wu, Yuning, and Adam Augustyn. "Chinese Exclusion Act." *Encyclopedia Britannica*. britannica.com/biography/chester-a-arthur.
Xu, Adam. "China-Owned Parent Company of Tik Tok Among Top Spenders on Internet Lobbying." VOA, February 13, 2023. voanews.com/a/china-owned-parent-company-of-tiktok-among-top-spenders-on-internet-lobbying-1696189/html.
"Yakuza." *Wikipedia.* en.wikipedia.org/wiki/yakuza.
Yam, Kimmy. "70% of Asian Americans Support Affirmative Action. Here's Why Misconceptions Persist." NBC News, November 14, 2020. nbcnews.com/news/Asian-America/70-asian-americans-support-affirmative-action-here-s-why-misconceptions-n1247806.
Yang, Jeff, Phil Yu, and Philip Wang. *Rise: A History of Asian America from the Nineties to Now*. New York: Mariner Books, 2022.
Yang, Lin. "Controversial Confucius Institutes Returning to U.S. Schools Under New Name." VOA, June 27, 2022. voanews.com/a/controversial-Confucius-institutes-returning-to-u-s-schools-under-new-name/6635906.htm.
Yang, Wesley. *The Souls of Yellow Folk: Essays*. New York: W.W. Norton and Company, 2018.

Yasir, Sameer, and Jeffrey Gettleman. "India Debates Skin-Tone Bias as Beauty Companies Alter Ads." *The New York Times,* June 28, 2020. nytimes.com/2020/06/28/world/asia/india-skin-color-unilever.html.

Yi, Se-Hyoung, and William T. Hoston. "Demystifying Americanness: The Model Minority Myth and the Black-Korean Relationship." *Journal of Ethnic and Cultural Studies* vol. 7, no. 2 (2020).

Yip, J., S. Ainsworth, and M.T.H. Hugh. "Beyond Whiteness: Perspectives on The Rise of the Pan-Asian Beauty Ideal." In G.D. Johnson et al., eds., *Race in the Marketplace: Crossing Critical Boundaries*, 73–85. New York: Palgrave Macmillan, 2019.

Yu, Charles. *Interior Chinatown: A Novel.* New York: Vintage, 2020.

Index

Abbott, Greg 195*n*19
Adrian, Jack 124, 200*n*40
affirmative action 149–54
African immigrant deaths 166
Agee, James 91
Aguinaldo, Emilio 32
Ahn, Philip 126
Ainsworth, S. 206*n*49
Alegria, Analycia A. 191*n*6
alien land laws 73–4, 106
aliens 209*n*34
Allyn, Bobby 211*n*59
Aloe, Ariel M. 191*n*7
American Association of Physicians of Indian Origin 30
American born Chinese aka ABC 67
American Homecoming Act 142
American Immigration Council 190*n*25
American Ninja Warrior 129
American Society of Plastic Surgeons 205*n*42
Americans United for the Separation of Church and State 208*n*25
Anand, Priya 202*n*77
Anderson, Carol 206*n*3
Angel Island 53
Animal Protection Act 131
anime 129–30
anti–Asian hate crimes 94
Anti-Defamation League (aka ADL) 96, 166, 197*n*7, 197*n*11
Apana, Chang 114
Aquilino, John C. 209*n*41
Arcidiacono, Peter 205*n*37
Arms Control and Export Control Act 179
Arnand, Priya 146, 204*n*10
Aronson, Joshua 203*n*82
Article 7 197*n*16
Aryan myth 137, 162

Aryans 27–8
Ash, Cay Van 200*n*38
Asian-American college attendance 149–50
Asian-American playbook 148–9
Asian: assimilation 11; continent 14; gangs 62; immigrants 4, 171; population 14; stereotypes 7–8, 113–158; wealth gap 137–8
Asian Pacific American Center 144
Asian Studies Review 157
Asians in U.S. labor force 146
"ATD Fourth World USA" 190*n*23
atom bomb 86
Augustyn, Adam 187*n*35

Babcock, Joseph 61
Badrinathan, Sumitra 188*n*47
Bae, Linda 157
Baehar, Peter 187*n*45
Bakula, Scott 139
Ballingrud, David 192*n*19
bamboo ceiling 9, 137, 145–8
Banga, Ajaypal S. 146
Bankhurst, Adam 201*n*50
Barnes, Julian E. 209*n*43
Barr, William 210*n*50
Basu, Moni 188*n*48
Bataan 88
Batalova, Jeanne 188*n*58, 209*n*36
Bateman, Jenna 138, 202*n*78
Battle Hymn of the Tiger Mother 9
Battle of Midway 71
Bee, Frederick 23
Belkiempis, Victoria 207*n*13
Berry, Shawn 98
Bhagavad Gita 90
Bhatia, Sabeer 30
Bhatt, Ajay 30
Bickers, Robert 124

227

Biddle, Francis 193*n*4
Biden, Joe 38, 180; administration 104, 197*n*4
Biggers, Earl D. 114, 122, 200*n*5
Bishop, Sanford 107
Black Korea 110
Black Lives Matter 111
blaming the victim 21, 162
blepharoplasty 154
Bollywood 31, 156
Borjas, George 190*n*15
Boston public schools 102
Boumediene, Houari 208*n*29
Boundless 190*n*19, *n*28
Bowers, Robert 166
Boxer Rebellion 4
Bradley, Tom 110
Braga, Anthony 192*n*28
Brahmans 28
Brennan Center for Justice 179
Breivik, Anders 166
Brewer, Lawrence 97–8
Brigham, Carl 48, 163–4, 190*n*26, 207*n*16
British 32
Brown, Abram 198*n*19
Brown, Michael 111
Brown v. Board of Education 152
BTS Army 111
Buck, Pearl S. 15, 186*n*8
Buck v. Bell 163
Budiman, Abby 185–6*n*4, 188*n*58
Burakumin 69
Bureau of Justice Statistics 100–1, 197*n*12
Burton, Jeffery F. 195*n*18
Bush, George H.W. 86, 110
Bushido 125
Butts, Dylan 209*n*42
Byrd, James, Jr. 97–8
ByteDance 104

Cameron, Donaldina 22
Campu podcast 80
Camus, Renaud 161, 165–7, 207*n*7, 207*n*14
Cantwell, Maria 211*n*59
Cao, Lan 117, 121, 200*n*15
Capoeira 125
Carradine, David 8, 115, 126
Carter, Jimmy 85
caste system 28
Cato Institute 50, 179, 190*n*24
Celebuski, Carin 202*n*74
Centers for Disease Control and Prevention 189*n*3
Central Pacific Railroad 20–21

chain migration 49, 164
Chamba (chamber) pots 78
Chamberlain, Houston S. 53, 161, 191*n*35
Chan, Alan K.K. 60, 191*n*9
Chan, Charlie 8, 114–120
Chan, Jackie 127
Chan, Peter 192*n*18
Chang, Gordon 20, 186*n*5, 204*n*16
chap ji kee 58
Chen, Meredith 209*n*42
Chen, Steve 8, 26
Cherlin, Andrew 202*n*74
Chew, Shou Zi 103
Chin, Ava 93, 159
Chin, Frank 114, 117, 200*n*2
Chin, Ko-lin 64–5, 67–8, 192*n*27
Chin, Margaret 148–9, 204*n*10
Chin, Vincent 94
Chinatowns 7, 21, 186*n*5
Chinese: agriculture 24–5; Communist party 103, 105; cuisine 26; employment in U.S. 24; exclusion act 5, 22–3, 89, 106, 120, 141, 181; fashion design 26; gangs 64–6; higher education 26; initiative 178–9; laundry 24; national intelligence law 103, 105; parenting 134–5; philanthropy 26; talent program 176, 178
Chinese Americans 15; economic impact 26; planning council 26
Cho, Ellen 210*n*50
Chopra, Deepak 31
Chou, Rosalind 10
Christian, Nicole 192*n*19
Chu, John 9
Chua, Amy 9, 134, 145, 201*n*62, 202*n*67–8
Civil rights movement 116
Clinton administration 50, 67, 81, 184
Club of Rome 209*n*33
Collins, Kris 105
Collisson, Craig 196*n*27
colorism 31, 157
Commission on the Wartime Relocation and Internment of Civilians 85–6, 196*n*26
Committee of 100 7, 24–5, 148–150, 178, 187*n*36, 204*n*162, 210*n*52, 210*n*55, 210*n*57
concentration camps 71–92; *see also* war relocation camps
Confucius Institutes 175–6
Congressional Record 191*n*38
conservative thought 207–8*n*22
coolies 17–18

Index

Covid-19 3, 7, 55, 93, 96, 102
Craft, Robert 142
Crazy Rich Asians 9
Crusius, Patrick 166
cultural lag 45
Cyrus Tang Foundation 26

dacoits 122
Dang, Laura 202n63
Davuluri, Nina 31, 157
De Brauw, Alan 190n15
De Gobineau, Alex Comte 53, 161, 163, 190n35
De Guzman, Chad 191n4
Delvalle, Laura 211n60
Densho Encyclopedia 79, 193n3
DeSantis, Ron 108, 160, 179, 195n19, 207n22, 209n39
Devereux, Stephen 182n2
DeWitt, John L. 83–5
Discrimination: against Chinese 25; of Asians in U.S. labor force 146–7
Dobbs, Lou 55
dog meat consumption 132, 201n53
Donegan, T.J. 201n50
Dr. Seuss 90, 196n44
Douglas, William O. 84
Du, Soon Ja 109
DuBois, W. E. B. 8, 190n17
Dunham, Carolyn B. 198n30
Dunnett, Madeline 200n49
Duryea, Bill 192n19

Eals, Clay 200n44
East Indians 27, 31
Eaton, Shirley 124
Ebers, Ronald 94
Economist Intelligence Unit 187n41
Edwards, Jonathan 187n45
effects of immigrant labor on American society 47
Ehrlich, Anne 189n4
Ehrlich, Paul 189n4, 208n31
Eisenhower, Dwight 87
Elfving-Hwang, J. 206n49
Ellis Island 20, 49, 54
Emmanuel, Kavitha 157
Emperor Hirohito 89
Encyclopaedia Britannica 186n11
Endo, Mitsuye 84–5
Enola Gay 88
epicanthic fold 4
"escape the corset" 157
Eshoo, Anna 103
espionage 175–81; of Japanese 75
ethnocentrism 16

eugenics 162–4
Eurasian Adam 13
exchange visitor program 33
Executive Order 9066 72, 83
Executive Order 9102 84
extortion 65

Fahy, Charles 83, 86
fair skin 156
Farago, Andrew 200n45
Fariver, Masood 211n60
Farrell, Mary M. 195n18
fascism 162
fat man 88
Feagin, Joe 10
Federal Bureau of Investigation (FBI) 99, 175, 178–9, 197n10
Fee, James Alger 83
Fetchit, Stepin 117
Fields, James A., Jr. 165
"The Fight for Representation: The State of Chinese Americans 2022" 187n37
Filipino Americans 32, 33
Fisher, Jamie 200n48
Floyd, George 111
Ford, Gerald 85
forever foreigners 158–60
"The Formation of Human Populations in South and Central Asia" 187n43
Fort Sill 82
Fortenberry, Jeff 107
FourPaws 132, 201n56
Fourteenth Amendment 74–5, 150–1
Fox, Stephen 194n7
Fox Movie Channel 117
Francis, Theo 198n19
Frayer, Lauren 206n48
Freeman, Abigail 198n19
Fresh Off the Boat 139–41
Frey, William 209n37
From Foundation to Frontiers 24
Fu Manchu 8, 200n39
Fuentes, Nick 195n19
Fuertes, Jairo N. 188n51
Fufeng Group 108
Fujii, Sei 106, 198n24
Fung, Yuan-Cheng 26

Gallardo, Lisa H. 188n58
Gamblers of the Old West 191n5
gambling 6, 56–70; in China 58
Gandhi, Mahatma 28
Gangnam Street 154–5
Gates, Robert 179
Gawande, Atul 31
Geary Act 23, 141

Gendron, Payton 166
Genpei War 128
gentlemen's agreement 73
German, Michael 179
Gettleman, Jeffrey 206n48
Global Chinese Philanthropy Initiative 187n38
"Gold Mountain" 20
Golden Venture 67
Goldstein, Dana 208n22
Graham, Jack 205n40
Gramlich, John 209n35
Grant, Madison 18, 48, 161, 190n16, 207n14
Great Leap Forward 4, 161
GREEN card 49
Gregg, Avani 105
Groves, Leslie R., Jr. 91
Guangdong province 21-2
Gupta, Prachi 202n62
gurdwara 30, 95
Gymdesk 200n42

Hadero, Haleluya 210n59
Haley, Nikki 182
Hamer, Fannie Lou 163
Hanamura, Wendy 195n18
Hanke, Ken 120, 200n23
Hanna, Mary 209n36
Hanna-Barbera 115
Hannah-Jones, Nikole 189n12
Hao, Karen 210n50
Harari, Yuval N. 207n6
Harijans 28
Harlins, Latasha 109
Harris, Kamala 182
Harth, Lauren 211n60
Harvard College 114
hatchet men 22, 65
hate crimes 7, Ch. 5, 95
hate groups 11, ch. 8
Hayes, Rutherford B. 18
Hazelhurst, Beatrice 205n39
He, Jingying 190n32
Hedges, Chris 189n1
Henderich, Holly 211n60
Henderson, Russell 98
Henley, D. 206n49
Herrnstein, Richard 137, 164, 207n18
Hersey, John 91
Herzig-Yoshinaga, Aiko 84
Hess, Abigail J. 189n14
Heyer, Heather 165
Hicks, George 60, 192n11
highbinders 22
Hilburn, Matt 201n60

Hillsborough Humanities Council 136
Hinduism 28-9
Hirabashi, Gordon 83, 86
Hiroshima 87-8, 91
Holloway, Kali 205n36
Hollywood Diversity Report 200n14
Holmes, Malcolm D. 138, 202n78
Holmes, Oliver W. 163
homo erectus 13
homo sapiens 13
Hong, Cathy Park 10, 11, 143-5
Hong Kong 64, 173-4
Hoover, J. Edgar 194n7
Horowitz, Adam 205n35
Horton Hears a Who 90
Hoston, William T. 111, 199n35
Houdini, Harry 123
Houston, Jean W. 194n12, 196n49
HR442 6
Hswen, Yulin 95, 197n5
Hu, Anming 177-8
Huang, Eddie 9, 140, 201n51, 202n81
Huang, Jensen 146
Huang, Yunte 113, 117-8, 200n12
Huawei 104
Huet, Ellen 146, 202n77, 204n10
Hugh, M.T.H. 206n49
huiguans 21
Hull, Cordell 193n1
Humane Society International 131
Hung Mun Triad 64
Hunt, Kasie 207n20
Hyun, Jane 146, 203n9

Ice Cube 110
immigrants 43-55; and crime 51-2; and illness 52; spending 51; and taxes 50-1
Immigration and Nationality Act of 1962 (aka McCarran-Walter act) 54
Immigration and Naturalization Act (aka Hart-Celler Act) 5, 23, 33, 37, 55, 63, 66, 143, 171
Indian American Attitude Survey 31
Inouye, Daniel 81
Institute for Taxation and Economic Policy 50
Intelligence Report 198n22
interethnic antagonism 108
International Organization for Migration 190n22
Interpol 211n60
Irish laborers 19, 21
Irons, Peter 84
Issei 39, 73, 79

Index

Jackson, Ketanji B. 151, 206n1
Jackson, O'Shea (aka Ice Cube) 199n34
Jain, Sunny 205n47
Jaisohn, Philip (aka Jae-Pil Seo) 37
Jalonick, Mary C. 210n59
Japanese Americans 38; contributions 40; reparations 75
Japanese internment 6, 7, 71–92
Japanese organized crime 68
Jayapal, Pramila 182
jeet kune do 126–7
Jensen, Arthur 137, 164, 207n16
Jensen, Gwendolyn 75–6, 193n5, 194n9
Jimenez, Thomas 205n35
Jindal, Bobby 182
Jirocho, Shimizu 69
Johnson, A. 192n30
Johnson, Lyndon B. 23
Johnson-Reed Act 89
Jones, Robert P. 208n25

Kagan, Elena 151
Kaiser Wilhelm III 19
Kang, Cecilia 198n18
Kang, D.B. 206n49
Kang, Jay C. 111, 113, 144, 199n36, 203n4
Kaplan, H. Roy 189n6, 189n13, 201n52, 202n73
Kapur, Devesh 188n47
Karim, Jawed 8
Karma 29
Kashiwagi, Sydney 210n55
Katyal, Neal 86, 196n28
Katzenelson, Ira 206n3
Kaur, Brahmjot 201n59
Kay, Jonathan 188n47
Kearney, Denis 23
Kharpal, Arjun 198n17
Khosla, Vinod 30
Kim, Cerrissa 203n83
Kim, David D. 199n32
Kim, John H. 189n61
Kim, Wooksoo 62, 192n12
King, John 97–8
King, Julian 105
King, Rodney 109
King Nala 57–8
Kinsler, Josh 205n37
Kodansha 130
Korean adoptions 141–2
Korean Americans 36; contributions 38, 109–11
Korean War 141
Korematsu, Fred 83–4
Koster, John 193n1
Kramer, Arnold 194n7

Kshatrya 28
Ku Klux Klan 94
Kuhn, Anthony 206n50
Kung Fu 126–7
Kung Fu (TV series) 8, 115
Kurusu, Saburō 193n1
Kwan, Chuck 201n60
Kwan, Kevin 137
Kwok, Sharon I. 64, 192n24

labor discrimination of immigrants 46
Lahiri, Jhumpa 202n75
Lai, Jimmy 174
land ownership in the U.S. 179
Langton, Lynn 197n12
Lapp, Ralph 88
Largent, Charles 200n39
Las Vegas, NV 58
Le, C.N. 192n14
Lederman, Doug 204n13
Lee, Aileen 26
Lee, Alex 205n39
Lee, Bill 22, 56
Lee, Brandon 127
Lee, Bruce 8, 126–7, 200n44
Lee, Christopher 123
Lee, Jenny K. 210n52
Lee, John H. 199n32
Lee, Julia 10, 13, 199n33
Lee, Lydia 189n6
Lee, Michele 197n15
Lee, Raymond 139
Lee, Wen Ho 178, 210n51
Lelling, Andrew 177
Leonhardt, David 191n40
Levy, Stuart J. 130
Li, Jet 127
Li, Xiaojie 210n52
Library of Congress 189n63, 193n3
Lieber, Charles 176–7
Lieu, Ted 27
Lifton, Robert J. 86–90, 196n30, 207n12
Light, Michael T. 190n32
Limehouse 122
Lin, Alfred 26
Lin, Tang-yen 25
Ling, Lisa 139
Linnaeus, Carolus 4
Lipman, Francine 51, 190n27
"Little Boy" 88
Liu, Dong 210n52
Liu, Simu 9, 139
Liu-Po 58
Livingston, Sigmund 96
Lo, T. Wing 64, 192n24
Long, Breckinridge 206n4

Long, Robert A. 105
Loo, Jasmine M.Y. 192n16
Lord, Florence B. 195n18
Lord, Richard W. 195n18
Los Alamos National Laboratory 178
Los Angeles riot 108–12, 144
Los Angeles Times 144
loyalty questions 79–80
Lu, Jackson G. 147, 204n15
Lu, Zhimin 177
Lucky Dragon Casino 61
lucky money 65
Luczak, Susan 59–60, 191n8
Luke, Keye 8, 115, 118–19, 126
Lunar new year 61
Lyons, Patrick 190n20

Macau 58, 191n4
MAGA (aka Make America Great Again) 159–60
Magnuson Act 23
Maheshwari, Sapna 205n45
Mahjongg 6, 60
Malthus, Thomas 43, 168, 208n30
Manchu, Fu 120–24
Manchu-Qing dynasty 63
manga 129–30, 200n49
Manhattan Institute 149
Manhattan Project 86, 89, 91
Manjeshwar, Sanjana 207n13
Manjiro (aka John Mung) 38
Manna, Jackie 200n46
Margolin, Cathy 201n58
Markel, Howard 53, 191n36
martial arts 125
Martin, Ross 115
Maruyama, Hana 78, 194n14–15
Maryvale treatment centers 60
Mathews, Mathew 62, 192n15
McCarran, Patrick 191n38
McCarthy, Joe 54
McIntosh, Peggy 209n39
McKinley, William 32
McKinney, Aaron 98
MD Anderson Center 177
Medicaid expansion 206n2
Mighty Morphin Power Rangers 129
migration out of Africa 13–14
Miller, Joan L. 75, 193n7
Miller, L. 206n49
Miller, Stuart C. 15–16, 186n9
Minetor, Randi 189n11
Mirage Studios 128
Mishra, Neha 188n56
Mishra, Reva 31
Mitchell, Greg 86–90, 196n30

Mitochondrial Eve 13
Miyakawa, Edward 194n16
Miyoshi, Nobu 76, 194n10
model minority 4, 9, 10, 117, 140, 143–158
Moffitt Cancer Center 177
Monk, Ellis P., Jr. 188n51
Moore, Annie 20
Moreland, Mantan 117
Morris, Michael W. 147, 204n15
Mountain of Gold 11
Moy, Michael 192n29
Mughals 32
mui tsais 22
Mukherjhee, Siddhartha 31
Muller, Eric L. 193n6
Munson, Curtis 85, 195n25
Murphy, Brian 30
Murphy, Francis 85
Murray, Charles A. 137, 164, 207n18
Murthy, Vivek 31
Mystal, Elie 205n36

NAACP (National Association for the Advancement of Colored People) 197n9
Nadella, Satya 30
Nagasaki 87
Nagata, Donna 76, 194n4
Naish, J. Carrol 115
Nam, Daniel 60, 192n11
Nanak 29
Narasimhan, Vagheesh 28
Narayen, Shantanu 30
National Archives 196n29
National Crime Victimization Survey 101
National Science Foundation 204n14
National World War II Museum 193n1
Native American protests 116
nature v. nurture 136–7
Neill, A.S. 135, 202n66
New Immigrant Survey 138
new immigrants 53
Newhouse, Dan 107
Ngai, Mae 186n6, 186n13–14, 186n19
Nicholson, Herbert 196n49
"A Night at the Garden" 207n11
Ninjutsu (aka ninpo) 128
Nintendo 130
Nisbett, Richard 147, 202n74, 204n15
Nisei 6, 39, 73, 76, 79–81
Nitz, Michael 94
no-no boys 79
Nomura, Kichisaburo 193n1
Northern Triangle 170

Index 233

Novas, Himilce 117, 121, 200n15
Nowak, Donald E. 191n7
Nowrasteh, Alex 51, 190n31

Oath Keepers 11
Obama, Barack 99
Occidental Board Presbyterian Mission House 22
Oei, Tian Poe S. 192n16
Office of Naval Intelligence 85
Office of the Historian 188n58
Ogburn, William 45, 189n2
Oh, Sandra 139
O'Keeffe, Kate 210n48
Oland, Warner 115, 117, 123
old immigrants 53
Olson, Steve 207n6
Ong, Paul 137
open society funds 97
Opium Wars 4, 17
Oppenheimer, Frank 89
Oppenheimer, J. Robert 89–90, 196n43
Orban, Viktor 97; administration 166
Organization for Economic Cooperation and Development 161
Organization of Chinese Americans 117
organized labor 19
Osaki, Paul 62
othering 2, 24

Page, Wade M. 30, 95
Page Act 22, 50, 121, 141
pai gow 62
Painter, Matthew A. 138, 202n78
Palmer, Alex W. 198n21
Palmeter, Ryan 166–7
Pan, Arnold 199n32
Pan, Deanna 197n14
paper sons 23
Parker, James A. 178
Patel, Kiran 188n54
Patel, Pallavi 188n54
Patraporn, R.V. 137, 202n76
Pearl Harbor 6, 71, 88
Pech, Chhandara 137, 202n76
Pei, I.M. 25
Pence, Charles W. 80
People's Republic of China (aka PRC) 173–76, 178–81
Perez, Evan 211n60
Peri, Giovanni 47–8, 190n15
perpetual foreigners 7, 10, 56, 139
Perrin, Linda 186n23, 186n26, 186n31
Peterson, Joel 203n84
Petrie, Doctor 122
Pettersen, William 143, 203n1

Pew Research Center 190n22
Phillip, Abby 191n39
Piazza, Thomas 102, 197n13
Pichai, Sundar 146
Pidgin English 118
Pierce, Walter 86
Pillalamarri, Akhilesh 188n50
Pinker, Steven 164, 207n19
Pisani, Joseph 198n19
Planty, Michael 197n12
plastic surgery 154–6
Poarch, Bella 104–5
Policy of Attraction 33
Polo, Marco 4, 15, 186n7
population growth 44–5, 168–73
Porath, N. 206n49
Potsdam Conference 87
Powell, Lewis 151
Power Rangers 200n47
Price, John A. 57, 191n3
Pringle, David 200n40
Promontory Point 20
Proud Boys 11, 165
Purple Heart Division (aka 442) 7, 80–1
Purush 28

QAnon 11, 167, 186n12
Qian, Nancy 180
Qing dynasty 64
Quammen, David 185n1

Rabinowitz, Hannah 211n60
racism 118, 123, 125, 165
racist theories 4
Racketeer Influenced and Corrupt Organizations Act (aka RICO) 67
Rae, Addison 104
Raftery, Erin 203n83
Ramaswamy, Vivek 183
Ransom, Tyler 205n37
Rao, Pavitha 205n46
Raphelson, Samantha 203n85
Raspail, Jean 185n2
Raylu, Namrata 192n16
Reagan, Ronald 86
RealSelf 205n39
Red Book 61
Red Notices 211n60
Regimental Combat Team (442) 80–1
Relethford, John 207n6
replacement theory 10, 11, 14, 160–7, 14n2
Report of the Immigration Commission 187n42
Republic of China 64
Republic Pictures 123

restrictive land laws 179
rhinoplasty 154
Richards, Josh 105
Ringle Report 85, 195n24
Rinker, Dipali V. 192n10
Rios, Edwin 185 n2
Roberts, John G., Jr. 150
Robey, George 122
Robey, Jason P. 190n32
Rodgers, Cathy M. 103
Rohmer, Sax 8, 120, 200n28
Rohwer Relocation Center 76
Romano, Renee 75, 194n8
Roof, Dylan 166
Roosevelt, Franklin 6, 71–2
Roosevelt, Theodore 32
Rosenfeld, Alan 194n7
Rotolo, Michael 208n25
Ruiz, Neil 185n4

Sa I Gu (aka Los Angeles riots in Koreatown) 109
Saban, Haim 129
Safeguard 211n60
Saffa, Joan 195n18
Samurai 125
San Francisco 16, 22
Sandholtz, Nathan 197n12
Sang-Hun, Choe 203n84
Sansei 39, 73, 76
Scheller, Alissa 209n35
Schumacher, E.F. 189n9
Schutze, Tye Leung 22
scientific racism 18
Sei Fugi v. California 74
self-fulfilling prophesy 4, 62
Shaadi.com 157
Shah, Rajiv J. 31
Shang-Chi 9
Shankar, Ravi 188n46
Shaolin monks 126, 200n43
Sharp, Abbie 206n50
Shepard, Mathew 97–8
Shima, George 40
Shockley, William B. 164
Shoowong, Molpasorn 209n42
Si-Fan society 121
Sic bo 58
Sikh American Legal Defense and Education Fund 188n48
Sikhs 29–30, 95
Silk Road 15
sing song girls 21, 121
Sinophobia 18–19, 108, 120, 178
Six Companies 21
skin-lightening 32, 156–7

Smith, Denis N. 122
Smith, Gregory 208n25
Smithfield Foods 107
Smithsonian exhibition 87–8
Sniderman, Paul 102, 197n13
Social Security Administration 204n23
Solomon, Harry 193n1
Sone, Monica 196n48
Soni, Saket 209n40
SONY Playstation 130
Soros, George 97
Sotomayor, Sonia 152
Spencer, Herbert 18
Sperber, Jonathan 189n3
Spratly archipelago 173
Steele, Claude 203n82
stereotypes 16, 17, 19, 22, 54–5, 61, 113–116, 118, 121
sterilization 162–3, 207n13
Stern, Alexandra M. 53–55, 191n36
Stoddard, Lothrop 18, 48, 161, 190n16
Stop AAPI Hate 3, 7, 95–6, 100, 102, 114, 150, 166, 197n6
Stop the Blame 210n58
Stovall, Tyler 49, 190n18
Strategic Bombing Survey 89
Students for Fair Admissions, Inc. v. University of North Carolina and the President and Fellows of Harvard College 149–54
Sudra 28
Sullivan, Jonathan 176
Summerhill School 135
Sumuru series 124
Sung, Betty Lee 63, 67, 192n20
Syngman Rhee 36
Szilard, Leo 89

Taft, William H. 33
Takei, George 76, 194n13
Tarrant, Brenton 166
Taylor, Bayard 18
technological imperative 44, 168
Teenage Mutant Ninja Turtles 128
Temporary Assistance to Needy Families (aka TANF) 50
Tevington, Patricia 208n25
Texas A&M University 172
Thomas, Clarence 151
Thorley, Martin 197n17
Thorp, Frank V. 207n20
Thrasher, Frederick 66, 192n26
Three Percenters 11
Tiananmen Square 211n60
Tien, Chang-lin 26
Tiger Moms 134–37, 149

Tik Tok 103–4, 176, 180–1
Till, Emmett 108
Tokyopop 130
Toler, Sidney 115, 117
Tondo, Lorenzo 208n24
tongs 6, 21–2, 63–5
Townsend, Matthew 201n49
Treaty of Nanking 17
triads 64
Trinity 90
Truman, Harry 36, 87, 89
Trump, Donald 3, 49, 55, 95, 97, 134, 164–5, 167, 176, 178, 182, 186n21, 195n19, 197n4, 201n61
Tuan, Mia 1
Tunell, Alex 205n39
Turner, Ben 209n33

umbrella revolution 174
UNHCR 190n21
Uniform Crime Report 191n1
Union Pacific Railroad 20
Unite the Right rally 165
United Nations World Health Organization 191n37
U.S. Bureau of Labor Statistics 204n11
U.S. Census Bureau 185n3
U.S. Department of Justice 179
University of North Carolina 114
University of Tennessee 178
Ustinov, Peter 115
Utoya Island 166
Utsch, Lorin 208n23

Vaishnav, Milan 188n47
Vaishya 28
Varnas 28
Vedas 28
Ventures for America 182
VerBruggen, Robert 149, 204n24
Verghese, Abraham 31
Verma, Seema 30
video games 201n50
Vietnamese accomplishments 36
Vietnamese adoptions 142
Vietnamese Americans 34
Viswantha, Aruna 210n48
Vitali, Ali 207n20
Volberg, Rachel 62, 192n15
VSHINE 131–2

Wagner, Richard 161
Waite, Ken 94, 165–7, 170, 197n2
Wall, Tamara L. 59–60, 191n8
Wallace, Henry 90
Wallace, Nina 194n14

Wang, Clifford C. 192n18
Wang, Francis Kai-Hwa 203n2
Wang, Philip 71, 197n3
Wang, Wayne 115
War Relocation Authority 72
war relocation camps 72, 75
Ward, Arthur Henry (aka Sax Rohmer) 121
Warrior, Padmasree 30
Watkins, Eli 191n39
Weber, Max 187n35
Wells, Spencer 207n6
Wen, H. 206n49
West, Cornell 152, 205n29
West, Kanye (aka Ye) 195n19
Western parenting style 134
White, Jessica 200n43
White Christian nationalism 165–6
White supremacism 95, 140, 145, 161–2
Whitfield, William 38
Wicks, Noah 198n26–9
Wikipedia 188n59, 189–90n60, 189n62, 192n23, 192n30, 193n3, 197n1, 200n43
Wilkerson, Isabel 187n45
Wilson, Darren 111
Wilson, Pete 110
Winters, Roland 115, 117
Wolf, Jessica 187n45
Wong, Christine 185n33
Wong, Edward 209n43
Wong, Huiyao 210n48
work-related injuries in the U.S. 46
World Health Organization 197n4
Wray, Christopher 175
Wu, Chien-Shing 25, 203n8
Wu, Frank H. 149, 179, 204n16
Wu, Yuning 187n35
Wuhan, China 95

xenophobia 178–9
Xi Jinping 58
Xu, Adam 198n20
Xu, Tony 146

Yakuza (aka gokudo) 6, 68–9
Yam, Kimmy 205n25
Yamamoto, Isoroku 71
Yang, Andrew 182, 200n48
Yang, Gene L. 129–30
Yang, Jeff 71, 197n3, 202n67
Yang, Jerry 25–6
Yang, Lin 209n47
Yang, Wesley 10, 203n7
Yasir, Sameer 206n48
Yasui, Minoru 82–3
Yellow Peril 19, 22, 121–3

Yen Press 130
Yeoh, Michelle 139
Yi, Se-Hyoung 111, 199n35
Yip, J. 206n49
Yonkers, NY 93

Yu, Charles 10, 43, 143, 145
Yu, Phil 71, 197n3
Yuan, Eric 26, 146

Zhengfai, Ron 104

www.ingramcontent.com/pod-product-compliance
Lightning Source LLC
Chambersburg PA
CBHW032038300426
44117CB00009B/1109